The Principalship: Dimensions in Instructional Leadership

LAWRENCE F. ROSSOW

The University of Oklahoma

Prentice Hall, Englewood Cliffs, New Jersey 07632

Library of Congress Cataloging-in-Publication Data

Rossow, Lawrence F. [date]

  The principalship : dimensions in instructional leadership /
Lawrence F. Rossow.
    p.   cm.
  Bibliography: p.
  Includes index.
  ISBN 0-13-712290-X
  1. School principals–United States. 2. Leadership. 3. School
management and organization–United States. I. Title.
LB2831.92.R67 1990
371.2′012′0973–dc20   89-33402
                    CIP

Editorial/production supervision: *Edith Riker/Sylvia Pafenyk*
Interior design: *Marjorie Shustak*
Cover design: *Lundgren Graphics*
Manufacturing buyer: *Peter Havens*

©1990 by Prentice-Hall, Inc.
A Division of Simon & Schuster
Englewood Cliffs, New Jersey 07632

Printed in the United States of America

10   9   8   7   6   5   4   3   2   1

ISBN   0-13-712290-X

PRENTICE-HALL INTERNATIONAL (UK) LIMITED, *London*
PRENTICE-HALL OF AUSTRALIA PTY. LIMITED, *Sydney*
PRENTICE-HALL CANADA INC., *Toronto*
PRENTICE-HALL HISPANOAMERICANA, S.A., *Mexico*
PRENTICE-HALL OF INDIA PRIVATE LIMITED, *New Delhi*
PRENTICE-HALL OF JAPAN, INC., *Tokyo*
SIMON & SCHUSTER ASIA PTE. LTD., *Singapore*
EDITORA PRENTICE-HALL DO BRASIL, LTDA., *Rio de Janeiro*

In Memoriam
Maria Antonia—with whom all things were possible

and
Dedicated to those three who make it all worthwhile
Nancy, Mara, and Marie Eileen

Contents

PREFACE   *ix*

1   THE NATURE OF INSTRUCTIONAL LEADERSHIP   *1*

Effective Schools Research   *2*
   High Level of Expectation 5   Safe and Orderly
   Environment 7   Clear and Focused Mission 9   Strong
   Leadership 10   Cautions 11
Leadership Theory   *11*
   Behavior Theory 12   Immaturity-Maturity 18
   Leadership Theory and Effective Schools 18
Motivation   *20*
   Theories of Motivation 23   Applying the Theories to
   Education 26
The Principal's Role as Leader in Effective Schools   *34*
   Principal as a Person: Personal
   Requisites 34   Modeling 34   Consensus
   Building 36   Feedback 37   Instructional Leadership:
   Functional Requisites 38   Instructional Leadership:
   Contextual Requisites 40
Summary   *42*
Selected Bibliography   *44*

2   RESEARCH IN EFFECTIVE TEACHING PRACTICES   *45*

Overview of Effective Teaching Practices   *46*
Teacher Attention to Student Characteristics 47   Teacher
Attention to Content Goals and to Knowledge and Skills
Assessed 59   Student Experience at
Success 53   Classroom Management 53
Applying Research to Practice   *55*
Direct-Instruction Model 55   Mastery Learning 56
Principal's Roles   *59*
Clinical Supervision 59   Observation
Instrumentation 65   Variables the Principal Can Control
from Outside the Classroom 69
Dealing with Resistance   *71*
Summary   *75*
Selected Bibliography   *78*

3   DECISION MAKING   *79*

Models of Decision Making 80   The Decision-Making
Process 85   Principal's Role in Decisions 91
Summary   *93*
Selected Bibliography   *94*

4   LEADERSHIP IN THE CURRICULUM   *97*

Basis for the Curriculum 98   Organizing the Curriculum
for Improved Instruction 104   Involving Others in the
Curriculum Process 114   Evaluation of the
Curriculum 119
Summary   *122*
Selected Bibliography   *122*

5   THE PRINCIPAL'S RELATIONSHIP WITH STUDENTS   *125*

The Principal's Direct Involvement in the Subject-Related
Curriculum 126   Extracurricular Activities 127   The
Principal's Supervision of Extracurricular
Activities 128   Problems Associated with Extracurricular
Activities 130
The Athletic Program   *134*
Principles and Goals for Athletics 134   Keeping Athletics
in Perspective 134   Student Government 137   Guidance
Services 140   Appraisal Service 142   Pupil
Data 146   Counseling Service 154

Summary *156*
Selected Bibliography *158*

6 THE PRINCIPAL'S RELATIONSHIP WITH SPECIAL EDUCATION *159*

Understanding Special Education Law *160*
Early Cases 160 Federal Legislation 162 Discipline of
Special-Education Students 168 Parents and Due
Process 169
The Principal and Special-Education Personnel *170*
The School Psychologist 170 School Social
Worker 171 Special-Education Teachers 172 The
Speech-Therapist 173 The Special-Education
Director 174
The Principal and the Special-Education Assessment
Process *174*
The Referral 176 The Referral Conference 178
Special Education-Regular Education Relationships *181*
Increasing Communication 182
Summary *182*
Selected Bibliography *183*

7 THE PRINCIPAL AND THE LAW *185*

Legal Literacy *186*
The Need for Legal Literacy 186 Establishing
Literacy 187 Evaluation of Legal Advice 188
Teacher's Rights *194*
Constitutional Rights of Teachers 194 Employment
Discrimination 196 Teacher Dismissal 206
Students' Rights *215*
Student Rights in Suspension and Expulsion 216
Preventive School Law *224*
Summary *225*
Selected Bibliography *226*

8 LEGAL ASPECTS OF THE INSTRUCTIONAL PROGRAM *229*

Legal Authority for the Curriculum 230 Minimum
Competency Testing 234 The Legal Status of
Homework 237 The Curriculum and Freedom of

Religion 237   Censorship 240   Copyright Law in
Education 244   Copying Music 248   Copying in the
Library 249
Summary *253*
Selected Bibliography *255*

9   BUSINESS MANAGEMENT IN THE PRINCIPALSHIP   *257*

Developing the School Budget 258   Administering the
School Budget 264   Accounting and the
Principalship 267   Facilities Management 270
Summary *273*
Selected Bibliography *273*

**10 SCHOOL-COMMUNITY RELATIONS FOR
INSTRUCTIONAL LEADERSHIP**   *275*

Developing a School-Community Relations Program *276*
    Analyzing the Community 276
Starting a School-Community Relations Program at the
    Building Level *283*
    Obtaining Community Support 284   School
    Volunteers 287   Parent Education 288   The Tools of
    Communication 289   Working with Parent and
    Community Groups 298
Summary *300*
Selected Bibliography *301*

11 THE PRINCIPAL AND EDUCATIONAL CHANGE   *303*

Planning for Change 304   Strategies for
Change 306   The Change Process 309   The Principal as
Change Facilitator 313   The Ideal Style? 314
Summary *314*
Selected Bibliography *315*

INDEX   *317*

Preface

After several years of teaching graduate courses on the principalship, the author became disenchanted with the books available on the topic. While the field was calling for a new kind of principal, that is, a principal who is an *instructional leader,* the books continued to address the principal's role as building manager. The gap between the need for the training of principals as instructional leaders and appropriate materials to support that need is the reason for this book.

The rationale for the book centers on the notion that today's school principal must be an instructional leader in order to implement what is known about "effective schools" and "effective teaching practices." Today's school principal must be a leader of people, not a manager of things. With this in mind, the book attempts to convert theory into practice by describing how the principal might better function as instructional leader. Pedagogically, the author believes that instructional leadership is not a born trait—*it can be learned.*

The book introduces a number of areas that have not been seen in works developed for the training of school principals. The first three chapters are devoted to understanding the basis for the principalship as instructional leadership. In those chapters the reader will be able to understand what is meant by effective-schools research and effective teaching practices, as well as how decision making can be used to enhance the possibility that the principal's building might be able to emulate current effective practices. Chapters 4, 5, and 6 deal with the principal's role in the curriculum and how that role impacts on students, including special education.

Recognizing that the modern school principal operates from an ever increasing knowledge base, chapters 7, 8, and 9 give a thorough presentation of law and finance. Chapters 10 and 11 expose the reader to the very human side of the principalship dealing with school/community relationship and how the principal might introduce change.

Regardless of the topic, the overall theme of instructional leadership pervades. Each area contains concrete examples of how the principal can relate the information to a practical situation in the field. In addition, the book includes such aids as charts, checklists, and diagrams to facilitate reading and understanding.

The content has been designed by an author with experience at all levels of education, including teaching, building level administration, central office administration, superintendency, school board membership, university administration and university professorship. The author has served as an educator in inner-city, suburban and rural settings throughout the United States.

The book is well suited for the training of those who wish to enter the principalship or assistant principalship at either the elementary or secondary levels. The book is useful for those already in the principalship who wish to know more about being an instructional leader. School superintendents and board members will find the book a valuable guide to making decisions about making their school system more responsive to instructional improvement.

The author wishes to thank all of those people who helped to make this project possible: Dr. Melvin Heller and Dr. Phillip Carlin, who were instrumental in preparing the author for a career in school administration; Dr. Gerald Gutek, who helped prepare me to become an author by sharing his expertise; Dr. Paul Salter, who encouraged me through the dark hours; Mark Rice and Lydia Buras for their fine technical assistance.

Lawrence F. Rossow
Norman, Oklahoma

1

The Nature of Instructional Leadership

The notion that school principals must also be instructional leaders is not new. The word *principal* was originally an adjective used to designate who among teachers was the one "in charge." Thus, the term *principal teacher* represented the notion that the person was truly a teacher, or even a "super teacher." With the rise of industrialization and the development of scientific management techniques, the term *principal teacher* became just *principal,* and the job took on a management focus. Recent demands for the principal to become more involved in the instructional program of the school call once again for a different and perhaps "return to roots" approach.

In this chapter, four important aspects of instructional leadership will be explored: (1) the impact of effective-schools research on the principalship; (2) theories that support instructional leadership; (3) the principal's use of motivation techniques in aiding leadership; and (4) the specific roles that the principal must assume within the leadership dimension.

EFFECTIVE-SCHOOLS RESEARCH

In discussing effective-schools research, we must begin by recognizing that the recent findings are a sharp departure from the findings of the mid-1960s and early '70s. Those early studies of schools painted a gloomy and pessimistic picture of our nation's schools. Coleman found that the strongest variable accounting for a student's level of achievement was the socioeconomic status (SES) of the student's parents.[1] The work of Jencks substantially confirmed Coleman's findings. In addition, he found that a student's future job success in terms of status and salary was related to the occupation of the parents.[2] In effect, these studies say that *schools don't make a difference.* No matter what the school does, the family backgrounds will determine success.

The impression was given that there are no schools that really make a difference in the academic lives of students. However, part of the problem with the studies by Coleman and Jencks is that they focused on schools as monolithic institutions. Coleman and Jencks pulled together data from many schools, looking for the overall influ-

[1]J. Coleman, E. Campbell, C. Hobson, J. McPartland, J. Mood., F. Weinfeld, and R. York, *Equality of Educational Opportunity* (Washington, DC: US Government Printing Office, 1966).

[2]C. Jencks, M. Smith, H. Acland, M. Bane, D. Cohen, H. Gintis, B. Heyno, and S. Michelson, *Inequality: A Reassessment of the Effect of Family and Schooling in America* (New York: Basic Books, 1972).

ences that schools have on students. When the majority of schools proved ineffective, the grouped results hid those schools that might have had positive results.

To the contrary, the effective-schools research of the mid-1970s and the 1980s has focused on individual schools that are exceptional because their students consistently achieve at a rate far higher than that of students in general. In composition of student body, location, socioeconomic setting, and financial resources, however, these schools do not differ from other schools. Whether they are in poor urban areas or in wealthy suburbs, they succeed while others fail. The researchers are looking for "human" variables, as opposed to "material" variables, that explain student success. What is it about schools that succeed? Might the determining variables be related to the principal's leadership and attitude about learning? These variables are within the educator's control to a greater degree than are such variables as the number of books in the library, teachers' salaries, and teacher–pupil ratios.

Summarizing the findings of effective-schools research is no easy task. Walberg has identified more than 2,700 research findings related to effective schools and effective classrooms.[3] On the basis of the research approach used, Purkey and Smith categorized some of the more widely respected studies into three groups: The outlier studies, case studies, and program evaluations.[4]

The outlier studies used highly effective schools (positive outliers) and unusually ineffective schools (negative outliers) to determine which sets of variables were associated with the schools' levels of achievement. Statistical treatments followed by an assessment of the school characteristics create composites that attempt to determine the reason for the positive or negative outcomes. Some of the noteworthy outlier studies were conducted by the New York State Department of Education,[5] the Maryland State Department of Education,[6] Lezotte,

---

[3]H. Walberg, D. Schille, and G. Haertel, "The Quiet Revolution in Education Research," *Phi Delta Kappa* (November 1979):179–183.

[4]S. Purkey and M. Smith, "Too Soon to Cheer? Synthesis of Research on Effective Schools," *Educational Leadership* 40 (December 1982):64–69.

[5]New York State Department of Education, *Reading Achievement Related to Educational and Environmental Conditions in 12 New York city Elementary Schools* (Albany: Division of Education Evaluation, 1974); New York State Department of Education, *School Factors Influencing Reading Achievement: A Case Study of Two Inner City Schools,* (Albany: Office of Education Performance Review, 1974); New York State Department of Education, *Three Strategies for Studying the Effects of School Processes,* (New York: Bureau of School Programs Evaluation, 1976).

[6]G. Austin, *Process Evaluation: A Comprehensive Study of Outlines* (Baltimore: Maryland State Department of Education, 1978).

Edmonds, and Ratner (model-cities elementary schools in Detroit),[7] Brookover and Schneider (Michigan elementary schools),[8] and Spartz (a Delaware school).[9]

Case studies of effective schools have generally dealt with urban elementary schools. Notable among these studies are Brookover (1979),[10] Brookover and Lezotte (1979),[11] and Rutter (1979).[12] Program-evaluation studies primarily focus on schools that are successful in raising students' reading scores. Armor's study is the one most often cited in the literature.[13]

In analyzing all of the studies across all methodologies, there appear to be common findings. Table 1-1 compares common findings among the effective-schools research studies.

Studies producing findings that were not replicated by other studies are not included in the table since the reliability of those findings would be relatively low. While none of the studies suggest that any one variable is more potent than another, a comparison of the common findings shows which variables appeared most often in the studies. Table 1-2 shows that "high expectation" appeared in every study.

The variables "safe and orderly environment," "clear and focused mission," and "strong leadership" appeared in two of the three groups of studies. The variables "monitoring of student progress," "staff training," and "staff control of instructional divisions" each appeared in one study. Having identified the more important variables associated with effective schools, we now turn to a more detailed explanation of each variable. We do this with the general assumption that in order to be an

[7]L. Lezotte, R. Edmonds, and G. Ratner, *A Final Report: Remedy for School Failure to Equitably Deliver Basic School Skills* (East Lansing: Michigan State University, 1974).

[8]W. Brookover and J. Schneider, "Academic Environments and Elementary School Achievement," *Journal of Research and Development in Education* (September 1975):82-91.

[9]J. Spartz, A. Valdes, W. McCormick, J. Meyers, and W. Geppert, *Delaware Educational Accountability System Case Studies: Elementary Schools Grade 1-4* (Dover: Delaware Department of Public Instruction, 1977).

[10]W. Brookover, C. Beady, P. Flood, J. Schweitzer, and J. Wisenbaker, *School Social Systems and Student Achievment: Schools Can Make a Difference* (New York: Praeger, 1979).

[11]W. Brookover and L. Lesotte, *Changes in School Characteristics Coincident with Changes in Student Achievement* (East Lansing: Michigan State University, 1979).

[12]M. Rutter, B. Maughan, P. Mortimore, J. Ouston, and A. Smith, *Fifteen Thousand Hours: Secondary Schools and Their Effects on Children* (Cambridge, MA: Harvard University Press, 1979).

[13]D. Armor, P. Conry-Osequera, M. Cox, M. King, L. McDonnell, A. Pascal, E. Pamly, and G. Zellman, *Analysis of the School Preferred Reading Program in Selected Los Angeles Minority Schools* (Santa Monica, CA: Rand, 1976).

TABLE 1-1. Common Findings Among Effective-Schools Research Studies.

TYPE OF STUDY	NAMES OF RESEARCHERS	COMMON FINDINGS (VARIABLES THAT SHOWED A HIGH CORRELATION WITH INCREASED STUDENT ACHIEVEMENT)*
Outlier	New York State Department of Education	Safe and orderly school environment
	Maryland State Department of Education	
	Lezotte, Edmonds, and Ratner	High level of expectation for student success
	Brookover and Schneider	
	Spartz	
Case	Brookover	Strong leadership
	Brookover and Lezotte	High level of expectation for student success
	Rutter	Clear and Focused School Mission
	Venezky and Winfield	
	Weber	Schoolwide training for teachers and staff
	California State Department of Education	Close monitoring of student progress
Program Evaluation	Armor	High level of expectation for student success
	Trisman	
	Doss and Holly	Considerable control by teachers and staff over instructional decisions
	Michigan Department of Education	Strong leadership
		Clear and focused school mission
		Safe and orderly school environment

*Each finding was collectively drawn out of all the research in that study type.

effective school, an equal percentage of the school's highest and lowest social classes will achieve minimum mastery of the basics.

HIGH LEVEL OF EXPECTATION

When teachers have high academic expectations of students, the students tend to achieve a high level of success. When teachers have low expectations, students achievement declines. The research points out that these expectations are communicated to students in the way

TABLE 1-2. Frequency with which Variables Appeared in Effective-Schools Studies Groups.

VARIABLE	FREQUENCY OF APPEARANCE IN THE THREE GROUPS
High expectation	3
Safe and orderly environment	2
Clear and focused mission	2
Strong leadership	2
Monitoring student progress	1
Staff training	1
Staff control of instructional decisions	1

teachers give assignments, comment on homework assignments, assign classroom responsibilities, require students to bring books and pencils to class, and provide students with leadership roles in the classroom. The principal can play an important role by supporting the teachers in their maintaining these high levels of expectation. It is unlikely that a teacher can pursue a path of high expectation unless it is a building-level value that is shared by all.

Squires, Huitt, and Segars have formulated Brookover's findings on high expectations into six questions that can be asked by those who are concerned with effective schools to see whether high expectations exist in their school:[14]

1. Do students master their academic work?
2. Do students feel that the school helps them to master their academic work?
3. Do principals and teachers believe and expect that students can master their academic work?
4. Do teachers and principals support the academic focus of the school by spending most of the school day on instructional activities?
5. Do teachers provide rewards for actual achievement?
6. Is there little differentiation among students or in the instructional program provided for them?

Mastery is the target of high academic expectation. While students have different levels of ability, and thus of achievement, at least a minimum mastery of the basics is expected for *all* students.

[14]D. Squires, W. Huitt, and J. Segar, *Effective Schools and Classrooms: A Research-Based Perspective* (Alexandria, VA: ASCD, 1985) p. 54.

SAFE AND ORDERLY ENVIRONMENT

A number of the studies cite a safe and orderly environment as a prerequisite to an effective school. Schools with high levels of violence and vandalism have difficulty focusing on academic goals.

In perhaps the most comprehensive study of school violence ever undertaken, the US Department of Health, Education, and Welfare analyzed data on schools throughout the country. The report *Violent Schools, Safe Schools: The Safe School Study Report to the Congress*[15] presented findings from a random sample of urban, suburban, and rural schools. Five indices were identified that account for a safe and orderly environment within the school: size and impersonality, systematic school discipline, arbitrariness and student frustration, reward structure, and alienation.

School Size and Impersonality

The *Safe Schools* study showed that the size and impersonality of a school are related to various forms of school crime. Larger schools tended to have greater property loss through burglary, theft, and vandalism. The larger schools were also associated with higher rates of personal violence, such as attacks against teachers and among students. Schools that had higher teacher–pupil ratios also had a greater incidence of violence. On the impersonality side, the results showed that the less students valued teachers' opinions of them, the greater the incidence of property loss.[16]

The findings seem to make sense. In larger schools, especially when classes themselves are also large, it is more likely that students can go unnoticed. In an impersonal school where teachers have relatively little personal contact with students, the students are less likely to be affected by teachers' opinions. Therefore, it is important for teachers to have personal contact with a limited number of students.

Systematic School Discipline

The *Safe Schools* study also noted that lower levels of property loss were found in schools with greater coordination between faculty and the principal in enforcing school rules. The strict application of

[15]US Department of Health, Education, and Welfare, *Violent Schools–Safe Schools: The Safe School Study Report to the Congress, Vol. 1* (Washington, DC: US Government Printing Office, 1978).
[16]*Ibid.* p. 132.

rules and control of classroom behavior were important. Also, lower levels of violence were found in schools in which the students perceived tight classroom control and a firm attitude on the part of the principal.[17]

To establish systematic school discipline, it may be necessary to have high levels of social interaction among faculty and principal so that consistent disciplinary policies can be developed and practiced. For the discipline variable, Squires, Huitt, and Segars suggest that the following questions be asked: (1) Has the principal built shared expectations and strong coordination about school rules? (2) Do students perceive congruence among the faculty in enforcing school rules and strictly controlling classroom behavior?[18]

Arbitrariness and Student Frustration

Higher levels of violence resulted when students perceived school rules as arbitrary. Higher rates of property loss resulted when students perceived that the faculty and principal were overly punitive in their discipline.[19] The student frustration may enter because of the cycle in which schools that have a weak discipline policy find themselves. Lax discipline policies tend to make students feel singled out when they are punished; this leads to increased crime. As teachers watch student crime increase, their attitudes about punishing students tend to become more authoritarian. Thus the cycle begins.

Reward Structure

The importance of the school's reward structure was brought out by four factors:

1. Schools in which students express a strong desire to succeed by getting achieving grades have less violence.
2. Schools in which students express a strong desire to succeed by achieving good grades have more property loss.
3. Schools in which students have a strong desire to be school leaders have greater property loss.
4. Schools in which teachers say that they lower students' grades as a disciplinary measure have greater property loss.[20]

[17]*Ibid.* p. 133.
[18]Squires, p. 51.
[19]Safe School Study, p. 134.
[20]*Ibid.* p. 135.

Surprisingly, the last three factors show an inverse relationship between the pursuit of grades and property loss. However, the same goal of achieving good grades, resulted in a decrease in violence. The study describes these facts as a phenomenon resulting from fewer rewards being available for the number of students in competition. This results in an uneven distribution, which is perceived by students as unfair. They react by destroying property.

In order to ensure that there are enough rewards to go around, the school should encourage rewards that go beyond the academic. Extracurricular activities can be a constructive source of rewards for students who cannot achieve academically.

Alienation

The alienation factor points to the importance of the school as a social institution. The *Safe Schools* study showed that student violence was higher in schools in which more students say that they cannot influence what will happen to them—that their future is dependent on the actions of others or on luck, rather than on their own efforts.[21] This finding would call upon school authorities to weave students, faculty, and principal together into the fabric of the school. The authorities should let personal interactions help students to see that they have the ability to control their environment.

CLEAR AND FOCUSED MISSION

Both the case-study and program-evaluation effective-schools research groups demonstrated the importance of a clear and focused mission. Faculty, administration, students, and parents should be aware of the *instructional goals* and *assessment procedures* for the school and for specific grade levels.

On the opening day of school, the principal should be able to answer the following question: What are the curriculum goals for each grade, and what is the management plan for carrying out these goals? If the faculty in a school building were polled, their answers to the following three questions should be very similar: What business are you in? How is business going? What evidence do you have for your answers?

[21]*Ibid.* p. 136.

STRONG LEADERSHIP

Case-study and program-evaluation effective-schools studies report that strong leadership from the principal is related to the effectiveness of schools. The most significant leadership dimension was in the relation to the school's instructional program. In large schools in which there are a number of assistant principals or vice-principals, it may be one of these second-level administrators who assumes the instructional leadership function. While exercising leadership in the school curriculum is of prime importance, the purposeful action of the principal was also seen as significant. Squires, Huitt, and Segar summarized the effective-schools research finding in this area by posing four questions:[22]

1. Does the principal have a purpose in mind in running the school?
2. Does the principal emphasize academic standards?
3. Does the principal provide a reliable system of support, appropriate inservice training for staff, and opportunities for staff to coordinate their actions in the areas of instruction and discipline?
4. Does the principal regularly observe classrooms and confer with teachers on instructional matters?

A more thorough discussion of leadership will follow in the next section.

Monitoring Student Progress

The case studies on effective schools demonstrated that frequent monitoring of student progress is associated with academic success. In these successful schools, several situations were noted: (1) Teachers expected to discuss results of their monitoring on a regular basis; (2) The expectations for students were communicated to students "up front"; (3) The faculty knew and used target dates for student progress; and (4) Teacher-made tests were developed with a view toward faculty teaching style.

Schoolwide Training

The case-study group of effective-schools research showed that the successful schools had used training programs for their faculty and staff. Programs focused on the instructional and student behavioral goals of the school.

[22]Squires, p. 55.

Local Involvement

The program-evaluation group of studies showed that the faculty and staff in the successful schools had a considerable degree of control over instructional and training decisions. This does not necessarily mean that teachers, rather than school administration, have to control the instructional program. Rather, there should be local control—faculty and principals working together to make instructional decisions, as opposed to decisions being made at a central office far away from the social unit of the school.

CAUTIONS

This section has only considered school-level factors in the effective-schools research. Interesting work has been done in the collateral area of effective teaching practices, which will be covered in the next chapter. The works cited represent correlational studies. This means that certain factors have been found to be "associated" with successful schools. This is not the same as causation. It cannot be assumed that an attempt to duplicate the characteristics of successful schools will guarantee results. It can only be said that improvements will *likely* result. In addition, the characteristics of successful schools have not been ranked. Researchers do not know which characteristics are more important than others. As Edmonds has pointed out: "We must conclude that to advance school effectiveness, a school must implement all of the characteristics at once."[23] While it does not provide a guaranteed recipe, effective-schools research can successfully be used as a broad framework for school improvement planning.

LEADERSHIP THEORY

Sergiovanni has defined the school leader as "the individual charged with the tasks of directing and coordinating the group activities necessary to achieve or change goals."[24] There can be no leadership position without a group from which the role of subordinate is created. In discussions of leadership theory, the interrelationship between leader

---

[23]R. Edmonds, "Programs of School Improvement: An Overview," *Educational Leadership* 40 (December 1982):4

[24]T. Sergiovanni and F. Carver, *The New School Executive; A Theory of Administration,* 2d ed. (New York: Harper & Row, Pub., 1980), p. 267.

and subordinate is constantly analyzed as the key to group functioning and the achievement of organizational goals.

Early studies of leadership focused on personal attributes. There was a belief that if traits of successful leaders could be identified, the selection of persons with those traits would ensure goal achievement. However, Stogdill found that it is not traits by themselves that make for leadership, but leadership behaviors in relation to the nature of the group to be led.[25] Other researchers such as Chris Argyris, have found that the maturity or immaturity of the worker will suggest the appropriate behavior.[26]

BEHAVIOR THEORY

Behavioral approaches to the study of leadership focus on the behavior of the leader in interaction with followers. More specifically, what activities or actions of the leader can produce an increase in the effectiveness of the group to be supervised? Perhaps the simplest approach to understanding the relationship between the behavior of leaders and the effect it has on followers was developed by Lipitt and White. They classified leadership behavior by three *styles:* autocratic, democratic, and laissez-faire.[27]

With the *autocratic* style, the leader would respond to poor work performance with close supervision and punishment. Task orientation would be a primary focus. Autocratic leadership has been found to produce the greatest results in terms of quantity but very poor results in terms of quality.

The *democratic* style focuses on participation of the group in the decision making. Subordinates are given responsibility for shaping their environment. They share part of the managing with the leader. The democratic style appears to be the most effective of the three approaches. Group performance produced results of high quantity and quality.

The laissez-faire approach is the opposite of the autocratic approach. The laissez-faire leader (almost a contradiction in terms) allows complete freedom within the group and sees the followers as being responsible for supervising themselves. This style produces results of both poor quantity and poor quality.

[25]R. Stogdill, "Personal Factors Associated with Leadership: A Survey of the Literature," *Journal of Psychology* 25 (January 1948):35–71.

[26]P. Hersey and K. Blanchard, *Management of Organizational Behavior,* 3d ed. (Englewood Cliffs, NJ: Prentice-Hall, 1977).

[27]J. Kaiser, *The Principalship* (Minneapolis: Bugess, 1985), p. 19.

Perhaps recognizing that describing leaders in terms of style tends to mask the interdependence of several dimensions, Hemphill and Coons, developed the Leader Behavior Description Questionnaire (LBDQ).[28] Halpin and Winer,[29] working from the original LBDQ, identified two dimensions that could be tested with this instrument: *initiation structure* and *consideration.* The relationship of these two dimensions are to be used to predict subordinate performance. It is Halpin's version of the LBDQ that has been most widely used by educational administrators.

Specifically, the initiation of structure dimension refers to the leader's behavior in delineating relationships with subordinates. Such relationships will establish patterns regarding the organization, channels of communication, and methods of procedure. On the instrument itself, the following fifteen questions attempt to provide the data base for initiating structure behavior. (Note: starred items were scored negatively.)

1. He makes his attitudes clear to the staff.
2. He tries out his new ideas with the staff.
3. He rules with an iron hand.*
4. He criticizes poor work.
5. He speaks in a manner not to be questioned.
6. He assigns staff members to particular tasks.
7. He works without a plan.*
8. He maintains definite standards of performance.
9. He emphasizes the meeting of deadlines.
10. He encourages the use of uniform procedures.
11. He makes sure that his part in the organization is understood by all members.
12. He asks that staff members follow standard rules and regulations.
13. He lets staff members know what is expected of them.
14. He sees to it that staff members are working up to capacity.
15. He sees to it that the work of staff members is coordinated.[30]

Behavior that would be classified on the consideration dimension refers to a leader's behaviors that are indicative of friendship with subordinates. Indicators include mutual trust, respect, and warmth of

[28] A. Halpin, "A Paradigm for Research on Administrative Behavior is Education," *Administrative Behavior in Education* R. Campbell and R. T. Gregg, eds. (New York: Harper & Brothers, 1957), p. 170.

[29] A. Halpin, *The Leadership Behavior of School Superintendents* (Chicago: Midwest Administrative Center, The University of Chicago, 1959).

[30] A. Halpin, *Theory and Research in Administration* (New York: Macmillan, 1966), pp. 88–89.

relationships. The following are questions on the LBDQ that assess the extent to which a leader exhibits consideration. (Note: starred items were scored negatively.)

1. He does personal favors for staff members.
2. He does little things to maᵃ.e it pleasant to be a member of his staff.
3. He is easy to understand.
4. He finds time to listen to staff members.
5. He keeps to himself.*
6. He looks out for the personal welfare of individual staff members.
7. He refuses to explain his actions.*
8. He acts without consulting the staff.*
9. He is slow to accept new ideas.*
10. He treats all staff members as his equals.
11. He is wiling to make changes.
12. He is friendly and approachable.
13. He makes staff members feel at ease when talking with them.
14. He puts suggestions made by the staff into operation.
15. He gets staff approval on important matters before going ahead.[31]

It is recommended that the LBDQ be administered in the following ways:

1. Leader on self (leaders complete LBDQ on their own perception of their own behavior).
2. Leader on ideal leader (leaders complete LBDQ on their own perception of how the ideal person in a leadership position ought to behave).
3. Subordinate on leader (subordinates complete LBDQ on how they perceive their leader as behaving).
4. Subordinate on ideal leader (subordinates complete LBDQ on how they perceive the ideal person would act in their leader's position).
5. Leader's superordinates on leader.
6. Leader's superordinates on the ideal person for that leadership position.[32]

When the LBDQ on the actual leader has been completed, it is referred to as the *LBDQ Real.* The respondents evaluate the actual leader on a five-point scale: always, often, occasionally, seldom, or never. When the LBDQ is completed on the ideal leader, it is referred to as the *LBDQ Ideal.* It is also possible for leaders to describe their own behavior as the behavior they think a leader should display. Scores on the two dimensions are obtained by summing the score for

---

[31]*Ibid.* p. 89.
[32]Kaiser, *The Principalship,* p. 20.

each item on a scale of 4 to 0. Consequently, the theoretical range of scores on each dimension is 0 to 60.

The initiating structure and consideration behaviors may range from low to high in any individual. As shown in Figure 1-1, the two types of behavior may be plotted on horizontal and vertical axes which intersect at the mean points to create cells. A leaders's scores placed in one of the cells illustrate the dual dimensions of the behaviors. If scores are below the mean in an initiating structure, the leader would be in a different cell than if the scores were above the mean on both dimensions.

Researchers such as Goldhaber[33] have had similar results as the LBDQ by using similar but simpler instruments. Kaiser's educational adaptation of Goldhaber's instrument is presented in Figure 1-2. The

FIGURE 1-1 Two-dimensional leadership grid.   Reprinted with permission of Macmillan Publishing Company from *The Principalship* by Jeffrey Kaiser. Copyright © 1985 by Macmillan Publishing Company.

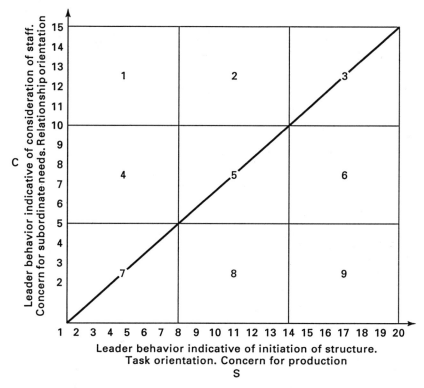

[33]G. M. Goldhaber, *Organizational Communication Instructor's Manual* (Dubuque, IA: W. C. Brown, 1974).

Structure-Consideration Intersect Instrument (SCII)

The following items describe many aspects of leadership behavior. Record the way you would probably act if you were the principal of a school. Circle whether you would be likely to behave in the described way always (A), frequently (F), occasionally (O), seldom (S), or never (N).

If I were the principal of a school . . .

1. I would most likely act as the spokesperson for the school.   A F O S N

2. I would encourage teachers to work overtime.   A F O S N

3. I would allow teachers complete freedom in their job.   A F O S N

4. I would encourage the use of uniform procedures.   A F O S N

5. I would permit the teachers to use their own judgment in solving problems.   A F O S N

6. I would try to encourage academic departments to compete with each other.   A F O S N

7. I would speak as a representative of the school.   A F O S N

8. I would needle teachers for greater effort.   A F O S N

9. I would try out my ideas in faculty meetings.   A F O S N

10. I would let the teachers do their work the way they think best.   A F O S N

11. I would be working hard for a promotion for myself.   A F O S N

12. I would be able to tolerate postponement and uncertainty.   A F O S N

13. I would speak for my teachers when visitors were present.   A F O S N

14. I would keep the work moving at a rapid pace.   A F O S N

15. I would turn the teachers loose in the classroom and let them go to it.   A F O S N

16. I would settle conflicts when they occur among teachers.   A F O S N

17. I would get swamped by details.   A F O S N

18. I would represent the school at outside meetings.   A F O S N

19. I would be reluctant to allow the teachers any freedom of action.   A F O S N

20. I would decide what should be done and how it would be done.   A F O S N

21. I would encourage better teaching.   A F O S N

22. I would let some teachers have authority that I keep.   A F O S N

23.	Things would usually turn out as I had predicted.	A F O S N
24.	I would allow teachers a high degree of initiative.	A F O S N
25.	I would assign teachers to particular tasks.	A F O S N
26.	I would be willing to make changes.	A F O S N
27.	I would ask to work harder.	A F O S N
28.	I would trust the teachers to exercise good judgment.	A F O S N
29.	I would schedule the work to be done.	A F O S N
30.	I would refuse to explain my actions.	A F O S N
31.	I would persuade others that my ideas were to their advantage.	A F O S N
32.	I would permit teachers to set their own pace.	A F O S N
33.	I would act without consulting teachers.	A F O S N
34.	I would urge teachers to constantly improve.	A F O S N
35.	I would ask that teachers follow standard rules and regulations.	A F O S N

Scoring:

1. Circle the item numbers for items 1, 4, 7, 13, 16, 17, 18, 19, 20, 23, 29, 30, 31, 33, and 35.
2. Write a 1 in front of the circled items to which you responded S (seldom) or N (never).
3. Write a 1 in front of the items not circles to which you responded A (always) or F (frequently).
4. Circle the 1s that you have written in front of the following items: 3, 5, 8, 10, 12, 15, 17, 19, 22, 24, 26, 28, 30, 32, and 34.
5. Count the circled 1s. This is your consideration orientation (C) score. Record the score in the blank following the letter C below.
6. Count the uncircled 1s. This is your task orientation (S) score. Record this number in the blank following the letter S.
7. C _____ S _____

Interpretation:

To locate yourself on the two-dimensional leadership grid, find your score on the consideration dimension (C) on the vertical axis of the graph. Next, move across the column corresponding to your C score to the cell that corresponds to your structure score (S). Place an X in the cell that represents your two scores.

FIGURE 1-2 Structure-Consideration Intersect Instrument. Reprinted with permission of Macmillan Publishing Company from *The Principalship* by Jeffrey Kaiser. Copyright © by Macmillan Publishing Company.

Structure-Consideration Intersect Instrument (SCII) is originally based on the work of Halpin, Goldhaber, and Blake and Mouton. After completing the SCII and obtaining a score, individuals can place themselves on the two-dimensional leadership grid. Locating oneself on the grid can increase self-awareness and be used as a goal for improvement.

IMMATURITY–MATURITY

Some theorists regard the behavior theories as an imcomplete explanation of the realities of leadership. Theoretically, individuals might adjust their behavior to suit the followers. Therefore, the leader would use a variety of styles in dealing with followers. Selection of the appropriate style would have much to do with the type of people the principal is asked to lead.

Argyris'[34] immaturity–maturity continuum, which includes the maturity level of employees, is one useful way of identifying a crucial characteristic among people. By knowing the maturity level of the followers, the leader can predict which style might work best. If one were to combine the use of the two-dimensional grid by behaviorists with Argyris' immaturity–maturity continuum, the following information would be revealed (see Figure 1-1).

The immature follower would be most productive under a leadership style as found in cell 9. Cell 9 is the *telling mode* for the leader. The goal is high performance at all costs. Follower needs are a low priority. As the follower matures (such as a beginning teacher now moving into the second or third year) the compatible leadership style would change from a cell 9 to a cell 3. Cell 3 is more of a *selling mode* for the leader. The next move would be to cell 1, the *participative mode,* and eventually to cell 7, a *delegating mode* type of leadership.

LEADERSHIP THEORY AND EFFECTIVE SCHOOLS

Sergiovanni has commented:

> The current focus in leadership theory and practice provide a limited view, dwelling expressively on some aspects of leadership to the virtual exclusion of others. Unfortunately, these neglected aspects of leadership are linked to excellence—a revelation now unfolding from recent research on school effectiveness and school excellence.[35]

---

[34]C. Argyris, *Integrating the Individual and the Organization* (New York: John Wiley, 1964).

[35]T. Sergiovanni, "Leadership and Excellence in Schooling," *Educational Leadership* 41 (February 1984):6

For Sergiovanni, leadership is defined in terms of the forces available to administrators, supervisors, and teachers as they influence the events of schooling. Five forces available, in hierarchical order of importance. Figure 1–3 shows each level.

The *technical* level is derived from sound management techniques. The *human* level focuses on the harnessing of social and interpersonal resources. The *educational* level is derived from expert knowledge about matters of schooling. The *symbolic* level comes from directing followers' attention on matters of importance to the school. The *cultural* level is derived from building a unique school culture.

Until recently, the technical, human, and educational forces have dominated the literature on leadership. Sergiovanni would maintain that the focus on these three levels ensure only that a school is *competent*. Their absence will contribute to ineffectiveness. However, the

FIGURE 1–3   The leadership forces hierarchy.   From Thomas J. Sergiovanni, "Leadership and Excellence in Schooling," *Educational Leadership* 41 (Feb. 1984)-9. Used with permission of the author.

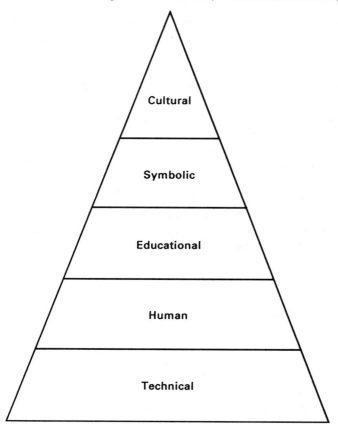

strength of their presence cannot provide *excellence*. Competent schools are those whose students are competent performers. That is, they perform up to minimum standards. Excellent schools are characterized by the following student behaviors *in addition* to the competency indicators:

1. interpersonal competence
2. creativity
3. curiosity
4. love of learning
5. critical thinking
6. problem solving
7. aesthetic appreciation

In order to provide for excellence, the leader must be able to marshal the symbolic and the cultural resources. The symbolic and cultural forces enable the school to be both tightly and loosely coupled at the same time. In one sense, the school should provide a tight structure around clear and explicit themes. Teachers, parents, and students should be able to answer these basic questions: What do we believe in? What is important here? What is the school about? Within this tight structure, the school community has the freedom and autonomy to pursue the school themes in ways that make sense to it.

Sergiovanni summarizes his position by proposing that a *leadership density* theory emerge as the viable replacement for earlier theories. Table 1-3 represents a coordinating schema that school leaders can use to plot their course toward being able to use higher levels of resources.

The ability of the five forces of leadership to bring about a combination of tight structure and loose structure corresponds very well to a number of important human characteristics associated with motivation. Motivation will be discussed in the next section.

MOTIVATION

In education, the term *motivation* is often associated with student motivation and with what teachers can do to increase it. However, this section will focus on motivation of teachers and on what principals can do to increase teachers' performance. In many ways the principal's knowledge of the factors that motivate teachers can be the key to effective leadership.

TABLE 1–3. Leadership Density Theory.

FORCE	LEADERSHIP ROLE METAPHOR	THEORETICAL CONSTRUCTS	EXAMPLES	REACTIONS	LINK TO EXCELLENCE
1. Technical	"Management engineer"	• Planning and time management technologies • Contingency leadership theories • Organizational structure	• Plan, organize, coordinate, and schedule • Manipulate strategies and situations to ensure optimum effectiveness	People are managed as objects of a mechanical system. They react to efficient management with indifference but have a low tolerance for inefficient management.	Presence is important to achieve and maintain routine school competence but not sufficient to achieve excellence. Absence results in school ineffectiveness and poor morale.
2. Human	"Human engineer"	• Human relation supervision • "Linking" motivation theories • Interpersonal competence • Conflict management • Group cohesiveness	• Provide needed support • Encourage growth and creativity • Build and maintain morale • Use participatory decision making	People achieve high satisfaction of their interpersonal needs. They like the leader and the school and respond with positive interpersonal behavior. A pleasant atmosphere exists that facilitates the work of the school.	
3. Educational	"Clinical practitioner"	• Professional knowledge and bearing • Teaching effectiveness • Educational program design • Clinical supervision	• Diagnose educational problems • Counsel teachers • Provide supervision and evaluation • Provide inservice • Develop curriculum	People respond positively to the strong expert power of the leader and are motivated to work. They appreciate the assistance and concern provided.	Presence is essential to routine competence. Strongly linked to, but still not sufficient for, excellence in schooling. Absence results in ineffectiveness.

TABLE 1-3. *Continued.*

FORCE	LEADERSHIP ROLE METAPHOR	THEORETICAL CONSTRUCTS	EXAMPLES	REACTIONS	LINK TO EXCELLENCE
4. Symbolic	"Chief"	• Selective attention • Purposing • Modeling	• Tour the school • Visit classrooms • Know students • Preside over ceremonies and rituals • Provide a unified vision	People learn what is of value to the leader and school, have a sense of order and direction and enjoy sharing that sense with others. They respond with increased motiviation and commitment.	Presence is essential to excellence in schooling though absence does not appear to negatively impact routine competence.
5. Cultural	"High priest"	• Climate, clan, culture • Tightly structured values—loosely structured system • Ideology • "Bonding" motivation theory	• Articulate school purpose and mission • Socialize new members • Tell stories and maintain reinforcing myths • Explain SOPs • Define uniqueness • Develop and display a reinforcing symbol system • Reward those who reflect the culture	People become believers in the school as an ideological system. They are members of a strong culture that provides them with a sense of personal importance and significance and work meaningfulness, which is highly motivating.	

From Thomas Sergiovanni, "Leadership and Excellence in Schooling," *Educational Leadership* 41 (Feb. 1984):12. Used with permission of the author.

THEORIES OF MOTIVATION

Among the most frequently cited motivation theories in educational administration are: Maslow's *needs hierarchy,* Herzberg's *motivation-hygiene theory,* and McGregor's *theory X and theory Y.* Each of these classic theories will be explained in this section, followed by an explanation of how the principal might apply the theories.

Maslow's Needs Hierarchy

In his classic work *Motivation and Personality,*[36] Maslow proposed a theory which essentially asserts that there are basic needs that everyone seeks to satisfy. The quest to satisfy these needs acts to motivate the individual. These needs are identified in Figure 1–4.

Four postulates coincide with understanding the hierarchy:

FIGURE 1–4   Maslow's needs hierachy.   Data (for diagram) based on Hierarchy of Needs from *Motivation and Personality, 2nd ed.,* by Abraham H. Maslow. Copyright © 1970 by Abraham H. Maslow. Reprinted by permission of Harper & Row, Publishers, Inc.

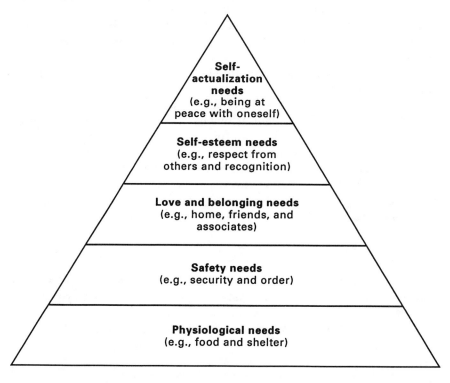

[36] A. Maslow, *Motivation and Personality* (New York: Harper & Brothers, 1954).

1. Once a need is satisfied, it is no longer an active motivator.
2. The most prepotent need will monopolize consciousness.
3. Less prepotent needs are minimized, and even forgotten or denied.
4. The higher one goes up the pyramid, the less the possibilities of satisfying that need.

Herzberg's Motivation-Hygiene Theory

In 1959 Frederick Herzberg proposed the motivation-hygiene theory in his book *The Motivation to Work*.[37] He theorized that the factors that satisfy employees and the factors that dissatisfy employees are mutually exclusive. The *satisfiers* and the *dissatisfiers* form two separate sets, as presented in Table 1–4.

The set of satisfiers are called *motivators,* and the set of dissatisfiers are called *hygienes.* The factors in the motivators set contribute to satisfaction if present but not to dissatisfaction if absent. They tend to affect employees' attitudes in a positive direction and can be related to increased performance. The factors in the hygienes set (so called because they prevent on-the-job trouble) lead to dissatisfaction if not present, but their presence does not contribute to satisfaction. In other words, their presence does not motivate. In the psychological sense, the hygienes are factors that take care of one's avoidance needs (basic animal needs), while the motivators take care of one's approach needs (basic human needs).

Herzberg's theory has important implications for management and labor. Even modern negotiations between the two parties focus on salary and working conditions. According to Herzberg's theory, raising salaries and improving working conditions will not produce higher levels of work performance; rather, they will help maintain current levels of performance. In other words, workers will be satisfied, but not motivated. To increase performance, managers must provide job factors related to one of the five motivation satisfiers.

McGregor's Theory X and Theory Y

In his 1960 work *The Human Side of Enterprise,*[38] McGregor proposes that human relations between manager and employee can be understood by knowing the manager's basic assumptions about workers. Basic assumptions can be distinguished by two very different

[37]F. Herzberg, B. Mausner, and B. Snyderman, *The Motivation to Work,* 2d ed. (New York: John Wiley, 1959).
[38]D. McGregor, *The Human Side of Enterprise* (New York: McGraw-Hill, 1960).

TABLE 1-4.   Herzberg's Satisfaction/Dissatisfaction Factors.

MOTIVATORS (SATISFIERS)	HYGIENES (DISSATISFIERS)
1. Achievement	1. Salary
2. Recognition	2. Possibility for growth
3. Work itself	3. Interpersonal relations with subordinates
4. Responsibility	4. Interpersonal relations with superiors
5. Advancement	5. Interpersonal relations with peers
	6. Status
	7. Supervision
	8. Company policy
	9. Working conditions
	10. Personal life
	11. Job security

From Frederick Herzberg, Bernard Mausner, and Barbara Snyderman, *The Motivation to Work, 2nd ed.* (New York: John Wiley & Sons, Inc., 1959). Copyright © 1959 by John Wiley & Sons, Inc. Reprinted by permission of John Wiley & Sons, Inc.

management views. McGregor called these views theory X and theory Y. The theory X manager assumes that

1. The average employee dislikes work and will make every attempt to avoid it.
2. In order to get work out of employees, the manager must direct, coerce, control, and threaten.
3. Average employees want security above all and therefore prefer to be directed and to avoid responsibility. They have little ambition.[39]

The theory Y manager assumes that:

1. The expenditure of physical and mental effort in work is as natural as play or rest.
2. External control and the threat of punishment are not the only means of bringing about effort toward organizational objectives. Humans will exercise self-direction and self-control in the service of objectives to which they are committed.
3. Commitment to objectives is a function of the rewards associated with their achievement.
4. The average human being learns, under proper conditions, not only to accept but to seek responsibility.
5. The capacity to exercise a relatively high degree of imagination, ingenuity, and creativity in the solution of organizational problems is widely, not narrowly, distributed in the population.
6. Under conditions of modern industrial life, the intellectual potential of the average human being is only partially used.[40]

[39]*Ibid.* pp. 33–34.
[40]*Ibid.* pp. 47–48.

APPLYING THE THEORIES TO EDUCATION

While the theories of Maslow, Herzberg, and McGregor were developed for management in general, they are easily applied to educational administration. The literature on educational administration contains many adaptations of the findings of business-related research for use by school principals.

Applying Maslow's Needs Hierarchy

When Maslow's theory is put into practice, prepotency postulate (the idea that a person cannot be motivated at a higher level unless he is satisfied at lower levels) seems to be overestimated. It may be more accurate to assume that hierarchies of needs are individually determined and vary from teacher to teacher. Each teacher, then, would have an individual pyramid, which the principal would use to aid in understanding that particular teacher.

Coffer and Appley suggest that in putting Maslow's hierarchy into practice, it is better to separate the five levels of need into two larger levels—*lower order* and *higher order*. Figure 1–5 shows how the pyramid would be divided into the two categories.

Expressions of higher-order needs will be dulled if the fulfillment of lower-order needs is deficient. However, it may be possible for a person to have some desire to fulfill higher-order needs while he is at the same time primarily fixed on the lower order. In addition, the fulfillment of a lower-order need does not mean that the need will not arise again some time in the future. It is as if no need can ever be fully satisfied forever. It may be more realistic to think of need fulfillment as need "appeasement." As Sergiovanni has put it, *"Need appeasement would suggest pacifying a need or causing a need to subside thus allowing attention to other needs and concerns but knowing that the appeased need will likely surface again."*[41]

Porter's[42] useful reformulation of Maslow's theory was later adapted by Sergiovanni and Carver for use with teachers. In this model, physiological needs have been dropped and autonomy needs have been added. Sergiovanni and Carver take the position that need deficiency is determined by ascertaining the difference between the *desired* level of need fulfillment in a particular area and the *actual* level of fulfillment. The lesser, the difference, the greater the satisfaction; the greater the difference, the greater the dissatisfaction.

[41]Sergiovanni, *The New School Executive,* p. 93.
[42]L. W. Porter, "A Study of Perceived Need Satisfaction in Bottom and Middle Management Jobs," *Journal of Applied Psychology* (December 1961):1–10.

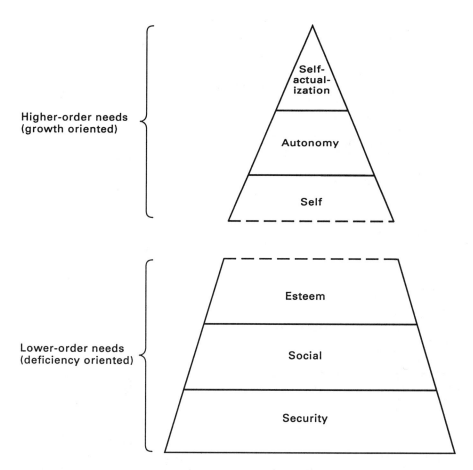

FIGURE 1–5. Maslow's hierarchy of needs in two categories. Figure from *The New School Executive: A Theory of Administration* by Thomas Sergiovanni and Fred Carver. Copyright © 1973 by Harper & Row, Publishers, Inc. Reprinted by permission of the publisher.

Applying Herzberg's Motivation-Hygiene Theory

Sergiovanni conducted a study of 3,382 teachers and discovered that many of the factors in Herzberg's original model did not apply to teachers as workers.[43] Table 1–5 shows a modified version of Herzberg's model based on Sergiovanni's findings.

It was discovered that achievement, recognition, and responsibility were the most important contributors to teacher satisfaction (motivators). Advancement was not found to be a motivator for teachers, while the work itself was found to be not only a motivator but

[43]T. Sergiovanni, "Factors Which Affect Satisfaction and Dissatisfaction of Teachers," *Journal of Educational Administration* (May 1967):66–82.

Basic Needs	Desired Fulfillment	Actual Fulfillment
• **Self-actualization:** the teacher perceived need for personal and professional success, achievement, peak satisfaction, and working at full potential.	_____	_____
• **Autonomy:** the teacher perceived need for authority, control, and influence.	_____	_____
• **Esteem:** the teacher perceived need for self-respect, respect by others as a person and as a professional.	_____	_____
• **Social:** the teacher perceived need for acceptance, belonging, friendship, and membership in formal and informal work groups. _Affiliation_ is another term for this need.	_____	_____
• **Security:** the teacher perceived need for money, benefits, and tenure associated with one's job.	_____	_____

FIGURE 1–6. Basic needs of teachers.   From L.W. Porter, "A Study of Perceived Need Satisfaction in Bottom and Middle Management Jobs," _Journal of Applied Psychology_ (Dec. 1961):1–10. Used with permission of American Psychological Association.

TABLE 1–5.   Herzberg's Factors Modified by Sergiovanni's Findings.

MOTIVATORS	HYGIENES
1. Achievement	1. Salary
2. Recognition	2. Possibility for growth
3. Work itself	3. Interpersonal relations with subordinates
4. Advancement	4. Interpersonal relations with superiors
	5. Interpersonal relations with peers
	6. Status
	7. Supervision
	8. Company policy
	9. Working conditions
	10. Personal life
	11. Job security
	12. Work itself

From Thomas Sergiovanni, "Factors Which Affect Satisfaction and Dissatisfaction of Teachers," _Journal of Educational Administration_. Reprinted with permission of _Journal of Educational Administration_.

also a hygiene. The factors that were contributors to teacher hygiene were poor relations with peers and students, unfair or incompetent administrative and supervisory policies and practices, and outside personal problems.

In an earlier, related work, Sergiovanni developed a list of characteristics that principals can use to identify *motivation seekers* and *hygiene seekers*. Table 1-6 outlines those characteristics. It is Sergiovanni's position that teachers can be generally thought of either as motivation seekers or as hygiene seekers. This position complements Herzberg's earlier notion that some individuals are motivated by hy-

TABLE 1-6. Differentiating Hygiene Seekers from Motivation Seekers.

MOTIVATION SEEKERS	HYGIENE SEEKERS
1. Emphasize the nature of the task.	Emphasize the nature of the environment.
2. Are primarily committed to the goals of the school or profession and work to pursue these goals.	Are primarily committed to private goals or extraschool goals and work for rewards from the school which help to pursue or purchase these nonschool or nonprofessional goals.
3. Show higher, *but not unlimited,* tolerance for poor hygiene factors.	Intermittent but chronic dissatisfaction with aspects of the work environment such as salary, supervision, working conditions, status, security, administrative policy, and fellow workers.
4. Show less reaction to improvement of hygiene factors.	Tend to overreact in satisfaction to hygiene factors.
5. Satisfaction is short-lived when hygiene factors are improved.	Satisfaction is short-lived when hygiene factors are improved.
6. Milder discontent when hygiene factors need improvement.	Tend to overreact with dissatisfaction when hygiene factors are not improved.
7. Realize great satisfaction from accomplishments.	Realize little satisfaction from accomplishments.
8. Genuinely enjoy the kind of work they do.	Show little interest in the kind or quality of work they do.
9. Profit personally and professionally from experience.	Do not profit personally or professionally from experience.
10. Have positive feelings toward work and life.	Generally cynical toward work and life.
11. Belief systems are sincere.	Prone to cultural noises—i.e., take extreme positions that are fashionable, superficially espouse management philosophy, act more like top management than top management does.

Figure from *The New School Executive: A Theory of Administration* by Thomas Sergiovanni and Fred Carver. Copyright © 1980 by Harper & Row, Publishers, Inc. Reprinted by permission of the publisher.

gienes but that this is not ordinarily the case. Healthy people respond to the satisfiers as motivator and to the dissatisfiers as hygienes. Healthy people that might be deprived of satisfactions from the motivator set tend to seek these factors elsewhere. For example, these individuals may be very involved in family activities, sports, church activities, or hobbies. While these "home life" activities are important to the well-rounded person, the workplace seems to be the more natural source of satisfaction in areas such as achievement and advancement.

As part of Sergiovanni's aforementioned study, he measured the extent to which teachers displayed motivation-seeking or hygiene-seeking tendencies. Two-thirds of the teachers were motivation seekers; one-fourth were hygiene seekers. The remaining eight percent were half way between motivation seeking and hygiene seeking. The responses did not vary with the sex, teaching level, or tenure status of the teacher.[44]

Applying McGregor's Theory X and Theory Y

Kaiser adapted McGregor's theories for education and combined them with a self-awareness instrument to be compiled by the school principal. The self-awareness instrument as shown in Figure 1-7 is easily scored. The higher the score is, the more likely it is that the principal supervises from the theory X position.

Interpreting the score for use in education requires some modification of the basic theory X and theory Y assumptions. Kaiser provides the following assumptions:

Theory X applied to education proposed the following:

1. The administration is responsible for organizing money, materials, equipment, and people toward the goal orientation of the organization.
2. Employees must be directed, motivated, and controlled. Their behavior must be modified by administration to fit the needs of the school system.
3. By nature, employees are passive, indifferent, and often employees must be persuaded, rewarded, punished, and controlled by administration so that efforts are uniformly directed. This is all necessary because teachers, like all employees,
   a. Lack ambition
   b. Dislike responsibility
   c. Prefer to be led
   d. Are self-centered
   e. Prefer to remain in old ruts
   f. Are gullible and less than bright

[44]T. J. Seriovanni, R. Metzcus, and L. Burden, "Toward a Particularistic Approach to Leadership Style: Some Findings," *American Educational Research Journal* 6, 1 (January 1969):62–79.

Administrative Style Analysis (ASA)

Check "Yes" or "No" for each item:	Yes	No
1. Although I provide my teaching staff and support staff with suggestions and guidance, they are responsible for setting and meeting most of their own goals.	_____	_____
2. I have frequent contact with all of my staff.	_____	_____
3. My staff come to me with criticisms and complaints, even about me.	_____	_____
4. I check almost all lesson plans of all the teachers in my school and closely monitor the work of my support personnel.	_____	_____
5. Many of my staff have recieved promotions to positions of greater responsibility.	_____	_____
6. I make or review almost all of the decisions in my school.	_____	_____
7. I give my staff as much responsibility as they can handle.	_____	_____
8. I plan almost everyone's work load in the school.	_____	_____
9. When I notice that I cannot provide staff members with sufficient challenge and opportunity, I help them get better jobs, even outside my school or school system.	_____	_____
10. My staff rarely come to me with their problems.	_____	_____
11. I encourage my staff to spend time on professional development.	_____	_____
12. My school has a greater turnover of staff than most schools.	_____	_____
13. Most of my staff are as concerned about challenge and interesting work as they are about their paychecks.	_____	_____
14. Teaching staff and support staff absenteeism is a problem in my school.	_____	_____
15. My school runs rather smoothly, even in my absence.	_____	_____
16. My school has more than its share of errors and waste.	_____	_____
17. My staff do not need me to make most of their day-to-day decisions.	_____	_____

18. More staff grievances are registered in my school
    than in others.   _____ _____

19. Several professionals in my school could replace me   _____ _____
    with little or no coaching.

20. I am frequently called on to "put out fires" in my   _____ _____
    school.

Scoring:
1. Total the number of *Yes* answers to even-numbered
   questions   _____

2. Total the number of *No* answers to the odd-numbered
   questions.   _____

3. Add the totals obtained in steps 1 and 2.   _____

Interpretation:
The higher your score, the greater chance that you administer from a
theory X assumption.

FIGURE 1–7. Administrative Style Analysis (ASA) Reprinted with permission of Macmillan Publishing Company from *The Principalship* by Jeffrey Kaiser. Copyright © 1985 by Macmillan Publishing Company.

Theory Y applied to education proposes the following:

1. The administration is responsible for organizing money, materials, equipment, and people toward the goals of orientation of the organization.
2. Employees are *not* by nature passive or resistant to organizational needs unless the organization has encouraged such passive or resistant behavior.
3. Employees are by nature self-motivated, have inherent potential for development and capacity for assuming responsibility, and are ready to direct their own goals toward those of the school system.
4. The essential task of the administration is to arrange for situations and methods of operation so that employees' personal goals are most easily achieved when efforts are directed toward school system goals.[45]

The National Association of Secondary School Principals developed a list of concrete motivators that could be used with teaching staff. While the list presents ideas in the form of a recipe, the suggestions are to be predicated on the theories that have been discussed in this section:

1. Create opportunities for teachers to have more contact with other adults. Establish and participate in a daily job, bike, or walk-a-thon, or exercise

[45]Kaiser, *The Principalship,* p. 5.

class. Find ways for teachers to visit the classrooms of peers in other schools, in other districts.

2. Create opportunities for teachers to gain recognition from other adults. Arrange for them to teach their peers or other adults. Invite teachers to testify on educational matters at school board meetings, to star in show-and-tell sessions for a districtwide audience.

3. Ask the superintendent or board members to visit your school and to take time to talk with individual teachers about what they are doing in their classrooms.

4. Select a panel of super teachers to go onstage at a districtwide get-together and be interviewed by administrators about their special teaching talents.

5. Write a note of commendation when a teacher accomplishes a particularly difficult job and put it in the teacher's mailbox.

6. Encourage and support teachers who want to try out new ideas.

7. Encourage teachers to attend professional meetings; pay all or part of their expenses, if possible.[46]

The NASSP also provides a motivation checklist for use by principals.

The role of the principal as motivator is one of the most significant among a wide range of roles to be assumed for effective instruc-

---

Motivation Checklist

Use the checklist to pinpoint ideas and motivators that may work with your staff:

_____ Do you invite participation in decisions that affect staff?

_____ Do you share the rationale for decisions made, except personal matters?

_____ Do you delegate challenging tasks and responsibilities?

_____ Do you regularly reinforce staff for positive job performance?

_____ Do you vary the approach you use with people?

_____ Do you operate on the premise that most people will work hard and be self-motivated?

_____ Do you accentuate the positive and eliminate the negative?

_____ Do you solicit employee suggestions, and then take them seriously?

_____ Do you look for ways to meet individual needs of teachers, when necessary, on a one-to-one basis?

_____ Do you stress team effort?

_____ Do you let *your* enthusiasm shine through?

_____ Do you frequently use these words: Good job; Well done; What do you think?; You count; Thank you[47]

---

[46]National Association of Secondary School Principals, "How to Motivate Staff," *Tips for Principals* (December 1981).

[47]*Ibid.*

tional leadership. In the next section, a number of important roles for the principal as instructional leader will be discussed.

THE PRINCIPAL'S ROLE AS LEADER IN EFFECTIVE SCHOOLS

Most researchers agree that the principal can be the key element in establishing an effective school. However, they diverge when attempting to isolate which areas of leadership are most responsible for a school's effectiveness. Some studies have focused on personal characteristics of principals. Other studies tend to view leadership for effective schools as the provision of necessary functions that could be carried on by any number of supervisors. Last, there is the view that the principal always works in some context and that a wide range of variables, both internal and external, in combination with the principal's behavior will ultimately produce a specific outcome.

This section will present the role of the principal as leader of an effective school from three requisites: (1) personal requisites, (2) functional requisites, and (3) contextual requisites.

PRINCIPAL AS A PERSON: PERSONAL REQUISITES

The ingredients of effective schools were discussed earlier in this chapter. Among the important variables were a climate for academic emphasis, a safe and orderly environment, and high expectations for success. While there are other variables associated with effective schools, these three are most controllable by the principal. Therefore, such researchers as Squires, Huitt, and Segars suggest that three personal areas be targeted: modeling, consensus building, and feedback.

MODELING

The behaviors of principals, as authority figures, communicate what is really valued to both teachers and students. Teachers and students will tend to imitate the actions, attitudes, and beliefs of those in authority, such as the principal. Figure 1–8 outlines questions that can

The Principal's Role

Modeling for an Academic Emphasis

Does the principal actively set the tone and focus of the school by observing classrooms, enforcing the discipline code in a "fair but firm" manner, and setting goals for the school that are supported by administration, staff, and students?

Does the principal regularly observe classrooms and confer with teachers on instructional matters?

Does the principal emphasize academic standards?

Modeling for an Orderly Environment

Are punishments delivered in a way that indicates firm disapproval of misbehavior while avoiding humiliation and avoiding modeling violence?

Is the building maintained and decorated to provide pleasant working conditions for students?

Is the principal perceived by students and faculty as modeling expectations of fair and equal treatment?

Do high proportions of students hold positions of responsibility?

FIGURE 1–8. Modeling behaviors role. From David Squires, William Huitt, and John Segars, *Effective Schools and Classrooms: A Research-Based Perspective* (Alexandria, VA: ASCD, 1985), p. 74. Reprinted with permission of the Association for Supervision and Curriculum Development. Copyright © by ASCD. All rights reserved.

guide the principal in the modeling role as directed toward goals related to academic emphasis and orderly environment.

Principals in effective schools model an academic emphasis by visiting classrooms, talking with teachers about their teaching, and setting goals that most teachers and students agree are important. The modeling role for maintaining an orderly environment can be accomplished in a number of ways. First, the rules that are established for student discipline communicate a deliberate message. Rules that are vague or too numerous for students to remember might communicate a lack of organization or an overly oppressive attitude. The way in which the rules for student conduct are administered is important. The principal should dole out punishments that avoid the semblance of violence or humiliation. In addition, it is important that the principal be perceived as fair rather than as a "hard nose."

The principal can also model an orderly environment by maintaining a well-decorated, clean, neat school building. A clean building communicates order.

CONSENSUS BUILDING

Some consensus, both explicit and implicit, is necessary for the achievement of academic emphasis, an orderly environment, and a sense of success. Therefore, behaviors that the principal displays that enhance consensus will improve prospects for an effective school. The questions in Figure 1-9 will guide the principal in attempting to build consensus around the three key elements for an effective school.

In building consensus for academic emphasis, the principal should encourage teachers to meet together to plan course content and sequencing of topics from grade to grade. More experienced teachers should be available to the new teachers for advice and guidance. The "buddy system" of experienced and inexperienced teachers helps the new teacher to understand both the formal and informal requirements for academic expectations of students. Research suggests that the principal should build consensus to limit the number of programs being offered to those considered essential. A curricular philosophy of wide course offerings seems to be somewhat detrimental to the status of an effective school.

Consensus for an orderly environment can be accomplished if the principal has periodic sessions with teachers concerning student behavior. What improvements can be made in certain areas of student conduct? Are there any recurring problems, such as class cutting or tardiness? Principal and teachers should operate under a theme of "working together."

Consensus for a high expectation of success is largely a matter of providing opportunities for interaction among students. Students must believe that their efforts will be rewarded and that success in life is not just a result of luck. They must be given the opportunity to feel as though they have some control over their own futures. Therefore, the principal should hold frequent assemblies where it is possible for a large number of students to be recognized for their accomplishments. Student activities should provide the opportunity for a large number of pupils to hold positions of responsibility. Teachers must understand the importance of their own belief that all students can achieve some success.

Consensus Building for an Academic Emphasis

- Is course planning done by groups of teachers?
- Do inexperienced teachers have extensive contact with a limited number of students in several aspects of their education?
- Is there little differentiation among students or in the instructional program provided for them?
- Do principals and teachers believe and expect that students can master their academic work?

Consensus Building for an Orderly Environment

- Have teachers and administrators come to a working consensus on patterns of acceptable behavior for staff, students, and administration?
- Has the principal built shared expectations and strong coordination about school rules?
- Do students perceive congruence among the faculty in enforcing school rules and strictly controlling classroom behavior?
- Do students perceive that discipline is unfairly administered?
- Does there appear to be a working consensus on how school life is organized?
- Are there structured opportunities for staff and administration to develop and reinforce consensus?

Consensus Building for Success

- Does the social structure of the school teach those who live there that their actions have some effect?
- Do students, faculty, administration, and the community feel that their own efforts govern their future?
- Do teachers have high expectations for all students, regardless of race or class?
- Are there provisions for school outings?
- Do a large number of students participate in assemblies?
- Do high proportions of students hold positions of responsibility?
- Are there out-of-class activities that bring students and teachers together to build toward common goals?
- Does the social structure of the school and classroom provide opportunities for students to practice leadership?

FIGURE 1-9. Consensus-building role. From David Squires, William Huitt, and John Segars, *Effective Schools and Classrooms: A Research-Based Perspective* (Alexandria, VA: ASCD, 1985); p. 76. Reprinted with permission of the Association for Supervision and Curriculum Development. Copyright © by ASCD. All rights reserved.

FEEDBACK

The role of the principal as a provider of feedback is as clear as basic stimulus–response psychology. All humans rely on feedback from the outside world in order to live peacefully within society. When we go to work, we are rewarded with a paycheck. If we were not rewarded, we would probably stop working. When we do something that disturbs the peace, such as running a red light, we are given a traffic ticket. If we never received tickets, we might continue to violate traffic laws. Teachers and students must be rewarded for things done correctly; this is *positive feedback.* For things done incorrectly, teachers and students must experience some penalty; this is *negative feedback.* As simple as this sounds, case studies have shown that many ineffective schools reward students' inappropriate behavior. Rutter found at least three times as many negative reinforcers as positive ones in the schools he studied.[48]

The questions presented in Figure 1-10 can help the principal provide feedback in the target areas of academic emphasis, orderly environment, and expectations for success.

Principals can support academic emphasis through such behavior as letting teachers know that homework is important and conferring with teachers about instructional matters. An orderly environment can be supported by feedback behaviors such as monitoring student discipline problems and assisting teachers with enforcing school rules. The principal communicates feedback that builds expectations for success when the rewards given student outnumber the punishments.

INSTRUCTIONAL LEADERSHIP: FUNCTIONAL REQUISITES

The uniqueness of each principal's situation make generalizations about personal characteristics and leadership styles difficult. Therefore, some researchers have focused on the common leadership functions that must be satisfied in schools. As a result of their 1981 study, Gerten and Carnine identified six administrative leadership functions that they consider essential to instructional improvement:

- Implement programs of known effectiveness or active involvement in curricular improvement.
- Monitor student performance.
- Monitor teacher performance.
- Provide concrete technical assistance to teachers as part of their inservice programs.

[48]M. Rutter, B. Maughan, P. Mortimore, J. Ouston, and A. Smith, *Fifteen Thousand Hours: Secondary Schools and Their Effects on Children* (Cambridge: Harvard University Press, 1979).

Feedback for Academic Emphasis

- Do teachers provide rewards for actual achievement?
- Do teachers praise students for work well done?
- Do teachers praise students' work in class?
- Is student work displayed on walls?
- Do teachers structure the classroom environment to permit students to succeed?
- Do teachers regularly give and mark homework?
- Does the principal check to see that teachers give homework?
- Does the principal regularly observe classrooms and confer with teachers on instructional matters?
- Do teachers and principals support the academic focus of the school by spending most of the school day on instructional activities?
- Do teachers feel their views are represented in decision making?

Feedback for an Orderly Environment

- Do students perceive congruence among the faculty in enforcing school rules and strictly controlling classroom behavior?
- Does the faculty express punitive or authoritarian attitudes toward students?
- Do teachers usually handle their frequent discipline problems themselves?
- Are punishments delivered in a way that indicates firm disapproval of misbehavior while avoiding humiliation and avoiding modeling violence?
- Is the principal aware of staff punctuality?

Feedback That Builds Expectations for Success

- Are rewards earned fairly by a large number of students?
- Does the feedback students receive in terms of rewards or praise outnumber punishments?
- Do high proportions of students hold positions of responsibility?
- Does the social structure of the school and classroom provide opportunities for students to practice leadership?
- Is inservice training provided that encourages self-reflection and skill building in areas promoting equal opportunity?
- Do students believe that luck is more important than hard work?
- Do students believe that they can get ahead without something or someone stopping them?

FIGURE 1-10. Feedback role. From David Squires, William Huitt, and John Segars, *Effective Schools and Classrooms: A Research-Based Perspective* (Alexandria, VA: ASCD, 1985); p. 77. Reprinted with permission of the Association for Supervision and Curriculum Development. Copyright © by ASCD. All rights reserved.

- Demonstrate visible commitment to programs for instructional improvement.
- Provide emotional support and incentives for teachers.[49]

These six support functions need not necessarily be carried out by the principal directly. Particularly in larger schools, the principal may have any number of vice principals, supervisors, or department heads who could actually direct those functions. The principal, should still remain somewhat involved, however, by monitoring the overall progress of those involved in the effort. Another approach might be for principals to delegate a certain number of functions to assistants while reserving selected functions for themselves.

INSTRUCTIONAL LEADERSHIP: CONTEXTUAL REQUISITES

Some researchers take an *integrated approach* to the view of the principal as instructional leader. In other words, they take the position that no one operates in a vacuum. A number of variables, both institutional and community, are "givens." It is only when interacting with these variables that the true effects of instructional leadership can be seen.

The idea of contextual influences on the principal as instructional leader emerged from a study by Dwyer and colleagues and the Instructional Management Program of the Far West Laboratory for Educational Research and Development.[50] The findings encouraged the development of a theoretical framework for examining instructional leadership. Dwyer presented a model that describes how the organization of the school and the community interact with the principal to produce the observed student outcomes. An adaptation of Dwyer's model is shown in Figure 1–11.

The community can be either a resource or a hindrance to the principal. To a large extent, the determination is a function of the principal's skills. Political savvy may be necessary if the principal is to find opportunity instead of problems. For the principal who possesses public relations skills and who can obtain volunteer time, philosophical support, and even financial help for the school from members of the community, there can be rewards. For the principal who has little public relations skill, community members can quickly become critics

---

[49]R. Gersten and D. Carnine, *Administrative and Supervisory Support Functions for the Implementation of Effective Educational Programs for Low Income Students* (Eugene: Center for Educational Policy and Management, University of Oregon, 1981).

[50]D. Dwyer, B. Rowan, O. Lee, and S. Bossert, *Five Principals in Action: Perspectives on Instructional Management* (San Francisco: Far West Laboratory for Educational Research and Development, 1983).

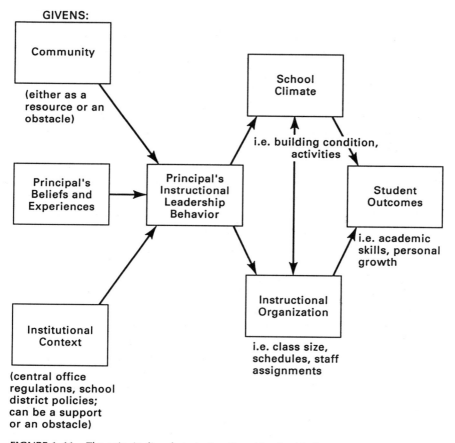

GIVENS:

FIGURE 1-11.   The principal's role in instructional leadership in context.   From D. Dwyer, et al, *Five Principals in Action: Perspectives on Instructional Managment* (San Francisco: Far West, 1983). Used with permission of Far West Laboratory for Educational Research and Development.

of the worst kind. Given enough ire, the community can doom even the best-intentioned principal.

Of course, the institutional context in which the principal works must be carefully evaluated. The institution, like the community, provides both constraints and opportunities. Perhaps the best example of institutional context is the principal's relationship with the central office. The extent to which the superintendent and district support staff share in the principal's views about instruction can determine success or failure. If the central office believes that each building should have autonomy, then differences in beliefs about instructional goals do not make a difference. However, if the central office believes that it must exercise a certain level of control over the affairs of the building principals, then similarity of instructional philosophy will be important. Dissimilarity of instructional approaches will require that the principal "lobby" the central office in an attempt to encourage a conversion of beliefs or more autonomy to pursue a course of action.

The principal's personal beliefs and previous experiences will influence his decisions and activities as an instructional leader. A principal with a background in counseling might be more apt to listen to constituents before making decisions. On the other had, a principal with a background in coaching might be more direct in assuming decision-making responsibility. A principal who values communication or democracy will display leadership behaviors that are different from those of a principal who does not share these values. Attitudes, values, and personal experiences enter into the mediation process between community and district demands. Taken together, community resources, institutional contexts, and personal backgrounds determine observed instructional leadership behavior.

Figure 1–11 shows two variables that the principal manipulates to produce the desired student outcomes—school climate and instructional organization. *School climate* refers to the overall character of the school. It is how the teachers and students "feel" about the school. It embraces both physical and social elements in its comprehensiveness. Climate can be altered by anything from a change in the color of the walls to an increase or decrease in the amount of recess time. The goal of the principal is to create a climate that communicates to students that the school is a pleasant place and that it can help them achieve success.

Instructional organization refers to the technical aspects of the school program, such as class size, schedules, and staff assignments. The principal can manipulate technical variables that can even include alterations in the scope and sequence of the curriculum or the distribution of instructional materials. As Dwyer has said about the interplay of climate and organization; "the elements of *climate* influence students' and staff members' feelings and expectations about the school, and that *instructional organization* delivers the reality."[51]

SUMMARY

Instructional leadership requires that the principal start with a knowledge of the research on effective schools. A synthesis of the research

[51] D. Dwyer, "The Search for Instructional Leadership: Routines and Subtleties in the Principal's Role," *Educational Leadership* 41, 5 (February 1984):36.

shows that at least seven variables are related to school effectiveness: (1) high expectations for student success, (2) a safe and orderly environment, (3) a clear and focused mission, (4) strong leadership, (5) monitoring student progress, (6) staff training, and (7) control of instructional decisions by staff.

Leadership theories can be grouped into two major approaches: behavioral and situational. Theorists who advance the behavioral theories would explain leadership in terms of the style of the leader. Those who hold to the situational theories would explain leadership in terms of the situation in which the leader is placed. No one style is best for all situations. The leader must be prepared to use any number of styles, depending on the situation.

More recently, researchers have attempted to take school effectiveness into specific account when analyzing leadership. Sergiovanni suggests that leadership be defined in terms of the forces available to administrators as they attempt to influence schooling. The forces available to the potential leader are technical, human, educational, symbolic, and cultural. The extent to which administrators are able to tap resources at the higher levels (symbolic and cultural) will determine their success as leaders of effective schools.

Teacher motivation can be an important element in the principal's success as a leader. Knowledge of the basic theories of motivation can help the principal motivate staff. Maslow's needs hierarchy, Herzberg's motivation–hygiene theory, and McGregor's theory X and theory Y can be applied to the educational setting for this purpose.

The principal can assume three distinct types of roles for leadership in effective schools: personal, functional, and contextual. Personal requisites demand that principals ask what behaviors they can display that will increase school effectiveness. The research suggests that principals model the behavior they wish teachers and students to emulate. Second, principals can build consensus for key school issues. Third, they should provide feedback for teachers and students. Functional requisites demand the principal ensure that certain leadership "jobs" get done regardless of the personal behaviors of leadership. These jobs include monitoring progress, implementing programs known to be effective, providing technical assistance, and showing support for programs. Contextual requisites demand that principals learn to operate within the variables of community and school district philosophies. Once adjusted to community and school district variables, the principal can ensure positive student outcomes by working within the school climate.

SELECTED BIBLIOGRAPHY

AMES, CAROLE AND RUSSELL AMES EDS., *Research on Motivation in Education, Vol 3,* San Diego, CA: Academic Press, Inc., 1988.

AMES, RUSSELL E. AND CAROLE AMES, *Research on Motivation in Education: Student Motivation, Vol. 1,* San Diego, CA: Academic Press, Inc., 1984.

ARGYRIS, CHRIS, *Integrating the Individual and the Organization,* New York: John Wiley and Sons, Inc., 1964.

BROOKOVER, WILBER AND LAWRENCE LEZOTTE, *Changes in School Characteristics Coincedent with Changes in Student Acheivement,* East Lansing, MI: Michigan State University, 1979.

COLEMAN, JAMES, E. CAMPBELL, J., J. MCPARTLAND, J. MOOD, F. WEINFELD, AND R. YORK, *Equality of Educational Opportunity,* Washington, DC: US Government Printing Office, 1966.

DWYER, D., B. ROWAN, O. LEE AND S. BOSSERT, *Five Principals in Action: Perspectives on Instructional Management,* San Francisco, CA: Far West Laboratory for Educational Research and Development, 1983.

GERSTEN, R. AND D. CARNINE, *Administrative and Supervisory Support Functions for the Implementation of Effective Educational Program for Low Income Student,* Eugene, OR: Center for Educational Policy and Management, University of Oregon, 1981.

GRIFFIN, ROBERT, *Off the Mark: Educating Underachievers in Secondary Schools,* Hillsdale, NJ: Lawrence Erlbaum Assocs, Inc., 1988.

HALPIN, ANDREW, *Theory and Research in Administration,* New York: MacMilllan, 1966.

HALPIN, ANDREW, *The Leadership Behavior of School Superintendents,* Chicago, IL: Midwest Administration Center, The University of Chicago, 1959.

HERSEY, PAUL AND KENNETH BLANCHARD, *Management of Organizational Behavior (4th ed.),* Englewood Cliffs, NJ: Prentice-Hall, Inc., 1982.

JENCKS, CHRISTOPHER M., M. SMITH, H. ACCLAND, M. BANE, D. COHEN, H. GINTIS, B. HEYNO, AND S. MICHELSON, *Inequality: A Reassessment of the Effect of Family and Schooling in America,* New York: Basic Books, 1972.

HERZBERG, FREDERICK, BERNARD MAUSNER, AND BARBARA SNYDERMAN, *The Motivation to Work (2d ed.),* New York: John Wiley and Sons, Inc., 1959.

KAISER, JEFFREY, *The Principalship,* Minneapolis: Burgess Publishing Company, 1985.

LEZOTTE, LAWRENCE, RON EDMONDS, AND G. RATNER, *A Final Report: Remedy for School Failure to Equitably Deliver Basic School Skills,* East Lansing, MI: Michigan State University, 1974.

MASLOW, ABRAHAM, *Motivation and Personality,* New York: Harper & Brothers, 1954.

MCGREGOR, DOUGLAS, *The Human Side of Enterprise,* New York: McGraw-Hill Book Company, Inc., 1960.

RUTTER, M., B. MAUGHAN, P. MORTIMORE, J. OUSTON AND A. SMITH, *Fifteen Thousand Hours: Secondary Schools and Their Effects on Children,* Cambridge, MA: Harvard University Press, 1979.

SERGIOVANNI, THOMAS AND FRED CARVER, *The New School Executive: A Theory of Administration (2nd ed.),* New York: Harper and Row, 1980.

SQUIRES, DAVID, WILLIAM HUITT AND JOHN SEGARS, *Effective Schools and Classrooms: A Research-Based Perspective,* Alexandria, VA: ASCD, 1985.

U.S. Department of Health, Education and Welfare, *Violent Schools-Safe Schools: The Safe School Study Report to the Congress, Volume I,* Washington, DC: US Government Printing Office, 1978.

2

Research in Effective Teaching Practices

The subject of effective teaching practices has increasingly become the focus of effective schools research. As researchers study differences among classrooms, the dynamic process that is led by the teacher is seen as a necessary unit of analysis. Attention has shifted from discussing general impressions of what every "good" teacher should be doing to identifying what th∩ successful teacher does to improve the achievement levels of stude..ts. Once successful-teacher behaviors are identified, the task becomes one of replicating those practices in other classrooms. Thus, the challenge of applying research to practice provides the framework for the role of the principal in the process. Perhaps more than any other task for the principal, changing teachers' instructional practices is essential to success.

OVERVIEW OF EFFECTIVE TEACHING PRACTICES

In 1972, Congress created the National Institute of Education. The institute has devoted its resources to research that attempts to identify characteristics of classrooms that contribute to instructional effectiveness. Most of the research describes those practices that will improve student performance in reading and mathematics. The preponderance of effective teaching practice data has been produced for the elementary level. Progress was slower in researching effective teaching practices in complex modern comprehensive high schools. However, the work of Stallings[1] and others does provide some guidance for effective practices at the junior high school and senior high school levels. The work of Brophy[2] cuts across all grade levels in suggesting that the key to effective teaching practice is *classroom management.*

At the elementary level, effective practices can be summarized in four characteristics. Specifically, effective classrooms are those in which

- teachers design and implement instruction in relation to specific student characteristics, such as prior learning and learning styles.
- teachers teach the knowledge and skills measured by the achievement tests used to assess student progress.
- students are engaged in learning activities for an appropriate amount of time per school day.

[1] J. Stallings, R. Cory, J. Fairweather, & M. Needels, *A Study of Basic Reading Skills Taught in Secondary Schools* (Menlo Park, CA: SRI International, 1978).

[2] J. E. Brophy, "Classroom Management and Learning," *American Education* 2 (1982):20–23.

- students experience a moderate to high level of success in their learning activities.[3]

TEACHER ATTENTION TO STUDENT CHARACTERISTICS

Awareness of the academic attainment that the student brings to the classroom at the beginning of the year coupled with some understanding of the student's learning style are important variables in effective teaching practices. Several researchers have provided insight into these areas.

Prior Learning

While teachers would like to assume that the students assigned to them have mastered the requisites of the previous grade, the fact is that each student enters the classroom with a very unique set of skills and knowledge. Bloom found that as much as 80 percent of the variance in posttest scores may be accounted for by pretest scores alone.[4]

The data point out that the knowledge that the student brings to the learning situation strongly affects how well the student scores on the year-end assessment. Students must be taught according to the level that they bring to the classroom at the outset. Unless the teacher proceeds in this fashion, the low achievement pattern is likely to be maintained. It has been shown that by attending to deficiencies in students' prior learning, the correlation between entering and ending achievement could be significantly reduced. Most of these studies compared the scores from one group of students who received corrective procedures after each learning task with scores from a group of students who did not. The correlation between entering and ending achievement for the first group was 0.36, while it was 0.68 for the latter group.[5] Bloom aptly summarized the importance of prior learning:

> If the school can assure each learner of a history of adequate cognitive entry in the first two or three years of the elementary school period, the student's subsequent history of learning in the school is likely to be more positive with respect to both cognitive and affective learning outcomes. Similarly, for each new set of learning experiences which start at later

[3]W. G. Huitt and J. K. Segars, *Characteristics of Effective Classrooms* (Philadelphia: Research for Better Schools, 1980).

[4]B. Bloom, *Human Characteristics and Student Learning* (New York: McGraw-Hill, 1976).

[5]Huitt and Segars, *Characteristics of Effective Classrooms,* p. 4.

stages of the school program (e.g., science, social studies, mathematics, second language), providing for adequate achievement and appropriate cognitive entry behavior in the initial and early stages of the new set of learning experiences is likely to have a strong positive effect on the learning of the later sets of tasks in the series.[6]

Learning Styles

In their article on teaching and learning styles, Fisher and Fisher defined learning as "a pervasive quality in the behavior of an individual, a quality that persists though the content may change."[7] The authors conceptualize two special styles: the damaged learner and the eclectic learner. The *damaged learner* is a student who is physically normal yet is not performing well because of deficiencies in other characteristics, such as lack of self-concept, social incompetency, or low aptitude. The *eclectic learner* is a student who can shift from one learning style to another, depending upon the situation. While eclectic learners may prefer one learning style over others, they are not bound to it.[8]

Dunn and Dunn developed a conceptualization of learning style wherein they identify eighteen elements of style. These elements are divided into four groups: environmental, emotional, sociological, and physical. Figure 2-1 shows how the teacher might use a schematic to diagnose a student's style.

The environmental elements relate to stimuli in a student's surroundings that are pertinent to his learning. For example, some students require absolute silence when studying, while others actually require sound. Still others are simply able to "block out" any extraneous noise.

The emotional elements concern such factors as whether a student is motivated to learn, whether a student will persist in a task and assume responsibility for its completion, and the amount of structure a student needs. Most teachers would probably agree that students who are highly motivated, persistent, responsible, and require little structure need to be taught differently than those who do not fit that description.

The sociological elements relate to how students respond to people while learning. Many students probably can learn in a variety of sociological patterns, while others are more limited. Some work best alone; others, with peers; still others, with adults.

[6]Bloom, *Human Characteristics,* p. 70.
[7]B. Fisher and L. Fisher, "Styles in Teaching and Learning," *Educational Leadership* 4 (1979):245.
[8]*Ibid.,* pp. 245–254.

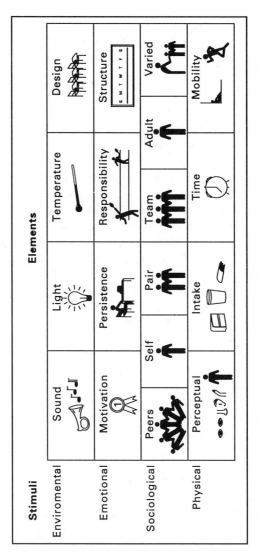

FIGURE 2-1. Diagnosing learning styles. From Dr. Rita S. Dunn and Dr. Kenneth J. Dunn, "Learning Styles/Teaching Styles: Should They—Can They—Be Matched?" in *Educational Leadership* 36 (Sept. 1979), 238–44. Reprinted with permission of the Association for Supervision and Curriculum Development. Copyright © by ASCD. All rights reserved.

The physical elements deal with senses that students use to process information as well as with the need to eat, drink, or move about when studying. Also important is the time of day when an individual's energy is at a peak; some people work best in the early morning, while others function optimally in the dead of night.

TEACHER ATTENTION TO CONTENT GOALS
AND TO KNOWLEDGE AND SKILLS ASSESSED

One of the basic requisites in establishing the teaching environment is to ensure that *what is tested is being taught.* Simple test validity would require that the test taken by students at the conclusion of their studies include items that were taught as part of their curriculum. In addition, the curriculum should have been developed as a result of desired objectives. Therefore, there should be some sense of the relationship among (1) the content goals or objectives that are desired, (2) the content actually taught by the classroom teacher, and (3) the content tested by an assessment instrument.

The need for teachers and supervisors to be alert to the congruence between content taught and the content tested was indicated in a study conducted by Brady involving 100 third graders learning reading and math. The study found that the overlap between content taught and content tested ranged from 4 to 95 percent. In other words, some teachers covered 95 percent of the content of the tests, while other teachers covered only 4 percent. In classes that covered more of the test content, students made greater gains in achievement. Achievement gains were more highly correlated with the difference in content covered than with any other classroom variable. In general, students must be taught at least 60 percent of the content tested if they are to attain expected levels of achievement.[9]

Written curriculum guides can help establish the necessary relationship that "what is taught is what is tested." However, principals should not assume that the mere existence of the curriculum guide is a guarantee. In his article on the subject, English contends that "the cycle of writing curriculum guides and buying or writing tests based on them may never influence the behavior of the teacher who constructs the real curriculum."[10]

---

[9]M. E. Brady, C. Clinton, J. M. Sweeney, M. Peterson, and H. Poynor, *Instructional Dimensions Study* (Washington, DC: Kirschner Associates, 1977).

[10]F. W. English, "Curriculum Mapping," *Educational Leadership* 37 (1980): 558–559.

AMOUNT OF PUPIL ENGAGEMENT TIME

How does time affect achievement levels? Researchers who study effective classrooms have devoted much attention to this question. The issue of time has two aspects. First, how much time is actually allocated to academics in the classroom? Second, what are students actually doing with the time spent? In other words, how much is spent doing academics versus other classroom activities or nonactivities, such as routines, socialization, or transition from one subject to another?

Wiley and Harnischfeger found that student achievement as measured by standardized tests is increased simply by increasing the number of days of annual attendance from 175 to 185.[11] The total influence of time appears to be greater for such subjects as mathematics, science, and literature, which are usually not taught outside school, than for such subjects as reading and language, which are heavily affected by the home environment.[12]

Table 2-1 shows data from some studies of time allocations for reading and mathematics in elementary schools as reported by Huitt and Segars. Teachers allocate from 55 to 106 minutes each day to reading, and from 37 to 52 minutes to mathematics. These ranges suggest that students may have triple the amount of time for some subjects than for others.

As to the question of time on task, Goodlad reported some interesting findings in his book *A Place Called School.*[13] Teachers spent their time on instruction, rather than on controlling students' behavior, managing classroom routines, and socializing. Table 2-2 summarizes Goodlad's data.

Analysis of the data suggests that if a classroom should be comparatively low in total school hours each day and low in time spent on instruction, the time spent on learning would be very low. In other words, some students could be experiencing levels of opportunities to learn which are quite different from others.

The Instructional Dimensions study,[14] conducted by Brady, showed that the average engagement rate (time on task) was about 60 percent for reading and mathematics. Comparing classroom-to-classroom differences provided an engagement time range of 4 to 90 per-

[11]D. E. Wiley and A. Hornischfeger, "Explosion of a Myth: Quantity of Schooling and Exposure to Instruction, Major Educational Vehicles," *Educational Researcher* 3 (1974):7–12.

[12]T. Husen and A. Purves, eds., *Literature Education in Ten Countries: International Studies in Evaluation, vol. 2* (New York: John Wiley, 1973).

[13]J. I. Goodlad, *A Place Called School* (New York: McGraw-Hill, 1984).

[14]Brady, *Instructional Dimension Study.*

TABLE 2–1. Average Time Allocations in Minutes for Reading Language Arts and Mathematics

	MANN STUDY (1926)	BEGINNING TEACHER EVALUATION STUDY PHASE II (MCDONALD & ELIAS, 1976)		INSTRUCTIONAL DIMENSIONS STUDY (BRADY ET AL., 1977)		WEISS STUDY (1977)	
	Grade 3	Grade 2	Grade 5	Grade 1	Grade 3	K-3	4-6
Reading	70.4	63.6	54.9	105.8	84.5	95	66
Math	39.2	37.5	48.0	48.6	52.6	41	51

From William G. Huitt and John K. Segars, *Characteristics of Effective Classrooms* (Philadelphia: Research for Better Schools, Inc., 1980, p. 9. Used with permission of Research for Better Schools, Inc.

TABLE 2–2. Observed Percentages of Five–Minute Intervals (FMI) Frames Spent on Instruction, Routines, Controlling Behavior, and Social Activity. Reported by Level of Schooling. (In Percent, Averaged Across Schools)

	INSTRUCTION	ROUTINES	BEHAVIOR CONTROL	SOCIAL ACTIVITY
Early elementary	73.27	18.99	5.52	2.27
Upper elementary	72.89	20.71	4.39	2.01
Junior high	77.42	18.02	2.88	1.68
Senior high	76.12	20.39	1.29	2.20

From John I. Goodlad, *A Place Called School* (New York: McGraw-Hill, 1984), p. 97. Used with permission of McGraw-Hill Book Company.

cent. Students' engaged time, or the amount of time students spend actively working on academics, is the result of considering both allocated time and the engagement rate.

Unless examined cautiously, the research in this area can be mistakenly interpreted as indicating that "more is better." It appears that the amount of engaged time reaches a saturation point. After a certain time is reached, achievement begins to decline. A good example of this phenomenon is shown by a reanalysis of the work by Stallings and Kaskowitz on first-grade mathematics.[15] Student achievement increased as student engaged time increased, up to about 95 minutes a day. Time in excess of 95 minutes related negatively to student gains, however.

[15] J. A. Stallings and D. Kaskowitz, *Follow Through Classroom Observation Evaluation 1972–1973* (Menlo Park, CA: Stanford Research Institute, 1974).

Another caveat in understanding engaged time has to do with the classroom as opposed to the individual student. Most of the research on engaged time focuses on the classroom as a whole, not on the needs of individual students. Bloom has estimated that the slowest 10 percent of students may need five to six times as much time to learn as the fastest 10 percent.[16] These findings imply that teachers should try to vary allocated time in relation to the time that different students need to learn. Varying allocated time would help to ensure that all students have the opportunity to master at least the basic skills.

STUDENT EXPERIENCE AT SUCCESS

As was noted earlier, the amount of time students spend on activities at which they are successful has a positive relationship to learning. Some of Skinner's theories suggest that optimal learning takes place when no errors are made. If this is true, then "errorless learning" might be a goal for teachers to consider.

Unfortunately, Fisher and Fisher have found that students spend only 50 percent of their time on tasks that provide a high degree of success. They define the highly successful student as one who makes only careless errors or who receives a score of 90 percent or better on written work.[17] Students who spent more than the average time in high-success activities generally had better-than-expected achievement in reading and mathematics.

CLASSROOM MANAGEMENT

In his article on classroom management and learning, Brophy refers to his 1979 research on teaching. He views the findings as suggesting that classroom management is a key variable:

> ... recent research on teaching has concluded that classroom management skills are associated not only with student attention and time on task but with student achievement in basic skills.[18]

Prevention, Not Remediation

While it is important for teachers to know how to deal with student misbehavior when it occurs, the preventive side of student

[16]Bloom, *Human Characteristics,* p. 84.
[17]B. B. Fisher and L. Fisher, "Styles in Teaching and Learning," *Educational Leadership* 36 (1979):245–254.
[18]Brophy, *Classroom Management,* p. 20.

control is more often associated with a positive learning environment. The research indicates that teachers' time is better spent on preparation and organization than on discipline and control. The major part of being an effective classroom manager involves active planning and decision making focused on setting up a functional physical environment and establishing efficient routines for handling logistics.

Teacher behaviors associated with effective management can be listed as follows:

1. *"With-itness."* This behavior involves the teachers' conveying a message to the students that they are aware of what is going on in the classroom; Any inappropriate behavior on the part of students is therefore perceived as easily detected. Teachers who display this behavior typically station themselves where they can see all parts of the classroom. They are able to scan all parts of the room continuously.

2. *"Overlappingness."* Effective classroom managers have the ability to conduct several activities at one time. For example, these teachers can instruct a small reading group while the rest of the class works on other projects at their desks.

3. *Continuity and momentum.* Teachers who display this behavior can move briskly and smoothly from one activity to another without disturbing the overall continuity of the classroom. Students are never confused about what to do next because routines are automatic. The teacher provides a continuous academic "signal" so that there is always an academic focus of which students are aware.

In short, the effective classroom manager minimizes the frequency with which students become disruptive in the first place.

Follow-up on Expectations

In addition to a focus on prevention, effective classroom managers are those who are thorough in following up on their expectations for students. Consequences for appropriate and inappropriate behavior are clear. In general, effective managers display three major clusters of behavior:

1. *Conveying purposefulness.* Effective classroom managers hold students accountable for completing work on time. They regularly circulate through the room during seatwork, checking students' progress. Completed papers are returned quickly with teacher feedback. Overall, the teacher's behavior sends a message to the students that academic work is important and has a purpose.

2. *Teaching proper behavior.* Effective classroom managers are very specific about what constitutes improper behavior for students. These teachers are willing to provide proscriptive instruction on "how-to" behavior when

students are reading or doing other independent work. In other words, the teacher spends time with the "do's" as well as the "don'ts" and models the "do's" for students.

3. *Diagnosing students' focus of attention.* The effective classroom manager is able to sense when students are confused or inattentive and thus calls for a shift in activity. This important teacher behavior is manifested in lesson plans that vary learning activities. These variations are developed with an understanding of the students' physiological as well as cognitive needs.

Being familiar with the literature on effective teaching practices is just the beginning for the principal. Applying the research to practice provides a formidable challenge, which will be considered in the next section.

APPLYING RESEARCH TO PRACTICE

Once the teacher is familiar with the research on effective classrooms, the task becomes one of implementing programs that will apply the research. Several investigators have proposed models of instruction that can effectively translate theory into practice. This section will review direct instruction and mastery learning, of the more respected application models based on effective-classrooms research.

DIRECT-INSTRUCTION MODEL

The *direct instruction* model was developed in 1979 by Rosenshine.[19] The model centers around four teaching strategies,

1. Matching instruction to students' abilities, though not necessarily to their learning styles
2. Establishing congruence between classroom tasks and achievement-test tasks
3. Allocating sufficient and continuous time for learning
4. Monitoring student performance and ensuring that students produce many correct responses

These strategies were experimentally applied by Leinhardt in

[19]B. V. Rosenshine, "Content, Time and Direct Instruction," in *Research on Teaching: Concepts, Findings and Implications,* P. L. Peterson and H. J. Walberg, eds. (Berkeley, CA: Cutchan, 1979).

1978.[20] A specific program was developed which incorporated the four strategies of the direct-instruction model. After reading a 45-page training manual and participating in an orientation workshop, teachers saw positive results with their students. A sample of the program is shown in Figure 2-2:

MASTERY LEARNING

In the late 1970s, Block and Burns[21] developed the *mastery learning approach,* which has two overlapping components. One component, *learning for mastery* (LFM), is both group-based and student-centered. The second component is the *personalized system of instruction* (PSI). This component is individually based and student-centered. The components address the two traditional modes of instruction: group teaching and individualization. Mastery learning does not suggest that one approach is superior to the other. Rather, the important condition is that the approach is student-centered.

The process of mastery learning, whether LFM or PSI, contains four basic elements:

1. *Course objectives.* Prior to actual instruction, specify a clear set of course objectives that students will be expected to master at a high level.
2. *Small learning units.* Break the course into many smaller learning units. Teach only a few objectives at one time.
3. *Unit mastery.* Teach each unit for mastery, and then test students' mastery of the objectives. Give additional instruction to those whose test performance is below mastery.
4. *Individual evaluation.* Evaluate each student's mastery of the course as a whole on the basis of what each has achieved individually, rather than "on a curve" or relative to classmates' achievement.

The Denver public schools have used the mastery-learning model successfully. In Denver, a three-year pilot study demonstrated that students taught according to the model showed significant increases in achievement over nonprogram students. Figure 2-3 outlines the Denver mastery-learning model.

[20]G. Leinhardt, "Applying A Classroom Process Model to Instructional Evaluation," *Curriculum Inquiry* 37 (1978):155–176.
[21]J. N. Block and R. B. Burns, "Mastery Learning," in *Review of Research in Education,* ed. L. S. Schulman (Itasca, IL: Peacock, 1976).

Summary of Key Instructional Behaviors

Daily Review (first eight minutes, except Mondays)

(a) Review the concepts and skills associated with the homework.
(b) Collect and deal with homework assignments.
(c) Ask several menial computation exercises.

Development (about 20 minutes)

(a) Briefly focus on prerequisite skills and concepts.
(b) Focus on meaning and promoting student understanding by using lively explanations, demonstrations, process explanations, illustrations, and so on.
(c) Assess student comprehension.
    (1) Using process/product questions (active interaction)
    (2) Using controlled practice
(d) Repeat and elaborate on the meaning portion as necessary.

Seatwork (about 15 minutes)

(a) Provide uninterrupted successful practice.
(b) Momentum—keep the ball rolling—get everyone involved, then sustain involvement.
(c) Alerting—let students know their work will be checked at the end of the period.
(d) Accountability—check the students' work.

Homework assignment

(a) Assign on a regular basis at the end of each math class, except Fridays.
(b) Should involve about 15 minutes of work to be done at home.
(c) Should include one or two review problems.

Special reviews

(a) Weekly review/maintenance.
    (1) Conduct during the first 20 minutes each Monday
    (2) Focus on skills and concepts covered during the previous week
(b) Monthly review/maintenance.
    (1) Conduct every fourth Monday
    (2) Focus on skills and concepts covered since the last monthly review

FIGURE 2–2. Example of the use of the direct instruction model. From G. Leinhardt, "Applying a Classroom Process Model to Instructional Evaluation," *Curriculum Inquiry* 37(1978): 155–176. Copyright © 1978 by John Wiley & Sons, Inc. Reprinted by permission of John Wiley & Sons, Inc.

Denver Public Schools' Mastery Learning Program Instructional Model

The mastery learning strategy being implemented in the Denver public schools is an adaptation of the mastery model described by James Block and Lorin Anderson in their book, *Mastery Learning in Classroom Instruction Planning,* and teaching to mastery can best be described through a flow chart.

I. Planning for mastery
   A. State overall objective.
   B. Task analyze overall objective.
      1. Identify prerequisite skills.
         a. Develop pretest to measure mastery of prerequisite skills.
      2. Identify component skills.
         a. Develop summative test to measure mastery of component skills and set mastery standard for that test.
         b. Write mini-learning unit objectives.
   C. Planning instruction.
      1. Develop lesson plans to teach mini-learning unit.
      2. Develop diagnostic/progress tests to measure mastery of mini-learning unit objectives.
      3. Develop correctives for each mini-learning unit.
      4. Develop extension activities for each mini-learning unit.

II. Teaching to mastery
   A. Orient students to your mastery strategy.
   B. Teach each mini-learning unit to mastery.
      1. Allow students adequate time to practice the skill.
      2. Administer diagnostic/progress tests to determine how students learning is forming.
         a. Students who do not master diagnostic/progress tests work with correctives until learning has been mastered.
         b. Students mastering diagnostic/progress test "extend" or "broaden" their thinking of that objective by working with extension activities.
   C. After each mini-learning unit has been mastered, administer the summative exam.
      1. Grade the exam based on your predetermined mastery standard.
      2. Report back to students what their grade really represents.
   D. Check on overall effectiveness of program.
      1. Evaluate success of program in terms of students mastering the final exam.
      2. Compare results of student success in mastery program with student success when you were teaching by traditional methods.

FIGURE 2-3. Example of the use of the Mastery Learning model.   From William Huitt and John Segars, *The Characteristics of Effective Classrooms.* (Philadelphia: Research for Better Schools, Inc., 1980). Used with permission of Research for Better Schools, Inc., and permission of *Phi Delta Kappa.*

PRINCIPAL'S ROLES

What is the principal's role in the effective classroom? The answer depends on the size of the school, the level of instruction, and the organizational pattern. For the elementary and smaller secondary schools where the principal is directly responsible for teacher supervision, the clinical supervision model for interaction with teachers might serve best. For the principal of the large secondary school, monitoring the amount of learning time being provided is a major step in improving student success. The principal of the large secondary school can also insist that those who are directly supervising teachers employ the clinical supervision model.

CLINICAL SUPERVISION

Supervision is the key to the principal's role in the effective classroom. While the many roles of the principal include management and administrative duties, the role of teacher supervisor presents the best possible opportunity for effecting a positive influence in the classroom. In their book on effective classrooms, Squires, Huitt, and Segars maintain that specific functions are crucial within the supervisory role.

> Every supervisor should be proficient in observing classrooms, conferencing, and planning with teachers to improve performance in these areas. Supervision that is practiced in this way *can* make a difference.[22]

Figure 2–4 depicts the supportive relationship that supervision can have with the effective classroom. The principal as supervisor has the major responsibility for communicating the overall school goals to the teachers as part of the evaluation process. The teacher's role is to provide students with time to learn and content to learn in ways that promote success. By observing students in the classroom, both the teacher and the supervisor can determine whether planned improvements have worked. It is the students' behavior that determines what teacher behavior is needed. Supervision, then, is focused on improving professional performance so as to deliver the valued outcomes of the school. One generally accepted value is increased student achievement.

---

[22]D. Squires, W. Huitt, and J. Segars, *Effective Schools and Classrooms: A Research-Based Perspective* (Alexandria, VA: ASCD, 1985) p. 25.

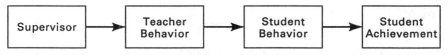

FIGURE 2-4. Supervisory relationship for the effective classroom.

Four-Step Cycle

Clinical supervision was popularized by Cogen in the mid-1970s.[23] Since then, its effectiveness has been documented by Sullivan,[24] and it has been found by Squires, Huitt, and Segars to be particularly suited to use in the effective conscious classroom.[25]

The model itself consists of at least four steps: (1) preconference, (2) classroom observation, (3) analysis and reflection, and (4) postconference. Before using the clinical supervision model, both teachers and principals should be trained in the format. Agreement should be reached on the use of the model by the teachers' organization and school authorities.

Preconference

The preconference is a "get acquainted" step, during which the supervisor and the teacher review the ground rules. Several conditions should be examined at this meeting. First, the goals for the upcoming classroom observation must be set. These goals should be consistent with the overall goals of the school and should be mutually agreed upon by the supervisor and the teacher. If this preconference is not the first meeting for the two parties, the goals should be consistent with those set at previous observation cycles. Second, specific data-collection methods are reviewed to determine whether they are appropriate for the goals to be accomplished. Third, a time should be set for the visit, with a view toward observing the problems discussed. Fourth, the place where the supervisor will be seated during the classroom visit should be determined. The seat should afford the supervisor maximum opportunity to see the whole class but should not be a distraction to the teacher and students.

Observation

During the observation, the supervisor collects student-based data. As Squires points out:

[23]M. Cogan, *Clinical Supervision* (Boston: Houghton-Mifflin, 1973).
[24]C. Sullivan, *Clinical Supervision* (Alexandria, VA: ASCD, 1980).
[25]Squires, *Effective Schools.*

Because students are generally the best source of evidence that learning is taking place, the supervisor is advised to spend time looking for and recording student patterns.[26]

The instrument used for data collection is important. It is a reflection of the specific student behaviors that the school system has identified as important to learning. Instruments that help to record the extent to which students attend to learning are most beneficial. An example of such an instrument will be discussed later in this section.

The supervisor should also note any ideas about the observation. These ideas can then be discussed with the teacher at the postconference. When leaving the classroom, the supervisor should remain as inconspicuous as possible. Comments about the observation should be reserved for the postconference, which can be scheduled by the teacher in the following few days. The supervisor should provide a copy of the collected data for the teacher. During the period between the observation and the postconference, both the teacher and the supervisor should be analyzing the data.

Analysis

The teacher should use two sets of notes to guide the analysis of the data; one set is provided by the supervisor as a result of his observation, and the other is the teacher's own set of notes on student patterns, made some time after the supervisor's visit. After carefully reflecting on both sets of notes, the teacher will have an informed basis for the postconference discussion.

Meanwhile, the supervisor should be conducting an analysis of the data with a view toward any positive patterns that appeared to assist student learning. Both teacher and supervisor should relate their analyses to the goals they identified at the preconference. If these steps are taken, a more productive postconference can be expected.

Postconference

Everything comes together during the postconference. The work of both parties is shared so that meanings of the observed behavior can be agreed upon. Once agreement is reached, the professional role performance of both teacher (as the students' leader in learning) and supervisor (as a helpful evaluator) usually improves. Because of the importance of the postconference step, it is advisable to use some

[26]*Ibid.*, p. 31.

specific format. The Champagne-Morgan conference strategy,[27] shown in Figure 2–5, is one example of a postconference format.

Five Phases of Long-Term Clinical Supervision

The four-step cycle in clinical supervision provides a framework for solving a specific instructional problem with a teacher or conducting an annual evaluation. But in the professional lives of principals and teachers, there will be many problems to be solved and many annual teacher evaluations. Just as the experiences of any colleagues change over the years, so do those of teachers and their supervisors. The supervisory experience, then, is made up of many four-step cycles. Over the long term, the teacher and the supervisor can be guided by a conceptual framework, which will assist them in making meaning out of the longer relationship. The conceptual framework "five phases of a supervisory experience," has been outlined through the work of Squires, Huitt, and Segars.[28] The five phases are (1) entrance, (2) diagnosis, (3) technical success, (4) personal and professional meaning, and (5) reintegration. Details of each phase follow.

Entrance

At the entrance phase, some structure for the supervisory process must be established. The four-step clinical supervision model is one such structure. Regardless of the model chosen, the supervisor and the teacher must understand the process. They must feel competent in applying the process to their situation—hence the importance of inservice training. The supervisor should make every effort to minimize the teacher's feeling of being overly subordinate throughout the process. The relationship should be that of colleague to colleague, rather than boss to underling. When the teacher's anxiety is lessened, there is a greater chance that the necessary changes will be made.

Diagnosis

The task of the diagnosis phase is for teacher and supervisor to agree upon an area of professional improvement for the teacher. Because this phase is a very sensitive point in the development of the teacher–supervisor relationship, the supervisor must exercise caution.

[27]D. Champagne and C. Hogan, "A Competency-Based Training Program for Middle Managers of the Educational System," *Supervisory and Management Skills* 2 (1978):423–436.
[28]*Ibid.,* p. 31.

Phase I: Setting Goals and Commitments to a Goal

Step 1.   Objectives are specified/reviewed: *"We decided to take a look at two patterns in your teaching."*

Step 2.   All data relating to objectives are shared: *"Let's talk for a few minutes about how you see this and how I see it given the data we already have, before we begin to suggest ways to deal with it."*

Step 3.   Agreement is made to focus on "key" objectives: *"This seems to be the key issue that we can begin to work on today."*

Step 4.   Agreement is made that some behavior changes are appropriate: *"Am I right that you want to try to do that differently?"*

Phase II: Generation and Selection of Procedures or Behavior

Step 5.   Positive, appropriate behaviors in the setting related to the objectives are identified and reinforced: *"What was that neat thing you did today? Perhaps we can build the new procedure on that."*

Step 6.   Alternative behaviors or reemphases are identified and examined: *"Before we decide what we are going to do, let's try to think of three or four different ways to approach this."*

Step 7.   An alternative behavior is selected: *"Which one of these ideas do you think seems the best one to begin working with?"*

Step 8.   Detailed implementation plans for the selected alternative are completed: *"Now that we've selected a way to go, our next step is to plan in detail what that means."*

Step 8a.   (If appropriate) Plans made are practiced or role-played. *"Try out Steps 1 and 3 of this process on me here, now. We may need more work on it."*

Phase III. Commitments and Criteria of Success Are Specified

Step 9.   Criteria for successful implementation of selected behavior are decided and agreed on: *"Will you suggest some ways we can measure or know whether our plans are working?"*

Step 10.   Feedback is shared on purposes, commitments, and perceptions of the conference: *"We have worked on _____ today. What do you think we have accomplished?"*

Step 11.   Commitments of both parties are reviewed: *"Okay, here is what I have promised to do, and here is what I think you have promised to do. Do you agree?"*

Conference Terminates.

FIGURE 2–5.   The Champagne-Morgan conference strategy.   From D. Champagne and C. Hogan, "A Competency Based Training Program for Middle Managers of the Educational System," *Supervisory and Management Skills* 2(1978): 423–36. Used with permission of the authors.

He must be aware that his definition of the problem will not simply be accepted by the teacher without question. The teacher must feel a part ownership in the identification of the problem. To avoid this pitfall, the supervisor should begin the diagnosis phase with only a general outline. The identification of specific problems should be left for joint sessions with the teacher in which mutuality can be established.

In addition to problem identification, the diagnosis phase includes data collection. Data is collected in order to validate the problem initially identified. The supervisor and teacher should not proceed until the data confirm that the problem exists. Data collection will typically focus on the teacher's interaction with students.

Technical Success

The third phase in the development of a long-term supervisory relationship is the recognition of technical success. At this phase the teacher actually implements the ideas that have been suggested through the teacher–supervisor relationship. As with previous phases, it is important that the teacher feel as though he is a major factor in deciding how the new teaching strategies will be applied. The supervisor initiates active interventions in areas where the teacher needs assistance. In addition, the supervisor brings to bear all of the resources at her disposal in order to give the teacher the best chance of succeeding with the improved instructional patterns.

Technical success is supported in an environment in which mistakes can be made without fear of failure, and in which feelings can be explored without questioning the worth of individuals. The relationship focuses on future improvements, rather than on detailed analysis of past mistakes.[29] Technical success centers on improving students' learning, and the supervisory experience should be judged on those terms.

Personal Meaning

At the fourth phase, the process changes from a focus on the teacher's interaction with students to an examination of the personal meaning that has come out of the improved professional practice. The recognition of personal meaning enables the teacher and the supervisor to deepen their relationship and thus provides for a richer professional practice in the future.

What has the teacher learned? What has the supervisor learned? This shift to the personal level helps both parties to use their experiences as a resource for improved performance. The exploration of personal meaning is a vehicle for professional growth. Professional growth, not personal growth is the end product.

[29]*Ibid.*, p. 38.

Reintegration

The final phase, reintegration, is the "capping off" phase. The teacher now can examine with satisfaction all that has been learned from the process. Improved classroom performance can be enjoyed. The supervisor can reflect on what has been learned about the supervisory process.

OBSERVATION INSTRUMENTATION

Earlier in this section, the importance of the classroom observation was discussed. Any classroom observation should center on the collection of data about students' behavior patterns—specifically those patterns that can affect learning. In making an observation, the supervisor must be aided by a well-constructed instrument that will serve the goals of the process.

Effective-classrooms research has identified students' *time on task* as an important variable in the improvement of instruction. Therefore, the systematic observation of time on task can be helpful to the supervisory process. Several researchers have developed instruments that are highly sensitive.[30] However, the extensive training required for the use of these instruments can be a drawback. Seifert and Beck[31] have introduced an instrument that is well suited to time-on-task observation and that can be put into use almost immediately. The supervisor can learn to use the instrument in a matter of minutes. Figure 2-6 shows the student observation form (SOF).

The SOF will collect data in six student behavior categories:

Strategy. This teacher behavior reflects the percentage of allocated time dedicated to each instructional strategy. For example, the recorded results of the instructional behaviors might indicate that 80 percent of the students' engaged learning time is being spent in the lecture/discussion setting.

Learning objective. This teacher behavior clarifies whether the teacher is teaching the identified objective.

Learner moves. The nine student behaviors identified in this category generate data about student engaged and nonengaged learning activities. The data will provide information about the number of minutes and

---

[30]See generally, D. Medley, H. Coker, and R. Soar, *Measurement-Based Evaluation of Teacher Performance: An Empirical Approach* (New York, NY: Longman, 1984), and J. Stallings, *Some How To's for Peer Observation and Observation Instruments* (Nashville: Peabody Center for Effective Teaching, 1985).

[31]E. H. Seifert and J. J. Beck, "Time-On-Task Observations: How Principals Can Improve Instruction," *NASSP Bulletin* (April 1984):29–34.

Teacher: _____ Date: _____ Time: _____

		CYCLE 1						CYCLE 2						CYCLE 3					
S		L	L	L	L	L	L	L	L	L	L	L	L	L	L	L	L	L	L
T		S	S	S	S	S	S	S	S	S	S	S	S	S	S	S	S	S	S
R		D	D	D	D	D	D	D	D	D	D	D	D	D	D	D	D	D	D
T		U	U	U	U	U	U	U	U	U	U	U	U	U	U	U	U	U	U
O		Y	Y	Y	Y	Y	Y	Y	Y	Y	Y	Y	Y	Y	Y	Y	Y	Y	Y
B		N	N	N	N	N	N	N	N	N	N	N	N	N	N	N	N	N	N
		R	R	R	R	R	R	R	R	R	R	R	R	R	R	R	R	R	R
	E	S	S	S	S	S	S	S	S	S	S	S	S	S	S	S	S	S	S
L		C	C	C	C	C	C	C	C	C	C	C	C	C	C	C	C	C	C
N		D	D	D	D	D	D	D	D	D	D	D	D	D	D	D	D	D	D
R		I	I	I	I	I	I	I	I	I	I	I	I	I	I	I	I	I	I
	N	W	W	W	W	W	W	W	W	W	W	W	W	W	W	W	W	W	W
M		O	O	O	O	O	O	O	O	O	O	O	O	O	O	O	O	O	O
V		X	X	X	X	X	X	X	X	X	X	X	X	X	X	X	X	X	X
E		T	T	T	T	T	T	T	T	T	T	T	T	T	T	T	T	T	T
		M	M	M	M	M	M	M	M	M	M	M	M	M	M	M	M	M	M
I		I	I	I	I	I	I	I	I	I	I	I	I	I	I	I	I	I	I
N		Y	Y	Y	Y	Y	Y	Y	Y	Y	Y	Y	Y	Y	Y	Y	Y	Y	Y
T																			

Codes:

Strategy (STRT)
L: Lecture/Discussion
S: Small Group
D: Directed Study (Self-Paced)
U: Other

Objectives (OB)
Y: On the objective
N: Not on the objective

Learner Moves (LNR MVE)
R: Engaged written
S: Engaged oral (spoken)
C: Engaged covert (listening, thinking)
D: Engaged receiving directions
I: Not engaged, interim activity
W: Not engaged, waiting for help
O: Not engaged, off-task
X: Waiting for lesson to start
T: Transition
M: Management

Interruptions (INT)
I: Interruptions from outside class-room
Y: Discipline problems in class

FIGURE 2–6. Student observation form.   From Edward H. Seifert and John J. Beck, "Time-on-Task Observations: How Principals Can Improve Instruction." *NASSP Bulletin,* (April 1984): 31. Used with permission of *NASSP Bulletin.*

the percentage of student time on task. For example, the data from the observation instrument will tell the principal and teacher how much time the student is spending writing, listening, waiting for help, and so on.

Interruption. Incidents such as intercom interruptions, class officer elections, candy sales, and discipline cases are recorded in this category as interruptive behaviors. Differentiation of discipline interruptions from other types of interruptions will provide more useful information for both teacher and principal.[32]

For purposes of analysis, it may be helpful to consider a hypothetically completed SOF. Figure 2–7 reveals at least five items of interest.

Analysis of Completed SOF

1. The teacher began the class with seven minutes of noninstruction. Students were left to their own imagination for something to do. Evidence: Three discipline interruptions during the seven minutes of off-task management.
2. The teacher varied the instructional strategy but used the small group activity ineffectively. Evidence: During the small group work, the teacher stood in the middle of the group instead of moving around the periphery of the groups.
3. The strategy of block-of-time seatwork in Cycle 5 does not fit the learning styles or ability levels of the students in the class. Evidence: The majority (five of six) of students are off task during the seatwork directions and at the beginning of the seatwork. Three incidents of discipline interruptions occurred during seatwork initiation.
4. The teacher was off the stated objective. Evidence: The teacher was off the objective for fourteen of the minutes in the example. Students were off task when the teacher was off the subject.
5. The teacher's classroom management techniques need to be improved. Evidence: A total of eight discipline interruptions occurred during the thirty-minute observation. Each time a discipline interruption occurs, the entire class is placed in an off-task mode.

The supervisor should collect using the SOF for a minimum of two student observations before discussing the results with the teacher. Once the data are gathered, it is the responsibility of the principal, in conjunction with the teacher, to identify strategies to solve the instructional problems.[33]

[32]*Ibid.,* pp. 32–33.
[33]*Ibid.,* p. 33.

FIGURE 2–7. Completed student observation form. From Edward H. Seifert and John J. Beck, "Time-on-Task Observations: How Principals Can Improve Instruction." *NASSP Bulletin,* (April 1984): 32. Used with permission of *NASSP Bulletin.*

The authors of the SOF suggest that the supervisor be guided by six steps in using the instrument.

- Identify the teacher's objective for the observation period. This information should be in the teacher's lesson plan.
- Identify five students in the class for concentrated observation. Each student should be observed for one minute on a rotating schedule so that each student is observed 10 times during the 55-minute class period. The students selected for observation should be average achievers.
- Chart the students' behavior from the beginning of the class period to the end of the class period.
- Use the observation form to chart the students' engaged learning time behavior.
- Analyze the results of the data collected during the classroom observation.
- Discuss the results of the time-on-task observation with the teacher.[34]

VARIABLES THE PRINCIPAL CAN CONTROL FROM OUTSIDE THE CLASSROOM

As was noted at the beginning of this chapter, not every principal operates as a classroom supervisor. However, there are ways in which the principal can help improve the instructional program without setting foot in the classroom. Again, the principal should attempt to increase the amount of time allotted to learning versus extraneous activity. Seifert and Beck have recommended the following:

- Reduce the use of intercom interruptions for messages to teachers and students. For each minute of such interruption, it takes five minutes for the students to return to on-task activities.
- Limit the number of personal interruptions by office aides, secretaries, and students. This requires principals to make sure that unnecessary classroom contacts are not made.
- Reduce the number of pep assemblies, entertainment programs, and special-interest programs. A great deal of learning time is lost during assemblies, and programs. For example, if ten 30-minute pep assemblies are held during football season, five hours of instruction are lost. This amounts to one day of allocated learning time just for football pep assemblies. The intention is not to suggest elimination of the activity program, but merely to point out an area that may need some consideration.
- Reduce student absenteeism by vigorously pursuing students whose attendance is less than desirable. Students cannot learn when learning time is reduced by classroom interruptions, assemblies, and absences. It

[34]*Ibid.,* p. 32.

is little wonder that the results of basic skill testing and achievement scores have declined. The average student learning time is reduced from 175 days to 135 days because of the aforementioned items. This amounts to a 33 percent loss in allocated learning time.[35]

In a paper presented at the national convention of the National Association of Secondary School Principals, Irwin outlined thirteen steps that principals can take to improve classroom instruction.

Planning Phase

1. Develop a model of goals for the clinical supervision of instruction to be used in classroom observations.
2. Increase the *number* of teacher-classroom observations per semester or year.
3. Work cooperatively with planning teams composed of department heads and teachers for the development of clear, precise long-range (general) and short-range (specific) instructional objectives based upon real and perceived needs.

Context for Assessment of Instruction

4. Make sure that classrooms are "clean, well-lighted" places for learning.
5. Encourage classroom displays that are current and that reflect the work of learning units developed cooperatively by teachers and students.

Observing Instruction

6. Emphasize and provide for in-service training.
7. Oversee the development of course syllabi by each and every teacher stemming from previously stated educational objectives; randomly review lesson plans.
8. Ensure the assignment of homework on a daily basis.
9. Introduce teachers to innovative teaching strategies.
10. Encourage teachers to take the time to work with students on test-taking skills.
11. Offer feedback to students and parents on test results (teacher-made or standardized).
12. Check on teachers' attendance-taking styles.
13. Make certain that the basic skills (reading, writing) are emphasized in all student work; insist upon accuracy and neatness.[36]

Use of the thirteen steps does not require that the principal actually perform in the role of classroom observer. These suggestions

---

[35]*Ibid.*, pp. 30–32.

[36]C. C. Irwin, "What Research Tells the Principal About Instruction" (Paper delivered at the annual convention of the National Association of Secondary-School Principals, Annual Convention, February 4, 1984), p. 16.

can easily be adopted by the principal of the larger secondary school. "Extra-classroom" variables can be used along with the clinical supervisory model by principals in smaller schools.

The role of the principal in the effective classroom is focused supervision. For those responsible for smaller schools, the clinical supervision model can be an effective method of improving instruction. Those who are responsible for much larger schools can require that department heads or assistant principals employ the clinical supervision approach. In addition, principals in both small and larger schools can use a number of "extra-classroom" controls that will enhance the learning experience. Principals of every type and in every setting have some opportunity to exert a positive influence on the effective classroom.

DEALING WITH RESISTANCE

In the preceding section, there was an assumption that teachers have already accepted the research on effective classrooms. However, some teachers will resist the change to the use of clinical supervision to improve teaching performance despite having participated in inservice programs on effective-classrooms research. The resistance simply may not have surfaced during the training sessions. How can the principal deal effectively with the teacher who will not cooperate? This section will explain the nature of resistance and explore techniques for dealing with the reluctant teacher.

The principal should view an expression of resistance as a warning sign. Resistance to change may be based on one or more of the following factors:

Habit: Habit is the human tendency to behave in the same way that one has always behaved. The familiar becomes a form of security. Proposed change challenges this security, and the challenge is frequently met with resistance.[37] Teachers are fearful of relinquishing familiar practices, particularly if they have used these practices for many years.

The simplest solution for the principal dealing with this factor is to help the teacher form new and more desirable habits to replace the old ones. The principal should assist teachers in discovering the sim-

[37] G. Watson, "Resistance to Change," in *Concepts for Social Change,* ed. G. Watson (Washington, DC: National Training Laboratory, 1966), p. 13.

ilarity between the old and the new procedures and should sincerely praise each accomplishment in the course of the supervision process.

Incentive: If teachers are to change their performance, they must have the right incentive. It is naive to assume that everyone will participate out of "dedication." Incentives might include additional pay, leadership status, inservice credits, scholarships for graduate courses, staff recognition procedures, professional counseling services, secretarial assistance, teacher aides, parent volunteers, or student teachers.

Incentives should be planned as part of an overall program toward change. Most desirable would be a policy at the school-board level that establishes incentives as part of the total instructional program. This commitment requires some budgetary provision.

Lacking support from higher levels, the principal can still provide incentives to teachers in order to assist change. *Time* is a potent incentive. Time is needed within the working day. Adequate time must be available to accommodate new performance skills in addition to necessary tasks. Time should be allocated as a regular part of the work day and year. The use of time must be creative, participatory, an integral to the individual.[38] Even if it's simply being relieved of playground duty or lunchroom supervision, time off for the classroom teacher will aid the principal in implementing a change in instruction.

Different Theories of Education: Many teachers have strong beliefs about educational procedures and are not willing to support practices that are contrary to their beliefs. Other teachers may simply have a different opinion about whether a change is needed. They may question whether it will accomplish all that the principal claims, or they may have a different assessment of how much improvement would actually occur if the change were implemented.[39]

The principal might convert "doubters" by presenting the conclusive literature on effective-classroom research. The principal might also cite other schools that have had success with the effective-classroom approach.

The teachers who are resisting change because of a difference in theoretical outlook are more difficult to persuade and require a more sophisticated approach. The principal can approach the problem by showing teachers that their espoused theory of education differs from

[38]L. J. Bishop, *Staff Development and Instructional Improvement* (Boston: Allyn & Bacon, 1976), p. 16.
[39]R. A. Gorton, *School Administration and Supervision* (Dubuque, IA: Wm. C. Brown, 1980), p. 301.

their actual classroom practice. The fact that these teachers may not be aware of the incongruence between their theories and their practice is the key to converting these teachers.

Incongruence between practice and espoused theory poses a dilemma. Teachers, for example, may share the same espoused theory regarding self-concept, but their pattern of questioning, their use of negative feedback, their marking on the bell curve, and their insistence on standard requirements may reveal a practice that is incongruent with the espoused theory. The social studies teacher who believes in and teaches a course in American democracy in a totalitarian manner represents another example of incongruency between practiced and espoused theory.[40]

Sergiovanni explains that incongruence between practice and espoused theory poses a dilemma to the teacher. Faced with the dilemma, the teacher becomes uncomfortable and begins to search for solutions. It is at this point that the principal stands the best chance of converting the teacher. The principal proceeds to provide the solution for the teacher by introducing effective-classroom innovations. Thus, the teacher uses the principal's theory to replace his own incongruent theory.

In order to understand the approach, it is helpful to conceptualize the relationship between what is known and not known about teachers' theories with the aid of the *Johari window* (Figure 2-8).

The Johari window depicts the relationship between the teacher and the clinical supervisor (the principal). The relationship revolves around aspects of the teacher's educational theories known to self and others, known to self but not others, not known to self but known to others, and not know to self or others. Four cells are depicted in the Johari window, each representing a different combination of what the teacher knows or does not know about his teaching as contrasted with what the supervisor knows and does not know about that teacher's performance.

In the first cell, the public or open self, the teacher's knowledge of his teaching behavior and other aspects of his professional practices corresponds with the supervisor's knowledge. This is the area in which communication is most effective and in which the need for the teacher to be defensive, to assume threat, is minimal. The clinical supervisor works with the teacher to enlarge this cell.

In the second cell, the hidden or secret self, the teacher knows about aspects of his teaching behavior and professional practice that

---

[40]T. J. Sergiovanni and R. J. Starratt, *Supervision Human Perspectives,* 3d ed. (New York: McGraw-Hill, 1983), p. 306.

	What the supervisor knows about the teacher	What the supervisor does not know about the teacher
What the teacher knows about himself	Public or open self 1	Hidden or secret self 2
What the teacher does not know about himself	Blind self 3	Undiscovered or subconscious self 4

FIGURE 2–8. The Johari window. From Joseph Luft, *Group Processes* (Mountain Veiw, CA: Mayfield, 1984). Used with permission of Mayfield Publishing Company.

the supervisor does not know about. Often the teacher conceals these aspects from the supervisor for fear that the supervisor might use this knowledge to punish, hurt, or exploit the teacher. The second cell suggests the importance of a supervisory climate characterized by trust and credibility to the success of clinical supervision. The teacher is encouraged in clinical supervision to reduce the size of this cell.

In the third cell, the blind self, the supervisor knows about aspects of the teacher's behavior and professional practice of which the teacher is unaware. This cell, though initially large is reduced considerably as clinical supervision develops and matures. This is the cell most often neglected by traditional teacher-evaluation methods.

In the fourth cell, the undiscovered self, aspects of teacher behavior and professional practice not known to either teacher or supervisor are hidden.

In his book *School Administration and Supervision,* Gorton suggests twelve generalizations for reducing the incidence of resistance among teachers:

1. Resistance will be less if administrators and managers [and, one might add, other participants] feel that the project is their own—not one devised and operated by outsiders.
2. Resistance will be less if the project innovation clearly has whole-hearted support from top officials of the system.

3. Resistance will be less if the participants see the change as reducing rather than increasing their present burdens.
4. Resistance will be less if the project accords with values already acknowledged by participants.
5. Resistance will be less if the program offers the kind of new experience which interests participants.
6. Resistance will be less if participants feel their autonomy and security is not threatened.
7. Resistance will be less if participants have joined in diagnostic efforts leading them to agree on what the basic problem is and to feel its importance.
8. Resistance will be less if the project is adopted by consensual group decision.
9. Resistance will be less if proponents are able to empathize with opponents, to recognize valid objections, and to take steps to relieve unnecessary fears.
10. Resistance will be reduced if it is recognized that innovations are likely to be misunderstood and misinterpreted, and if provision is made for feedback of perceptions of the project and for further clarification of need.
11. Resistance will be reduced if participants experience acceptance, support, trust and confidence in their relations with one another.
12. Resistance will be reduced if the project is kept open to revision and reconsideration if experience indicates that changes will be desirable.[41]

Perhaps the most comprehensive synopsis of factors that affect the introduction of change in teaching practice was developed by Lippitt in 1967. Figure 2–9 categorizes much of what has been discussed in this section.

It should be evident that most factors related to change resistance are personal characteristics. The wise principal knows all staff members well, understands their individual differences, and gauges the growth of each teacher in terms of his own peculiar growth pattern rather than by comparing it to that of the group.

SUMMARY

The research on teaching has produced several factors that can be considered essential for an effective classroom: (1) teacher attention to student characteristics, (2) teacher attention to content goals and to

[41]Gorton, *School Administration,* pp. 302–303.

Facilitating Forces	*Hindering Forces*

1. Characteristics of the Practice

A. Relevant to universal student problems	A. Does not meet the needs of a class
B. Can be done a little at a time	B. Requires a lot of energy
C. Consultant and peer help available, needed skills are clearly outlined	C. Requires new skills
D. Clearly aids student growth	D. Requires change in teacher values
E. A behaviorial change with no new gimmicks	E. Requires new facilities
F. Built in evaluation to see progress	F. Won't work
G. Innovation has tried a new twist	G. Not new
H. Student, not subject, oriented	H. Not for my grade level or subject
I. No social practice can be duplicated exactly	I. Effectiveness reduced if practice gains general use

2. Physical and Temporal Arrangements

A. Staff meetings used for professional growth, substitutes hired to free teacher(s) to visit other classrooms, lunchtime used for discussions, students sent home for an afternoon so teachers can all meet together	A. No time to get together
B. Extra clerical help provided	B. Too many clerical duties to have time to share ideas
C. Staff meetings for everyone to get together, occasionally; grade level or departmental meetings	C. Classrooms are isolated
D. Meetings held in classrooms	D. No rooms to meet in

3. Peer and Authority Relations

A. Sharing sessions or staff bulletins become a matter of school routine	A. Little communication among teachers
B. Public recognition given to innovators and adopters: innovation-diffusion seen as a cooperative task	B. Competition for prestige among teachers
C. Sharing ideas is expected and rewarded; norms support asking for and giving help; regular talent search for new ideas	C. Norms enforce privatism

D. Area team liaison supports new ideas

D. Colleagues reject ideas

E. Principal or superintendent supports innovation-diffusion activity

E. Principal is not interested in new ideas

F. Principal helps create a staff atmosphere of sharing and experimentation

F. School climate doesn't support experimentation

G. Staff meetings used as two-way informing and educating sessions

G. Principal doesn't know what's going on

H. Teachers influence the sharing process

H. Teacher ideas don't matter

4. Personal Attitudes

A. Seeking new ways

A. Resisting change

B. Seeking peer and consultant help

B. Fearing evaluation and rejecting failure

C. Always open to adapting and modifying practices

C. Dogmatism about already knowing about new practices

D. Public rewards for professional growth

D. Feeling professional growth not important

E. See groups as endemic and relevant to academic learning

E. Negative feelings about group work

F. Understand connection between mental health and academic learning

F. Mental health is "extra"

G. Optimism

G. Pessimism

H. Test ideas slowly

H. Afraid to experiment

I. Suiting and changing practice to fit one's own style and class

I. Resistance to imitating others

FIGURE 2–9. Forces relevant to the facilitation and hindrance of innovation and diffusion of teaching practices.   From Ronald Lippitt, "The Teacher as Innovator, Seeker, and Sharer of New Practices" in *Perspectives on Educational Change,* ed. Richard I. Miller (New York: Appleton-Century-Crofts, 1967), 310–311. Used with permission of Richard I. Miller.

knowledge assessed, (3) student engagement time, (4) student experience at success, and (5) classroom management.

In order to apply effective-classroom research, instructional models must be used to guide teachers' performance. Two such models are *Direct Instruction,* by Rosenshine, and *Mastery Learning,* by Block and Burns.

The principal's role in the effective classroom is one of clinical supervisor. As clinical supervisor, the principal will use the four step cycle of (1) preconference, (2) classroom observation, (3) analysis and reflection, and (4) postconference. The four-step cycle supports the many short-term relationships the principal must have with teachers.

However, long-term relationships require a different operational framework. Squires, Huitt, and Segars have recommended five phases to the development of the long-term supervisor–teacher relationship. These phases are (1) entrance, (2) diagnosis, (3) technical success, (4) personal and professional meaning, and (5) reintegration.

The principal will discover that some teachers will resist using the findings of effective-classroom research. In dealing with this kind of teacher, it is helpful for the principal to identify the source of the resistance. Teacher resistance may be based on habit, lack of incentive, or differences in theories of education. The principal's approach to converting the resistant teacher must be psychologically astute. One approach is to show these teachers that the theory they espouse is different from the theory that they practice. The principal may be aided in the analysis of what the teacher knows about his own practice by the use of the Johari window.

SELECTED BIBLIOGRAPHY

BLOOM, BENJAMIN, *Human Characteristics and Student Learning,* New York: McGraw-Hill, 1976.

BRADY, M. E., C. CLINTON, J. M. SWEENEY, M. PETERSON AND H. POYNOR, *Instructional Dimensions Study,* Washington, DC: Kirschner Associates, Inc., 1977.

COGAN, M., *Clinical Supervision,* Boston, MA: Houghton-Mifflin, 1973.

GORTON, RICHARD A., *School Administration and Supervision,* Dubuque, IA: Wm. C. Brown Co., 1980.

GUTHRIE, JAMES W. AND RODNEY J. REED, *Educational Administration and Policy: Effective Leadership for American Education,* Englewood Cliffs, NJ: Prentice-Hall, Inc., 1986.

HUITT, WILLIAM G. AND JOHN K. SEGARS, *Characteristics of Effective Classrooms,* Philadelphia, PA: Research for Better Schools, Inc., 1980.

MEDLEY, DONALD, HOMER COKER AND ROBERT SOAR, *Measurement-Based Evaluation of Teacher Performance: An Empirical Approach,* New York: Longman, 1984.

MORPHET, EDGAR L., ROE L. JOHNS, AND THEODORE L. RELLER, *Educational Organization and Administration: Concepts, Practices and Issues (4th ed.),* Englewood Cliffs, NJ: Prentice-Hall, Inc., 1982.

REBORE, R. W., *Educational Administration: A Management Approach,* Englewood Cliffs, NJ: Prentice-Hall, Inc., 1985.

SERGIOVANNI, THOMAS J., *Educational Governance and Administration (2nd ed.),* Englewood Cliffs, NJ: Prentice-Hall, Inc., 1987.

SERGIOVANNI, THOMAS J. AND ROBERT J. STARRATT, *Supervision Human Perspectives (3rd ed.),* New York: McGraw-Hill Book Co., 1983.

SQUIRES, DAVID, WILLIAM HUITT, AND JOHN SEGARS, *Effective Schools and Classrooms: A Research-Based Perspective,* Alexandria, VA: ASCD, 1985.

STALLINGS, JANE, *Some How To's for Peer Observation and Observation Instruments,* Nashville, TN: Peabody Center for Effective Teaching, 1983.

SULLIVAN, C., *Clinical Supervision,* Alexandria, VA: ASCD, 1980.

3

Decision Making

The importance of decision making in the administration of organizations was recognized as early as 1938 in the writings of Barnard.[1] In 1947, Simon conceived of decision making as the most critical aspect of administration:

> If any "theory" is involved, it is that decision making is the heart of administration and that the vocabulary of administration theory must be derived from the logic and psychology of human choice. . . . The task of "deciding" pervades the entire administrative organization quite as much as the task of doing—indeed, it is integrally tied up with the latter. A general theory of administration must include principles of organization that will insure correct decision making, just as it must include principles that will insure effective action.[2]

Knezevich has provided a simple but useful starting point for understanding decision making. He, too, defined decision making as: *a conscious choice from among a well-defined set of often competing alternatives.*[3] In making educational decisions, the principal should address *what* is the subject of the decision, *who* must be involved in making the decision, and *how* the decision should be made.

Knowing the *what* is a matter of accurately identifying an administrative functional area, such as personnel, curriculum and instruction, finance, or school–community relations. Identifying *who* should be involved requires that the principal know whether any combination of teachers, parents, students, or other administrators need to be consulted. The *how* of the decision concerns the actual process used by the principal to arrive at an ultimate solution.

This chapter will explore the variety of aspects that the principal must consider in decision making. First, appropriate models of decision making will be introduced (what). Second, these models will suggest which process might be used given the type of decision to be made (how). Finally, the specific roles that the effective principal might assume in decision making will be analyzed as the "principal-as-a-person" is considered.

MODELS OF DECISION MAKING

We must discuss models of decision making before we can examine the actual process of making the decision. The model that is used can

---

[1]C. Barnard, *Functions of the Executive* (Cambridge, MA: Harvard Press, 1938).
[2]H. Simon, *Administrative Behavior* (New York: Macmillan, 1950) p. XIV.
[3]S. Knezevich, *Administration of Public Education,* (New York: Harper & Row, Pub., 1975), p. 32.

explain why certain administrators proceed by "shooting from the hip" while others retire to a state of solemn contemplation. The model provides the philosophical base for establishing certain decision-making practices.

A review of the literature suggests that there are as many as six decision-making models. In their book on educational administration, Sergiovanni and colleagues point to the following possible models: calculative (or rational), collegial, incremental (or muddling through), political bargaining, charisma, and garbage can.[4] Each model assumes a certain position on the extent to which the decision-making participants agree or disagree on the "means" and the "ends" of the process. Certain models can be more useful than others, depending upon which combination of agreement or disagreement toward the means and ends exist. Table 3-1 outlines which model might be used with which situation.

Calculative Model

The calculative model has its roots in the concept of rationality. It can be traced to Dewey's work on the scientific approach to solving problems. Briefly, the decision maker decides what needs to be done, looks at all the possible choices, compares the consequences of each choice, then chooses the best alternative. The calculative model assumes that

1. Problems can be clearly defined.
2. Alternatives can be described as a result of a sufficient search.
3. Consequences of each alternative can be discovered.
4. The relative success of each alternative can be weighted.
5. The weighting of alternatives can produce a ranking of the benefits of each possible choice.

TABLE 3-1. Decision Models and Agreement/Disagreement on Means/Ends.

MODEL	SITUATION
1. Calculative	Agreement on means and ends
2. Collegial	Disagreement on means, agreement on ends
3. Incremental	Agreement on means, disagreement on ends
4. Political bargaining	Agreement on means, disagreement on ends
5. Charisma	Disagreement on means and ends
6. Garbage can	Disagreement on means and ends

[4]T. Sergiovanni, M. Burlingame, F. Coombs, and P. Thruston, *Educational Governance and Administration* (Englewood Cliffs, NJ: Prentice-Hall, 1980), pp. 354–368.

While the calculative model is perhaps "the original," it has come under a great deal of criticism. Scholars have maintained that the model does not accurately describe how school administrators make decisions. Perhaps the requirement that the participants agree on both the means and the ends is too much to expect in today's schools. Simon and March have found that (1) principals have limited time to devote to calculative-type deliberations; (2) a high degree of uncertainty exists in the educational environment, and the calculative model depends on accurately knowing conditions; and (3) the behavior of the educational institution is sufficiently clouded as to frustrate the calculative process.[5] Speaking to this last point more specifically, Dill has noted:

> In organizations, lines of authority and responsibility frequently become clouded. Sometimes this confusion is created by different ways people see problems; sometimes confusion is a deliberate device to generate new and different solutions. Regardless of the intent, organizational members and organizational leaders lose control of the calculative process. Factors such as informal processes or special committees upset normal calculative procedures. Often, these organizational processes appear more political than calculative, more bent on gaining power than on finding right answers.[6]

Disappointment with the calculative model provided the catalyst for a number of other models. They will be considered in the sections that follow.

Collegial Model

As Table 3-1 shows, the collegial model would be appropriate when participants disagree on the means but can agree on the ends. For example, teachers are professionally trained to accept certain goals for the sake of educating our nation's youth; however, the method of attaining these goals often differs from teacher to teacher because of experience and teacher-training programs.

Davis found that an important aspect of the collegial model is the use of mutual contributions of the participants.[7] The principal using the collegial model can anticipate that participants will disagree about how to make a choice. Therefore, the goal of the principal would be to

---

[5] J. March, "Business Decision Making," *Readings in Managerial Psychology,* ed. H. Leavitt and L. Pondy (Chicago: University of Chicago Press, 1964), pp. 447–456; and H. Simon, "Thesis of Decision Making in Economics and Behavioral Science," *American Economic Review* 49 (June 1959), pp. 253–283.

[6] Sergiovanni, *Educational Governance,* p. 360.

[7] K. Davis, "Evolving Models of Organizational Behavior," in *Organizational Behavior: A Book of Readings,* ed. K. Davis (New York: McGraw-Hill, 1974), pp. 4–15.

establish integration of thought through teamwork. This might require encouraging people to work in smaller groups or in pairs, with
sharper ideas on how to proceed.

Thompson and Duden found that the collegial model is closely
aligned with the position that employees have a right to participate in
decisions that might influence the profession. This approach is particularly suited to the educational environment. Teachers tend to look
upon themselves as professionals who spend a great deal of time
working independently in their classrooms. While there are both district and building-level requirements for working behavior, the
teacher retains some discretion in carrying out the goals of the institution.

Incremental Model

The incremental model, also known as the "muddling through"
model, suggests that decision making is not a rational science. Formulated by Lindblom,[8] the approach views decision making as a series of
compromises and bargains made in order to reach a solution to a
problem. The original goals in reaching some decision go through
incremental changes. Even the goal itself may change several times
before a solution is reached.

The incremental model is appropriate when there is agreement
on means but disagreement on ends. The approach can be successfully
used in complex situations in which effort to define a single goal tends
to result in disagreement.

Political-Bargaining Model

Ironically, the model that seems to fit teachers and principals
best does not fit those who control from the top—school boards. In
analyzing the Cuban missile crisis, Allison discovered that the decisions of representative organizations, such as Congress, state legislatures, city councils, and school boards, are the result of political bargaining.[9] Solutions are found not by calculation, but rather through
conflict, compromise, and confusion.

As is the case with the incremental model, the political-bargaining approach is typical of a situation in which there is agreement on
means but disagreement on ends. There is an assumption that groups

[8]C. Lindblom, "The Science of Muddling Through," *Public Administration Review*
19–20 (Spring 1959):79–88.

[9]G. Allsion, *Essence of Decision: Explaining the Cuban Missile Crisis* (Boston:
Little, Brown, 1971), pp. 10–38.

can find reasonable means (like parliamentary procedure) while ignoring or deemphasizing differences over goals. Perhaps the divergence in the backgrounds of school board members supports the possibility of disagreement on goals. This phenomenon is less likely among teachers, who have more congruence because of their similar training.

Charisma Model

The notion of charisma can be traced to the turn of the century to the works of sociologist Max Weber. Charisma is a key ingredient of leadership. The charismatic leader is able to change people's views about the world and thus alter their decision-making pattern. This asset would be invaluable in the situation in which there is disagreement about both means and ends. Charisma might be the only thing that would convert a stalemate into a viable solution.

Unfortunately, few principals can rely on charisma, because they often simply don't have it. Those who have the gift of charisma would do well to recognize the utility of the charisma model in successfully resolving what otherwise would prove to be an impossible situation.

Garbage-Can Model

Another approach to dealing with situations in which neither means nor ends can be agreed upon was developed by Cohen and his associates.[10] Cohen recognized that educational organizations have very diverse groups which demand a certain degree of participation. Teachers, parents, students, and administrators all wish to be represented in the decision-making process. How can decisions be reached when there is such divergence? Cohen suggests that problems and solutions are simply dumped into a "garbage can." The mix of problems and solutions in the garbage can is constantly being organized and reorganized.

Solutions in this setting are generally arrived at with ease. Thus there is a tendency to adopt the first available remedy. Cohen calls this "oversight." At times, the garbage-can model supports ignoring a problem until a solution for a different problem appears. The potential for success in solving any problem draws attention away from failures in the unsolved areas. Cohen calls his phenomenon "flight."

The garbage can model can even produce a solution before there is a problem. For example, let's say that the teachers in a particular

---

[10]M. Cohen, J. March, and J. Olsen, "A Garbage Can Model of Organizational Choice," *Administrative Science Quarterly* 17 (March 1972):1–15.

building want a photocopying machine installed in their lounge. Searching for a rationale for this new convenience, the teacher group decides to present the principal with a set of facts that portrays the lack of a photocopying machine as leading to increased frustration among faculty members. In turn, this frustration will have a negative affect on morale. The principal, of course, wishes to prevent this morale problem (real or not) and gives the teachers their copying machine. Therefore, the existence of the solution (copying machine) preceded the problem (lack of morale). The teachers had a solution that was in search of a problem.

Regardless of which decision-making model seems indicated, the principal must be able to apply the model to a particular set of circumstances. In the next section, the detailed process of decision making will be discussed.

THE DECISION-MAKING PROCESS

Dewey's classic work, *How We Think*[11] outlined six steps in making a decision:

1. There must be a situation that calls for a decision before there can be decision making (felt need).
2. It is imperative to define or diagnose the nature of the problem (location and clarification).
3. The problem can be analyzed by gathering data pertinent to it (further clarification).
4. Alternative courses of action must be generated or preferred solutions formulated (suggestion of possible solutions).
5. Each alternative course of action should be appraised, preferably through the use of a model that portrays the essential properties of the phenomenon under study (hypothesizing).
6. Consequences of each possible choice must be examined through sophisticated processes such as cost–benefit analysis or informal consideration of what might happen after the decision is made (mental elaboration).
7. After the choice is rendered and the decision is put into effect, the decision should be evaluated (experimental corroboration).

Modern application of decision-making theory to the field of educational administration was made by Griffiths in his often-cited 1959 book, *Administrative Theory*. Most writers on the decision-making process use Griffith's "six steps" as a foundation for discussion. The steps are as follows:

[11] J. Dewey, *How We Think* (Boston: Heath, 1910).

1. Recognize, define, and limit the problem.
2. Analyze and evaluate the problem.
3. Establish criteria or set standards.
4. Collect data.
5. Select a solution.
6. Put the solution into effect.[12]

Step 1: Recognize, define, and limit the problem.   The first step in the process is to recognize that a problem exists. The principal must avoid reacting too quickly. As the situation is first presented, there is typically inadequate information, coupled with only one person's perception. Once the principal is fairly certain that a problem exists for which a decision may be necessary, the focus can shift to defining the problem with precision.

Gorton has provided some suggestions for aiding the principal in setting the limits of the problem:

1. What is known and unknown about the situation? What other factors must be clarified before a decision can be made?
2. Can anyone else provide additional information or a different perception of the situation? To what extent is the administrator's bias or the biases of others influencing his perception of the circumstances necessitating a decision?
3. Who will be affected by the decision?
4. How serious is the problem or question? How soon must a decision be made?[13]

Step 2: Analyze and evaluate the problem.   After the problem is defined, a thorough analysis of possible alternatives is necessary. One of the alternatives should be to *do nothing*. Leaving the problem alone can be one of the wisest choices. Barnard observed: "The fine art of executive decision making consists of not deciding questions that are not pertinent, in not deciding prematurely, in not making decisions that cannot be made effectively, and in not making decisions that others should make.[14]

The principal must be careful not to fall into the "either–or trap." The inexperienced principal can mistakenly assume that only two alternatives exist, since that is the way the problem is often presented. For example, let's say the Parent–Teachers Association (PTA) presents a proposal to the principal for an elaborate fund-raising carnival to

---

[12]D. Griffiths, *Administrative Theory* (New York: Appleton, 1959), p. 94.
[13]R. Gorton, *School Administration and Supervision,* (Dubuque, IA: Wm. C. Brown, 1980), p. 231.
[14]Barnard, *Functions of the Executive,* p. 194.

take place in the spring. On the surface, it might appear as though the principal must either accept or reject the PTA proposal. However, creative thinking can uncover several other alternatives. The principal might present a counterproposal for a less complicated approach to raising money, such as a bake sale. Further, the principal might decide to buy more time by establishing a committee to study the matter.

Brainstorming with fellow administrators or trusted staff can be an effective way to generate alternatives. Assessment of the feasibility of each alternative should not be part of the brainstorming activity. Rather, assessment of alternatives should come in the next step, after all possible alternatives, no matter how unusual, have been posed. Many potentially fruitful ideas are stifled by premature evaluation.

Step 3: Establish criteria or set standards. After all the options are generated, criteria and standards of judgment must be set so that the success of a decision can be evaluated. The criteria are simply clear statements of the values that must be addressed by an acceptable solution. The criteria should be set in separate categories and then prioritized. One category can be labeled "musts"; another, "wants." All solutions would have to meet the "musts" criteria, while those satisfying the "wants" would be considered nice, but dispensable. It is important to include criteria that are often hidden, such as "group popularity." While the principal does not want to make a decision based solely on its popularity, it is an important variable to keep in mind.

Once the criteria are set, the process of carefully assessing each alternative can begin. Here the principal must try to forecast the possible consequences of each alternative. The consequences must be viewed from two perspectives: (1) How will the alternative be received by those who will be affected? (2) Are the necessary competencies, skills, and resources available to carry out a particular alternative? Predicting the reactions of individuals or groups to a particular alternative can be difficult. In some cases, it may be necessary to "run it up the flagpole" in order to elicit reactions. The question of sufficient competencies may even be more crucial than that of reaction. There is nothing so unpleasant as making a decision to follow a course of action, only to discover later that the idea cannot be fully implemented.

Step 4: Collect data. At this step, the principal must collect reliable and bias-free information from as many sources as possible. This is when the principal's listening and interpersonal communication skills will be important. Partin has suggested that four questions be posed throughout the data-collection process.[15] These questions improve information gathering:

1. What are the facts I already have?
2. What else do I need to know?
3. Whom can I ask?
4. What should I ask?

Asking trusted colleagues what their experience has been in solving similar problems can be helpful. If the principal has kept up with the professional literature, the increased knowledge can provide a reliable backdrop for information gathering on the specific problem.

Step 5: Select a solution.   If the previous steps have been properly followed, the principal can begin evaluating each of the alternatives with an eye toward choosing the best. There will be no perfect solution. Most often, the best solution is the one alternative that can maximize gains and minimize losses.

Throughout step 5, the use of imagination and intuitive hunches about certain alternatives cannot be overlooked. The principal should try to identify these hunches in more specific terms and convert them for systematic use in making the selection. While intuition and previous experience can enter the picture, the principal must not allow personal biases to significantly affect the decision. The principal's preconceived attitude about a person or situation should not be allowed to distort the reality of the current problem.

Step 6: Put the solution into effect.   Implementing the solution may seem automatic, but it can be the most crucial aspect of the decision-making process. The implementation step must begin with a carefully drawn plan. Prior to devising the plan, however, the principal must determine the extent to which those expected to follow the decision will indeed do so. It does the principal no good to make a decision that no one will follow. The principal's ability to persuade others to comply with the decision depends on a number of factors. One factor is the perceived legitimacy of the principal's position within the organization as a decision maker for the particular problem. Those who must follow the decision must perceive the principal as one who has the *right* to make the decision. The *perception* of the followers is what is key—not whether the principal can show that he has the right to decide by pointing to his job description, for example. However, it is possible that

[15]R. Partin, "A Dozen Ways to Enhance Your Decision Making," *NASSP Bulletin* 63 (March 1979):17.

the decision may be followed despite objections, if it is felt that nothing can be done to stop implementation.

Provided that the principal genuinely wishes to have the decision willingly accepted, several options are open for countering resistance. One option for the principal is to either modify or abandon the decision. Another option is to try to change the attitudes of those who must follow the decision. Knowing the exact source of the resistance can help the principal in deciding a course of action for dealing with the problem. Gorton has suggested five avenues to explore in tracing the source of resistance. He believes that resistance can result from

1. The individual's or group's feeling about the administrator as a person, or about the way in which the decision was made.
2. An inaccurate understanding of the way in which the decision will affect the individual or group.
3. Inadequate skill or competency on the part of those who are to carry out the decision.
4. A perception by the individual or group that the decision will cause more personal disadvantages than advantages.
5. An honest disagreement about the merits of the decision, despite the fact that those involved may not feel that they would be adversely affected.[16]

Once resistance, if any, has been handled, the principal can proceed with the implementation plan. Who needs to do what and how must be outlined. Involving support personnel is helpful, as is delegating some of the responsibility for implementation so that the principal's role can be limited to coordination. Gorton has suggested that an effective implementation schedule should include the following:

1. **Planning.** Working out in broad outline the things that need to be done and the methods for doing them to accomplish the purposes set for the enterprise.
2. **Organizing.** Establishing the formal structure of authority through which work subdivisions are arranged, defined, and coordinated for the specific objective.
3. **Staffing.** Selecting and training the staff and maintaining favorable conditions of work.
4. **Directing.** Making decisions and embodying them in orders and instructions; serving as the leader of the enterprise.
5. **Coordinating.** Interrelating the various parts of the work.
6. **Reporting.** Keeping those to whom the executive is responsible informed as to what is taking place; keeping himself and his subordinates informed through records, research, and inspection.

[16]Gorton, *School Administration and Supervision,* p. 235.

7. **Budgeting.** Fiscal planning, accounting, and control.
8. **Evaluation.** Formative and summative.[17]

Throughout the process of decision making, the involvement of others is crucial. The next section will explore the varieties of activities that the principal might consider in involving others in decision making.

How to Involve Others

The quickest and simplest way to encourage group involvement is to call a meeting to discuss the decision to be made. The principal can assemble those who might be most affected by the outcome of the decision. If the principal involves too many who do not have a stake in the decision, the process may be hampered by apathy and the principal may wind up talking to himself.

Even if the correct assembly of people is present, there is always a possibility that those who feel insecure will not fully share their thoughts. By the same token, some people may dominate the meeting, thus preventing shared input to the principal, who must guide the group to a decision.

In recent years, formalized approaches to group decision making have helped minimize some of the negative aspects of discussion meetings. Two such approaches are the Delphi technique and the Nominal Group technique.

Delphi Technique

This technique involves four steps to generating information that can be used to make a group decision:

1. Define the problem to which group response is required.
2. Identify those individuals who need to be in the decision-making group.
3. Solicit responses from the identified group through a questionnaire constructed by the principal.
4. Summarize their responses and share input with the group, asking members to change their responses until there is reasonable consensus.

Since the responses to questions are in writing (and perhaps are even anonymous if the principal so chooses), the quality of information provided is increased. Status and conformity pressures are eliminated. On the other hand, the lack of face-to-face interaction with participants is a criticism of the Delphi Technique.

[17]*Ibid.*, p. 236.

Nominal Group Technique

The Nominal Group Technique (NGT), developed by Delberg and Van de Ven, is a fairly simple approach to the group decision-making process. It usually involves seven steps:

1. Present the problem to the group, either orally or in writing.
2. Ask the group to individually list responses to the problem, taking only a specified amount of time. (During this time, group members keep their responses private.)
3. Ask each member of the group to present one idea from his list and record the idea on a chalkboard or overhead projector.
4. Solicit one idea from each member of the group until all ideas are recorded.
5. Discuss each idea listed.
6. Ask each group member to privately (on paper) rank the listed ideas.
7. Pool rankings to obtain the best ideas from the entire group.

Whether a group decision-making process is used may ultimately depend on the degree of autonomy that is afforded the principal. Group decision making is more often seen in situations in which the superintendent has given the principal ultimate responsibility for coming up with a decision.

Perhaps the greatest advantage of group decision making is that it has the potential to enhance the professionalization of education on every level from the superintendent to the classroom teacher.

PRINCIPAL'S ROLE IN DECISIONS

Griffiths has an interesting perspective on the role of the principal as a decision maker:

> If the executive is personally making decisions, this means there exists malfunction in the decision process. . . . It is not the function of the chief executive to make decisions; it is his function to monitor the decision-making process to make sure that it performs at the optimum level.[18]

Griffiths's point of view emphasizes the need for the principal to consider "deciding not to decide." The role of the principal in nondecision making can be just as crucial as decision making. Whether the principal actually makes the decision or assumes the role of "monitor"

---

[18]Griffiths, *Administrative Theory,* p. 73.

of decisions may depend on the innate decision-making styles of the individual administrator.

Jung's classic works on perception and judgment provide the conceptual base for an approach that the principal might tend to prefer from a personal standpoint. In a redescription of Jung's theory of psychological types, Read and colleagues point out that people differ in *perception* and *judgment*.[19] Perception is how one becomes aware of something. Judgment is reaching conclusions about the perception. Figure 3-1 shows that perception is of two types—sensing and intuitive. Those who prefer *sensing* like well-defined problems with concrete facts. These people are good with routine work and with details, and are present-oriented. Those who prefer the *intuitive* will gravitate toward problems that are more mysterious and require a creative solution. These people are future-oriented.

In the area of judgment, two types are prominent—thinking and feeling. *Thinking* types evaluate by logic and approach problems by searching for facts. The goal of completing the "project" is more important than the resulting effects on people. *Feeling* types approach things on the basis of feelings and values. They are more philosophical, are good listeners, and relate well with staff.

The four ordered pairs of decision styles are the result of Jung's conceptual approach. In a study done by Brightman,[20] it was shown that a majority of school administrators fall into the *sensing/thinking* style, while the *intuitive/feeling* style is less common. Mintzberg's work in leadership roles provides ten categories of behavior that could apply to the principalship. Table 3-2 shows the ten roles grouped into three areas: *interpersonal, informational,* and *decisional.*

FIGURE 3-1. Jung's perception/judgment conception.

		Ordered pairs create observed style
Perception <	Sensing	Sensing/Thinking Style
	Intuitive	Sensing/Feeling Style
		Intuition/Thinking Style
		Intuition/Feeling Style

Judgment < Thinking
            Feeling

[19]H. Read, M. Fordham, and G. Adler, *Carl Jung: Collective Works* (Princeton, NJ: Princeton University Press, 1970).

[20]H. Brightman, "Improving Principals' Performance Through Training in the Decision Sciences," *Educational Leadership* 41 (February 1984):51.

TABLE 3–2. Mintzberg's Leadership Roles.

ROLES	DESCRIPTIONS
Interpersonal	
Figurehead	Obliged to perform routine duties of a legal, ceremonial, or social nature.
Leader	Train and motivate subordinates to perform up to their potential.
Liaison	Maintain network of outside contacts who provide information that cannot be obtained from traditional sources, such as the school's management information system.
Informational	
Monitor	Seeks both written and oral information to understand his internal organization and external environment.
Disseminator	Transmits information, facts, and values from outsiders or subordinates to other members of the organization.
Spokesman	Transmits internal information, facts, and values to outsiders. Speaks on behalf of his organization or discipline.
Decisional	
Entrepreneur	Searches for opportunities to initiate "improvement projects." Is a proactive manager.
Disturbance handler	Solves crisis problems—problems that are characterized as deviations from expectations. Is a reactive manager.
Resource allocator	Makes (or approves of) significant decisions and allocates necessary resources to accomplish improvement projects.
Negotiator	Represents organization at major negotiations within and outside the organization.

From H. Brightman, "Improving Principals' Performance Through Training in the Decision Sciences," *Educational Leadership* 41 (Feb. 1984):51.

While only four of the ten roles bear directly on decision making, those roles under the interpersonal and informational areas can serve as a guide for the principal as "nondecision maker."

SUMMARY

There are at least six recognized models of decision making: calculative, collegial, incremental, political bargaining, charisma, and garbage can. Different models are effective depending on whether the problem situation can be identified for agreement on the needed ends or solution and the means to the end. If there is agreement on the ends to be achieved and the means to get there, then the calculative model should be used. If there is disagreement on both ends and means, then the charisma model or the garbage-can model should be used. If there is disagreement on ends but agreement on means, then the incremental or political-bargaining approaches should be used. If there is agreement on ends but disagreement on means, then the collegial model should be used.

The process of decision making should include six steps: (1) recognize, define, and limit the problem; (2) analyze and evaluate the problem; (3) establish criteria or set standards; (4) collect data; (5) select a solution; (6) put the solution into effect.

Involving others in the decision making is essential. Group decision making can enhance the effectiveness of the ultimate decision. Several techniques for group decision making are available for the principal to consider. The Delphi technique provides all group members with an equal chance to participate, regardless of the group members' personalities or speaking skills. The Nominal Group technique is a similar approach to group decision making that strives for concensus.

The principal's role in decision making is largely predicated on the personal disposition revealed by four style possibilities: sensing/thinking style, sensing/feeling style, intuition/thinking style, or intuition/feeling style.

SELECTED BIBLIOGRAPHY

A Historical Perspective: School Based Management/Shared Decision Making—A Pilot Program, Miami, FL: Office of School Based Management, Dade County Public Schools, 1987.

BARNARD, C. *Functions of the Executive,* Cambridge, MA: Harvard Press, 1938.

BLUMBERG, ARTHUR, "School Organizations: A Case of Generic Resistance to Change," Mike M. Milstein, ed., *School Conflict and Change,* New York: Teachers College, Columbia University, 1980.

BOLMAN, L. G., AND TERRANCE E. DEAL, *Modern Approaches to Understanding and Managing Organizations,* San Francisco, CA: Jossey-Bass, 1984.

DAVIS, CREATH, *How to Win in a Crisis,* Grand Rapids, MI: Zondervan Corp., 1987.

DAVIS, M., *The Art of Decision-Making,* New York: Springer-Verlag, 1985.

DEAL, TERRENCE E., "Effective School Principals: Counselors, Engineers, Pawnbrokers, Poets . . . or Instructional Leaders," William Greenfield, ed., *Instructional Leadership: Concepts, Issues, Controversies,* Boston, MA: Allyn & Bacon, 1987.

DEWEY, J. *How We Think,* Boston, MA: Heath, 1910.

FOX, WILLIAM M., *Effective Group Problem Solving: How to Broaden Participation, Improve Decision Making and Increase Commitment to Action,* San Francisco, CA: Jossey-Bass, 1987.

GREEN, JOSELYN, ED., *What Next? More Leverage for Teachers,* Denver, CO: Education Commission of the States, 1986.

GRIFFITHS, D., *Administrative Theory,* New York: Appleton, 1959.

LIEBMANN, ANN, ED., *Building a Professional Cutlure . . . ,* New York: Teachers College Press, 1988.

MARCH, J., "Business Decision Making," H. Leavitt and L. Pondy, ed., *Readings in Managerial Psychology,* Chicago, IL: University of Chicago Press, 1964.

MORRIS, VAN CLEVE, R. C. CROWSON, E. MANNY HURWITZ, JR., AND C. PORTER-GEHRIE, *The Urban Principal: Discretionary Decision Making in a Large Educational Organization,* Chicago, IL: University of Illinois, 1981.

READ, H. M. FORDHAM AND G. ADLER, *Carl Jung: Collective Works,* Princeton, NJ: Princeton University Press, 1970.

SERGIOVANNI, T., M. BURLINGAME, F. COOMBS AND P. THURSTON, *Educational Governance and Administration,* Englewood Cliffs, NJ: Prentice-Hall, 1980.

SIMON, H., *Administrative Behavior,* New York: Macmillan, 1950.

4

Leadership in the Curriculum

The school principal will find it difficult, if not impossible, to be an effective leader without a thorough grasp of the curriculum. It is the curriculum that serves as a support to the instructional program and operationalizes the goals that are to be accomplished. The effective school principal will have an understanding of the basis of the curriculum, how it can be organized, how to involve people in the process, and how to evaluate the product of the process. In this chapter, each of the important aspects of the curriculum for the effective school principal will be explored.

BASIS FOR THE CURRICULUM

Defining *curriculum* is a most difficult task. Curriculum experts are not in agreement, as evidenced by the plethora of definitions available. Nevertheless, two representative views of curriculum have lasted long enough to be included in most modern conceptions of the term.

As a result of the eight-year study, a study by the Progressive Education Association from 1933 to 1941, curriculum was seen as "the total experience with which the school deals in educating young people."[1] Tyler saw curriculum as "all of the learning of students which is planned and directed by the school to attain its educational goals."[2] In a more practical vein, Glickman defines curriculum as "the content of instruction; what is intentionally taught to students in a district, school, or classroom; the guides, books, and materials that teachers use in teaching students."[3]

Regardless of definitions, curriculum is more than a schedule of courses at a particular time in a particular school. The concept of curriculum must include the ways in which subject matter relates to other knowledge and to students' life and society. This formulation of curriculum is similar to Dewey's notion that education is the reconstruction of experiences.[4]

It Starts with Philosophy

The elements of a curriculum stem from a philosophical decision about the purpose of schooling. Curricula have been developed to

[1]H. H. Giles, S. P. McCutchen, and A. N. Zechiel, *Exploring the Curriculum* (New York: Harper & Row, Pub., 1942), p. 293.

[2]R. W. Tyler, "The Curriculum: Then and Now," in *Proceedings of the 1956 Invitational Conference on Testing Problems* (Princeton, NJ: Educational Testing Service, 1957), p. 79.

[3]C. D. Glickman, *Supervision of Instruction* (Boston: Allyn and Bacon, 1985), p. 307.

[4]J. Dewey, *Democracy and Education* (New York: Macmillan, 1916) pp. 89-90.

embrace several philosophies of life and, therefore, education. Predominant among the prevailing philosophies are essentialism, experimentalism, and existentialism. Each of these philosophies can form the rationale and resulting format for the school curriculum. *Essentialism* is the basis for the fundamental skills/literacy rationale for the curriculum. The "back-to-basics" movement has its conceptual roots here. A typical format for the essentialism philosophy–fundamental skills/literacy rationale is the behavioral-objective approach. *Experimentalism* forms the basis for social growth–general education rationale, which in turn is reflected in a format such as "webbing," or "mapping." The *existentialist* philosophy has its rationale in creativity, self-awareness, and the growth of the individual. No particular format follows from this approach. Rather, the curriculum becomes highly teacher–student centered.

Essentialism and the Fundamental Skills/Literacy Approach

The philosophy of essentialism has its roots in the *idealism* of Plato. Plato believed that the world as we know it is really an *idea* of the world, and that nature is higher than humanity. The best people can do is glimpse nature, which is outside of the human consciousness. In the late 1930s, Bagley developed essentialism as an educational philosophy. Its emphasis is on the training of the mind.

As the United States was becoming industrialized, it became apparent that the masses needed to have some knowledge of the "three R's." Therefore, schooling was focused on basic literacy. The essentialism philosophy, and its companion emphasis on fundamental skills, seemed necessary. However, while basic education was recommended for the masses, *liberal education* was developed for the elite. It was felt that the upper class must have the opportunity to be well-rounded. Some of the greatest thinkers of that time warned that schooling the masses only in the basics could have long-lasting, negative effects. In Dewey's words:

> He who is poorly acquainted with the history of the efforts to improve elementary education in our large cities does not know that the chief protest against progress is likely to come from successful business men. They have clamored for the three R's as the essential and exclusive material of primary education—knowing well enough that their own children would be able to get the things they protest against. Thus they have attacked as fads and frills every enrichment of the curriculum which did not lend itself to narrow economic ends. Let us stick to business, to the essentials, has been their plea, and by business they meant enough of the routine skills in letters and figures to make those leaving the elementary school at about the fifth or sixth grade useful in their

business, irrespective of whether pupils left school with an equipment for advance and with the ambition to try to secure better social and economic conditions for their children than they themselves had enjoyed.[5]

The literacy rationale for curriculum is not only a historical phenomenon. The "back-to-basics" movement of the late 1970s and early 80s was very popular. The public became discontent with what it saw as a curriculum with too many "frills." Going back to basics seemed to be a solution.

A current outgrowth of the fundamental skills/literacy rationale is the minimum competency requirements that now prevail in all parts of the country. Many states require that students pass minimum competency tests for promotion and graduation. Even within the classroom, students are required to show literacy at various stages of progress (or lack thereof) throughout the school year.

Calls for educational reform by a number of commissions have included consideration of basic literacy as a necessary element of the curriculum. For example, the 1983 Task Force on Education for Economic Growth of the Education Commission of the States recommended a broadened conception of basic education. Their intent was to upgrade the American labor force so as to better compete with foreign nations.[6]

An excerpt from the report reveals the reliance on basic literacy for American schools:

> What we consider the basic skills today can be described fairly simply. In most states and communities that have established minimum competency requirements, "basic skills" are defined in minimal, rudimentary terms as follows:
>   First, the ability to comprehend literally a simple written passage.
>   Second, the ability to compute with whole numbers.
>   Third, the mastery of writing mechanics.
>   When state or local assessment projects test students for minimum competency it is these minimal skills that are examined. We expect our schools to impart much more than these basic skills; we demand that they impart no less . . . [7]

Experimentalism and the Social Growth/General Education Approach

As the United States grew, so did its confidence in the ability of humankind to control nature. The philosophy of Pierce and Jones

---

[5]Dewey, "Learning to Earn," *School and Society* 5 (March 24, 1947):332.
[6]Task Force on Education for Economic Growth, *Action for Excellence* (Denver: Education Commission of the States, 1983), p. 9.
[7]*Ibid.*, p. 15.

became recognized. Experimentalism focused on what people can do to nature rather than on what nature does to people. For the experimentalist, what works *is* reality. There are no unchangeable truths; there is only what we know at a certain point. For example, Newtonian science gave way to the theories of relativity. Knowledge is a result of the interaction between people and the environment. Working with the group to achieve growth is the goal of a human society.

As the growth of society became recognized, so did a dissatisfaction with basic education. People were interested in a wider world of choice. Why should the majority be given only a basic education while the elite were given a liberal education? The compromise became known as *general education.* In 1945, the Harvard Committee on General Education in a Free Society reported on the importance of providing a general education. They defined it as "that part of the curriculum that is designed to provide for a common universe of discourse, understanding and competence."[8] The purpose of general education was believed to be the development of "autonomously thinking, socially responsible citizens of a free society."[9]

Experimentalist educators such as Dewey saw general education as the means through which the common need for democratic citizenship among students of diverse backgrounds would be met—a true curriculum for a "melting pot" society. In the 1970s, general education was popularized as the conceptual base for *core curriculum.*

The *Report on the Core Curriculum*[10] was developed on the campus of Harvard University in 1978. It proposed that students take a common "core" of courses which together would represent that part of a student's education devoted to general learning. After general education requirements were met, students could undertake *specialized education.* Only once education for citizenship (general education) was satisfied should students pursue education for an occupation (specialized or vocational education).

Existentialism in Education

The philosophy of existentialism is evident in the writings of some of the great continental thinkers, such as Kierkegaard, Sartre, and Heidegger. The existentialist believes that the individual is the source of all reality. If humans were removed from the face of the

---

[8]Report of the Harvard Committee, *General Education in a Free Society* (Cambridge, MA: Harvard University Press, 1945), p. 51.

[9]*Ibid.,* p. 54.

[10]H. Rosovsky, *Report on the Core Curriculum* (Cambridge, MA: Harvard University Press, 1978).

earth, the earth would cease to exist. Without humans to experience the "existence" of things, things do not exist. In answer to the familiar riddle "If a tree falls in the forest and there is no one there to hear it, does it make a sound," the existentialist would say no. If no one is present to hear the tree fall, then the tree makes no sound.

As a philosophy of education, existentialism could be the basis of curricula that emphasize teacher and student choice. In essence, teachers, together with their students, make their own curriculum. The freedom for the individual to discover himself is paramount in an existentialist-centered curriculum.

A Curriculum Format for Each Philosophy

Philosophical emphasis can be detected in the format used in developing the curriculum. A common format used to express the essentialism outlook in the behavioral-objective approach. The webbing, or conceptual mapping, approach is associated with experimentalism, and the results-only format with existentialism.

Behavioral-objective Format.   In the behavioral-objective format, the knowledge and skills to be acquired are predetermined. What is to be learned is stated in behavioral terms—that is, in terms of the behaviors that students are expected to display. The learning activities in which students can engage in order to accomplish the objective are also specified. Finally, the way in which students are to be evaluated is outlined. Figure 4–1 gives an example of the objective-activity-evaluation approach to using the behavioral-objective format.

Webbing/Conceptual Mapping.   The webbing approach can be described as a series of interrelated activities centered around one theme. Conceptual mapping is an interpretation of webbing and behavioral

FIGURE 4–1. Behavioral-objective format.

1. *Behavioral objective:*	By the end of the week, students will be able to add fractions with a common denominator.
2. *Activities:*	1. Teacher will demonstrate on the chalkboard the steps for adding fractions.
	2. Students will come to the board for practice.
	3. Students will work problems at their seats.
	4. Students will be assigned homework each night during the week.
3. *Evaluation:*	At the end of the week, students will take a paper-and-pencil test on adding fractions.

objectives. An example of each approach is provided in Figure 4–2. As the figure shows, the webbing format for a social studies unit might resemble a spider's web. The varieties of activities that can be combined to shape the students' understanding of the topic is very much aligned with general-education thinking.

The conceptual map is a more moderate approach to the general-education theme but, nevertheless, is clearly not an essentialist's approach to curriculum. The following five components of mapping, as developed by Posner and Rudnitsky, best summarize the approach:

FIGURE 4–2. Webbing format.

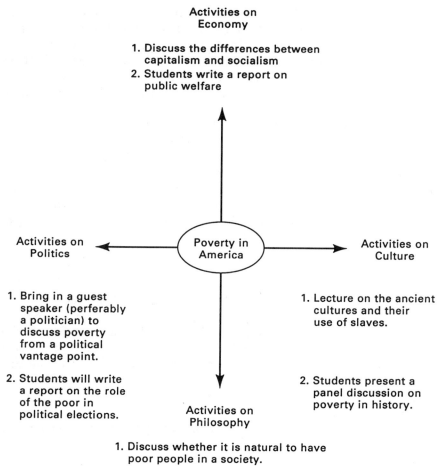

Activities on
Economy

1. Discuss the differences between capitalism and socialism
2. Students write a report on public welfare

Activities on
Politics

Poverty in
America

Activities on
Culture

1. Bring in a guest speaker (perferably a politician) to discuss poverty from a political vantage point.

2. Students will write a report on the role of the poor in political elections.

1. Lecture on the ancient cultures and their use of slaves.

2. Students present a panel discussion on poverty in history.

Activities on
Philosophy

1. Discuss whether it is natural to have poor people in a society.
2. Students survey other student classes to determine attitudes about poverty.

1. Rationale for the course, including the overall educational goals.
2. List of intended learning outcomes for the course, categorized according to type of learning.
3. Conceptual maps depicting the relationship among the important ideas to be learned in the course.
4. Instructional plan describing (1) what each unit is about, (2) what learning outcomes each unit is intended to accomplish, and (3) what general teaching strategies could be used in each unit to accomplish the intended learning outcomes.
5. Evaluation plan describing behavioral indicators for each high-priority intended learning outcome (main effects), together with a list of some unintended, undesirable learning outcomes (side effects) to be on the lookout for.[11]

Results-Only Format.   The existentialist philosophy is best served by the results-only format. Simply put, this approach would only *suggest* certain skills or content areas to be learned in connection with a certain concept. It would be entirely up to the teacher to decide what activities should be used to accomplish the learning task. The teacher is responsible for the *results* of learning. The route to be taken is up to the teacher.

The answer to the question "What is the basis for curriculum?" must depend on the philosophical outlook of the curriculum developer. If the outlook is essentialistic, then a focus on basic education would be expected, and a behavioral-objective format would be compatible. If the philosophy is experimental, then an affinity for general education would be natural, with a webbing or conceptual map approach to formatting. Finally, if existentialism is dominant, a high degree of teacher latitude in developing learning directions would be expected, and the results-only approach would prevail.

ORGANIZING THE CURRICULUM FOR IMPROVED INSTRUCTION

We have noted that a particular philosophical bent might direct the way in which a curriculum will function along the lines of general education, basic education, specialized education, and so on. The curriculum formats that might follow the adoption of a particular function were also discussed. In this section, the step-by-step process of developing a curriculum will be addressed.

The *Dictionary of Education* defines *curriculum development* as:

---

[11]G. J. Posner and A. N. Rudnitsky, *Course Design: A Guide to Curriculum Development for Teachers,* 2d ed. (New York: Longman, 1982), p. 8.

a task of supervision directed toward designing or redesigning the guidelines for instruction; includes development of specifications indicating what is to be taught, by whom, when, where, and in what sequence or pattern.[12]

The sequence of events in curriculum development are shown in Figure 4–3. The activities include evaluation of the curriculum. This activity will be discussed in detail in the last section of this chapter.

Assessment

Whether the curriculum to be developed is a new addition or a change in the existing curriculum, the need for development must be assessed. Of course, any change must begin with an *awareness* that change is welcome. Later in this section, the issue of involving others in the curriculum-development process will be addressed. Involving others is a key to heightened awareness. For now, it will be assumed that there is sufficient agreement among faculty and community for the principal to begin the process by assessing needs.

Gorton has synthesized a number of criteria for assessing curriculum by posing ten questions.[13] The answers to these questions would provide some direction for development.

1. Has the school established clearly stated, operationally defined education objectives?
2. Is each course in the curriculum related to and supporting the achievement of school objectives?
3. Does the planned curriculum take into consideration sufficiently the "hidden curriculum" of the school?
4. Does the curriculum meet the needs of all students? Is it comprehensive?
5. Does the curriculum reflect the needs and expectations of society, as well as the needs of the students?
6. Does the content of the curriculum provide for the development of student attitudes and values, as well as knowledge and skills?

FIGURE 4-3. Sequence of events for curriculum development.

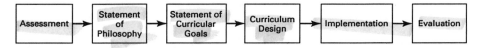

[12]C. V. Good, ed., *Dictionary of Education,* 3d ed. (New York: McGraw-Hill, 1973), p. 158.

[13]R. A. Gorton, *School Administration and Supervision,* 2d ed., (Dubuque, IA: Wm. C. Brown, 1983), pp. 303–307.

7. Are the curriculum materials appropriate for the interests and abilities of the students?
8. Are the educational objectives for each subject in the curriculum clearly stated and operationally defined?
9. Is there subject matter articulation between grade levels, and correlation among the various subjects of the curriculum?
10. Are the various subjects in the school curriculum achieving their proposed objectives?

In a more "how to" fashion, Oliva provides a checklist of six specific steps that he found being used by the Georgia Department of Education (Figure 4–4).[14]

Statement of Philosophy

Writing a school's philosophy can be a unique experience for those involved. Educators often resist this task. Writing philosophy is seen as an impractical and abstract exercise. Given this general reluctance, how can the task be best approached?

To begin, the school's statement of philosophy should be composed by a committee with broad representation. Membership might include faculty, staff, administrators, and parents. The meetings of the committee should allow for open discussion. Oliva has recommended that discussions might focus on beliefs concerning

FIGURE 4–4. Checklist for conducting a curriculum needs assessment.

Step 1.   **Initiate the needs-assessment process**

This step entails gearing up for the needs assessment: selecting needs-assessment committee members, orienting them, and making tentative plans.

[ ] **Task 1.   Establish a needs-assessment committee**
- Select a coordinator
- Identify a resource person
- Outline required committee functions/prerogatives
- Choose a committee with cross-sectional representation

---

[14]W. Crouthamel and S. M. Preton, *Needs Assessment: User's Manual Resource Guide; Needs Assessment: Checklist of Steps* (Atlanta: Research and Development Utilization Project, Georgia Department of Education, 1979) in *Supervision for Today's Schools,* 2d ed., ed. P. Oliva (New York: Longman, 1984), pp. 320–322.

[ ] **Task 2.   Orient the committee to the overall needs-assessment process**
  • Brief committee on strategies, recommendations
  • Identify current resources and constraints

[ ] **Task 3.   Make tentative plans**
  • Review specific needs-assessment components
    Determine desired comprehensiveness of the local plan
  • Determine individual committee member responsibilities
  • Set tentative timelines

Step 2.   **Conduct perceived needs assessment**

School publics are surveyed to determine what they view as the top school needs. It is recommended that the publics surveyed include administrators, teachers, and students, and that approximately five top needs of each group be identified and then merged into one list.

[ ] **Task 1.   Review/finalize the perceived needs assessment process**
  • Specify target individuals or sample sizes
  • Finalize instruments
  • Detail administration procedures
  • Define points to be made to each target group
  • Finalize data-analysis mechanics

[ ] **Task 2.   Conduct the perceived needs assessments**
  • Conduct school **administration** assessment
  • Conduct a **teacher/school staff** assessment
  • Conduct a **student** assessment

[ ] **Task 3.   Identify sets of top needs**
  • Score the instrument(s)
  • Determine top needs by group
  • Merge into one cross-system list

Step 3.   **Verify perceived needs by objective means**

The aim of Step 3 is the verification by objective means of each of the top perceived needs to determine that a major problem, limitation, or discrepancy does in fact exist. That is, do test data, structured observations, interview data, or other means (existing or new) bear out the identified needs? Thus, the list is further delineated.

[ ] **Task 1.   Plan for verification**
  • Orient committee on possible verification tools
  • Select objective means to verify each need (existing or new)

- Plan for administration (procedures, timeline)

[ ] **Task 2.   Validate the perceived needs**
- Collect/compile existing or new data
- Analyze all data
- Compare perceived needs with analysis of objective measures
- Finalize the cross-system perceived needs list

Step 4.   **Determine systemwide need priorities**

One cross-system survey instrument is developed and administered during Step 4. A discrepancy-type instrument is suggested for surveying everyone's perception of (1) the importance of addressing a need and (2) the degree to which this need has been met to date. From these perceptions, needs can be rank ordered, resulting in a systemwide list of priority needs.

[ ] **Task 1.   Organize for a systemwide ranking of needs**
- Review the plan for determining systemwide priorities
- Develop one cross-system survey instrument
- Determine groups to respond/sample sizes
- Determine procedures for ranking resulting needs
- Specify administrative mechanics

[ ] **Task 2.   Conduct the assessment**
- Administer the instrument (distribute/collect)
- Score the instrument

[ ] **Task 3.   Place cross-system needs in priority order**
- Rank order the needs
- Compile priority list of cross-system needs

Step 5.   **Choose need to be addressed by improvement efforts**

Step 5 involves deciding which of the systemwide needs is to be the focus of improvement. It is recommended that one (or possibly two if they are closely related) be identified by weighing what is most desirable to address and what resources are available. Obtaining school system approval and communicating undertakings to the educational public are also parts of the step.

[ ] **Task 1.   Determine which need is to be improved**
- Estimate the resources required to tackle each need
- Select need(s) to address

[ ] **Task 2.   Obtain school system approval**
- Obtain central administrative approval
- Obtain school board approval

[ ] Task 3. **Communicate findings/undertaking to the public**
- Decide on points to be made to various publics/ presentation modes
- Present information within the system (faculty, students)
- Communicate information to parents/community

Step 6. **Conduct a causal analysis of the need to be improved**

This step requires a look at factors that might have caused the identified need. Six factors are recommended for analysis in relation to the need: students, teachers, curriculum, resources, management, and the community. The causal analysis study is to delimit or redefine the need with respect to possible causal influences. A master list of causes is generated and ranked, and a report published.

[ ] Task 1. **Organize to conduct the causal analysis**
- Review the process
- Assemble/orient representatives for the need area(s) affected
- Determine additional support required
- Set timelines, responsibilities

[ ] Task 2. **Analyze the need in relation to six causal areas**
- Decide which of the six causal areas to investigate
- Describe desired conditions in each area
- Examine interrelationships across the six areas
- Select analysis tools or techniques for data collection
- Collect and analyze data

[ ] Task 3. **Place causal factors in priority order**
- Generate a list of primary causal factors
- Decide which have the greatest impact on the system
- Place the causal factors in priority order
- Choose final areas to attack through an improvement effort

[ ] Task 4. **Evaluate Your needs-assessment process using needs assessment checklist of steps**

[ ] Task 5. **Develop a report of causal factors**
- Submit report to central administration and board for approval
- Communicate report to educational community and public

- the purpose of education
- the nature of learning
- the nature of the learner
- the nature of society[15]

The national Study of School Evaluation has recommended that philosophy statements be shaped by twelve elements:

1. Relevance of the statement of philosophy to the larger purposes of the American democratic commitment
2. Attention to intellectual, democratic, moral, and social values basic to satisfying the needs of the individual and his culture
3. Recognition of individual differences
4. The special characteristics and unique needs of elementary school pupils
5. Concern for the nature of knowledge and for the nature of the learning process as they apply to learners and their total development
6. Consistency of philosophy with actual practice
7. Identification of the roles and relationships expected of the community, the pupil, the teacher, and the administration in the educational process of the school
8. The role of the elementary school program of the school district and the importance of articulation with the other elements of the overall educational program
9. The responsibility for making a determination as to a desirable balance among activities designed to develop the cognitive, affective, and psychomotor domains
10. The relationship of the school to all other educational learning centers
11. The responsibility of the school toward social and economic change
12. The accountability of the school to the community it serves[16]

Once the statement of philosophy has been drafted, it should be presented to the entire faculty (perhaps even to a parent group such as the PTA) for ratification. The next step in curriculum development can now be taken.

Statement of Curriculum Goals

Specifying curriculum goals is the first step in applying the school's statement of philosophy. Curriculum goals are expectations of the learners as they encounter the curriculum. They should take into consideration three sources: the student, the larger society, and the "state of the art" in particular subject disciplines. Curriculum goals are

---

[15]Oliva, *Supervision for Today's Schools,* p. 268.
[16]*Ibid.*

stated in general terms. The following is an example of goals for an elementary school's mathematics education program.

Mathematics Education: Students will acquire the skills and knowledge of mathematics necessary for being responsible consumers.

1. Students acquire knowledge of basic arithmetic, including addition, subtraction, multiplication, division, fractions, and decimals.
2. Students will develop and use arithmetic skills in solving consumer-oriented problems.
3. Students will acquire a rudimentary knowledge of mathematical concepts involving algebra and geometry.

Once the curriculum goals are written, the decisions concerning *curriculum design* can be made. At this point, some authors would suggest that curriculum behavioral objectives be written, before the design is established. However, as we have noted, the behavioral-objective format is only one approach to curriculum development. It is an approach that is consistent with an essentialistic view of education. Admittedly, the behavioral-objective approach to curriculum has become so popular that the average educator hardly thinks of curriculum without behavioral objectives. Nevertheless, the position forwarded here is that there are a number of legitimate ways to approach curriculum formatting. The most important point to remember is that the formatting should be consistent with the school's philosophy of education. This is not to say that *instructional objectives* are not used. Instructional objectives differ from behavioral objectives in that they are typically written by an individual teacher or are written as a curriculum guide to help the teaching process.

Curriculum Design

At the design stage, decisions must be made about the *content* of the curriculum. Can the curriculum goals be translated into specific instructional objectives? One of the most respected mechanisms for helping to make decisions about goals and instructional objectives is the Tyler rationale (Figure 4–5).

The rationale suggests that work begins with a thorough understanding of the three sources for curriculum goals. Once goals are established, they must be checked against the school's philosophy and against what is known about sound educational psychology. Once modifications have been made, specific instructional objectives can be written in the form of a curriculum guide.

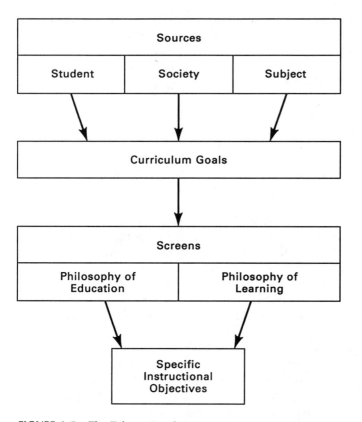

FIGURE 4-5. The Tyler rationale. Based on Ralph W. Tyler, *Basic Principles of Curriculum and Instruction* (Chicago: University of Chicago Press, 1949).

Implementation

Some curriculum experts choose to make the implementation of the curriculum a separate issue—so separate that implementation is often left out of the development process altogether. However, the implementation step is so crucial that it should not be thought of as a step. It is a process.

The implementation process may have as many as three stages: the communication (or proposal) stage, the teacher inservice stage, and the instructional application stage.

1. Communication (Proposal).   At the communication stage, a proposal must be prepared. It is at this time that the fruits of the curriculum committee's labor must be revealed to the larger educational community for their consideration. A curriculum proposal might include the following six parts:

1. description of the proposed plan, including a time schedule for its implementation
2. rationale and justification for the plan or program
3. summary of the research related to the plan or program, with information on the success or failure of similar plans or programs elsewhere, if any
4. human and material resources needed, including facilities necessary
5. estimated costs of the plan or program
6. a plan for evaluating the success of the innovation[17]

Once the proposal is developed, several methods should be used for communicating the content. A number of written versions of the proposal should be prepared. Not every parent is interested in or should receive a copy of the full proposal. An abbreviated handout summarizing the main features of the project could be prepared for the PTA. The handouts can also serve as an introduction to the upcoming staff meetings on the subject. A form for requesting a copy of the full proposal can be included as part of the handout. In this way, those who are interested in more details can be satisfied.

Bulletins can be prepared for the general public that briefly touch on the contents of the proposal and explain how to obtain more information. Once the various written materials have been prepared, meetings can be organized. A general faculty meeting followed by inservice workshops and small-group meetings should be arranged. Following staff orientation, general parent meetings, perhaps sponsored by the PTA, should be held. In addition, the use of support services can facilitate communication. Virgilio and Virgilio have recommended three possible support services: (1) the development of training programs for administration and staff personnel given by the curriculum writing committee, (2) the use of college courses, such as for-credit "special topics" classes designed for teaching curriculum change, and (3) release time for teachers so that they can have study groups in the library for the purpose of reviewing new curriculum materials.[18]

2. Teacher Inservice. The inservice phase of implementation is more than a teacher's meeting. Ongoing staff development needs must be addressed. It must be understood that the new curriculum repre-

---

[17]*Ibid.,* p. 281.
[18]S. J. Virgilio and I. R. Virgilio, "The Role of the Principal in Curriculum Implementation," *Education* 104 (Summer 1984):348.

sents a change in the lives of teachers. This calls for both reeducation and resocialization—reeducation so that faculty can acquire any additional competencies necessary to reaching the new curriculum, and resocialization so that faculty has an opportunity to change attitudes and habits. At this point, bringing in "experts" to assist with the process might be considered. A consultant from a university can help with the ongoing staff development needs.

Teachers should be encouraged to discuss the new curriculum among themselves. The interaction can help create an atmosphere of participation. Heightened participation has been associated with greater success in curriculum implementation.[19]

Instruction Planning.   Until teachers actually begin lesson planning with the new curriculum, it is difficult to determine whether the process has been successful. All necessary components of the curriculum should be available as teachers plan for putting the curriculum into action. Teachers will be quickly frustrated if supplies such as audiovisual equipment, workbooks, and supplementary materials are not available.

The curriculum development process can be long and complex. Because both patience and sacrifice are necessary for all concerned, it is important for those affected to be involved in the process, as we will discuss in the next section.

INVOLVING OTHERS IN THE CURRICULUM PROCESS

Who should decide the curriculum? The answer to this question depends on the community. However, situations in which the administration makes the decision in a vacuum are becoming increasingly rare. Some degree of faculty involvement, and even parent and community involvement, are more common. The extent of involvement will depend on the level of experience of faculty and on community custom in becoming involved in school affairs. Depending on the nature of the curriculum improvement, the decision may be left entirely up to the faculty. For example, the first-grade teacher makes the principal aware that the students are having difficulty with addition of whole numbers. In response, the principal might simply ask the teacher to research and then choose some appropriate supplementary materials to provide extra drill.

[19]F. English, *Fundamental Curriculum Decisions* (Alexandria, VA: ASCO Yearbook, 1983).

How many others are involved in the curriculum process can be determined by the choice of a *districtwide* or *school-site* approach. Choosing the appropriate level of faculty involvement can be important to successful participation. Whether the entire community or only the faculty is involved, the most common organizational method is the committee. The usual route for a curriculum decision of at least school building–level significance is outlined in Figure 4-6.

Districtwide versus School-Site Approach

The districtwide approach to curriculum development is typically organized around a central curriculum committee on which representatives from different schools within the district serve. Depending on the size of the school district, this arrangement can be either realistic or unwieldy. The districtwide approach, with its central curriculum committee, can limit its membership to faculty and administrators (building level and central office) or can include parent representatives and the community at large.

There are a number of advantages to the districtwide approach. First, it can provide greater coordination among offerings throughout the district. This makes curriculum monitoring more efficient. Second, bringing together representatives from around the district can foster greater unity.

There are disadvantages. Because the decisions are being made at the district level, there is a risk that building identity will be sacrificed. Because they feel removed from the curriculum development process, teacher apathy can develop.

The school-site approach has gained much popularity in recent years with the rise of effective-schools research. This approach is from the bottom to the top, as opposed to from the top, down. The ideas for change and improvement come from the individual classrooms of each building rather than from the central office. The advantage of the

FIGURE 4-6. Route for curriculum decisions.

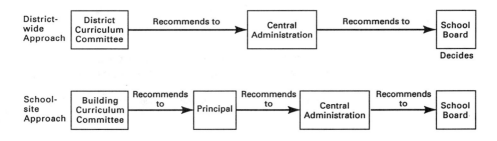

school-site approach is that teachers can feel much more a part of the curriculum development process. In addition, the unique community served by each school can be taken into account when planning for a curricular change.

Unless the faculty and staff at the building level are both competent and self-motivated, however, curriculum development can be poor. The principal of a large school may be too busy to run curriculum committees. Or, the principal may feel insufficiently trained to undertake a curriculum project outside his area of expertise.

Both districtwide and school-site approaches have something to offer. Wisdom would dictate that one approach not be used exclusively. Both approaches can be used effectively as long as the goal is to capitalize on the strengths of each method while minimizing the disadvantages.

Levels of Faculty Involvement

While the point has been made that involvement of faculty in the curriculum development process is especially important, not every teacher is prepared to be involved. Tanner and Tanner have explained that teachers function at one of three levels with regard to curriculum development.[20]

Level I is the *imitative-maintance*-level. Teachers at this level are interested in maintaining the status quo. When a change in the curriculum is made, they rely on the principal to tell them what to do. Level II is the *mediative* level. This teacher can be expected to have some notion of the need to integrate curriculum with the evolving conditions of society. However, a teacher on this level still falls short of being able to participate in reconstructing the curriculum by using problem-solving methods, for example. Level III, the *creative-generative* level, is the most desirable in terms of participating in curriculum development. This teacher is capable of taking a macrocurriculum view supported by cooperative planning for vertical and horizontal articulation. Table 4-1 compares the three levels by character, activities, and capabilities.[21]

The Curriculum Committee

The curriculum committee is an integral part of curriculum development work. If the school-site approach to curriculum development

[20]D. Tanner and L. Tanner, *Curriculum Development: Theory into Practice,* 2d ed. (New York: Macmillan, 1980).
[21]*Ibid.,* p. 637.

TABLE 4-1. Levels of Teacher Involvement in Curriculum Development.

LEVEL	LOCUS	TASKS & ACTIVITIES	PRINCIPAL RESOURCES
Level I: Imitative-maintenance	Microcurriculum Established conditions Segmental treatment	Rudimentary Routine Adoptive Maintenance of established practice	Textbook, workbook, syllabi (subject by subject), segmental adoption of curriculum packages, popular educational literature School Principal
Level II: Mediative	Microcurriculum Established conditions Segmental treatment Awareness of emergent conditions Aggregate treatment Macrocurriculum	Interpretive Adaptive Refinement of established practice	Textbook, courses of study (subject by subject, with occasional correlation of subjects), multimedia, adaptation of segmental curriculum packages, professionsl literature on approved practice Pupils, teacher colleagues, helping teacher, supervisor, curriculum coordinator, parents, community resources, school principal, inservice courses
Level III: Generative-creative	Macrocurriculum Emergent conditions Aggregate treatment	Interpretive Adaptive Evaluative problem-diagnosis problem-solving Improvement of established practice Search for improved practice	Textbook, courses of study (across subjects and grade levels), alternative modes of curriculum design, professional literature on research and approved practice, multimedia, projects Pupils, teacher colleagues, helping teacher, supervisor, curriculum coordinator, parents, community resources school principal, inservice courses, outside consultants, experimental programs, professional conferences and workshops

Source: D. Tanner and L. N. Tanner, *Curriculum Development: Theory into Practice,* 2d ed., p. 637. Copyright © 1980 by Macmillan Publishing Co., Inc., New York.

is followed, the committee members will be teachers in the building who have some subject-matter expertise in the curriculum area under consideration. Typically, the building principal or assistant principal will sit on the committee. The principal may even chair the committee. If the districtwide approach to curriculum development is followed, the curriculum committee will be composed of members representing different buildings and grade levels throughout the district, the district curriculum director, and the superintendent or assistant superintendent.

The administrator's role on the curriculum committee is that of consultant and facilitator. Administrators can expect that there will be members of the committee who possess grater knowledge of the subject than they do. Therefore, administrators will be of greatest assistance when helping the members to define their function and follow an orderly process. Administrators can also help to facilitate the work of the committee by securing necessary resources and removing obstacles.

Parent and Community Involvement

Parents and the community can be a valuable resource in helping to reach curriculum decisions. Parent and community involvement can help to (1) strengthen the bond between school and community, (2) convey information from schools to parents, (3) help develop public confidence in the school curriculum, and (4) encourage community residents to evaluate schools in terms of students' needs.[22]

The selection of particular parents or community members can be a delicate decision. One approach is to determine whether the curriculum to be developed is more controversial for professional educators or for the community. If the subject area is more controversial for the community (sex education, for example), the administrator should opt for a broad spectrum of representation. One method for obtaining broad representation is to ask for volunteers to participate. All people who volunteer would then become members of the committee.

If the curriculum to be developed is more controversial for the teachers and staff (the reading program, for example), then the administration must carefully control which members of the community or parents are invited. Parents known to be interested in the subject area or "experts" in the community might be individually approached. The administration may wish the staff to select the committee. The staff, in

---

[22]D. Else, "Productive Advisory Committees Keep Parents Happy and Curriculums Current," *The American School Board Journal* 170 (June 1983):34.

turn, will invite parents and community members it believes to have interest or expertise in the subject.[23]

The work of the committee itself can take a number of directions. It is best for the administrator in charge to outline the steps that the committee will follow throughout the process. Gorton has suggested nine steps for curriculum committee work:

1 → Identify and define the need for curriculum improvement (needs assessment).

2 → Identify or develop proposed curriculum change alternatives that meet the need for improvement.

3 → Analyze the advantages, disadvantages, and costs of different proposals for improving the curriculum. Select the best alternative.

4 → Identify and define what kinds of activities, resources, time, and other changes will be needed in order to implement the curriculum improvement.

5 → Prepare written document detailing proposed curriculum improvement and seek approval from appropriate individuals or agencies.

6 → Plan and initiate pilot project to test the validity of the proposed curricular improvement and to identify the need for revision before final implementation. Agree on evaluation criteria and methods before implementation of the pilot project.

7 → Determine the success of the pilot project and decide whether or not to revise the curriculum improvement proposal, implement "as is," or reject it.

8 → Implement the curriculum improvement change on a broader scale if the pilot project was successful. This step should include inservice education for those who are to implement the proposal and orientation for others who will be affected by the change.

9 → Evaluate the curriculum improvement change (using criteria and methods agreed upon prior to the implementation of the change) periodically after its implementation, to ascertain the need for further refinements.[24]

EVALUATION OF THE CURRICULUM

The evaluation that will be discussed here should not be confused with the kind of evaluation that was presented earlier in this chapter. Curriculum evaluation is conducted initially as a form of needs assessment. The principal should determine at the outset whether curricu-

---

[23]J. P. Clement, "Parents—Essential to an Effective Curriculum," *NASSP Bulletin* 64 (January 1980):56–61.

[24]D. L. Stufflebeam et al., *Educational Evaluation and Decision Making* (Itasca, IL: Peacock, 1971), p. 216.

lum change is necessary. This determination can only be made through evaluation.

Another time for evaluation occurs when the curriculum development process has been completed. The principal and others who were involved in the process should know whether the curriculum was successfully implemented. Are the teachers actually using the new curriculum? Are they using it correctly? This type of evaluation might be called *outcome* evaluation or *project evaluation.* In order to properly conduct a product or outcome evaluation, a number of variables must be considered. Operating from a model is a wise approach in proceeding with the evaluation.

Evaluation Models

The purpose of the evaluation model is to help in decision making. The evaluation provides data that administrators, teachers, parents, and the community can use to decide what to do about the curriculum just implemented.

A general model of evaluation was introduced by Stufflebeam and colleagues that shows the relationship between evaluation and decision making. Three steps are included in the evaluation process: *delineating* what is to be collected, *obtaining* the data, and *providing* the information to the decision makers. (Figure 4–7).

The method of product evaluation is to assess whether the objectives of the curriculum innovation were achieved. Therefore, operational definitions must be developed along with criteria to be used in measuring the objectives. Once the criteria are applied, a choice can be made: Are the results good enough that the curriculum implementation can be considered a success? Or do the results indicate that modifications are needed? Perhaps the results are so bad that the curriculum choice originally made should be abandoned and the process started over.

The design of the evaluation should focus on producing data that can be used by various decision makers. More than just administrators are involved in making decisions about the curriculum. Teachers, parents, and the larger community should be considered curriculum decision makers. It is the "user" constituents who may ultimately determine whether the curriculum innovation is a success. The data that are collected in the evaluation process are not all the same, nor can they be properly used by all levels of decision makers.

A teacher's evaluation of the curriculum is one level of decision

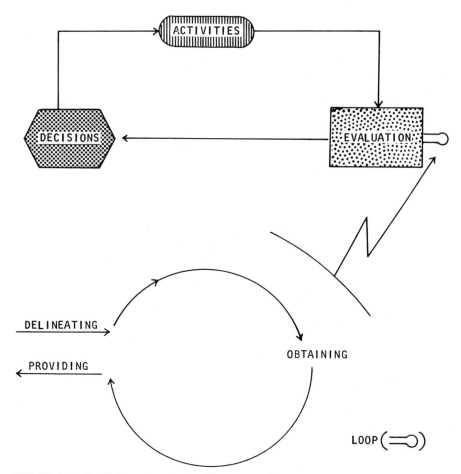

FIGURE 4-7. Stufflebeam's evaluation/decision-making model.

making. The principal's evaluation is another level. The parent's and the teacher union's evaluations are still more levels. Each of the decision-making levels will be concerned with a somewhat different set of alternatives. Therefore, their data needs will differ. The wise evaluator will produce data that each decision-making group can appropriately use for their specific interests. One data set is not appropriate for all decision-making groups.[25]

[25]W. J. Gephart, "Who Will Engage in Curriculum Evaluation?" *Educational Leadership* (January 1978):255–258.

SUMMARY

Before the principal can assume a leadership role in the school curriculum, a knowledge of the basis for the curriculum should be acquired. Three primary philosophies of education should be considered: essentialism, experimentalism, and existentialism. The philosophy that is adopted will dictate which curriculum format is used. The behavioral-objective format is consistent with the essentialism philosophy. Webbing is closely aligned with experimentalism. Those who subscribe to existentialism would use the results-only format.

Once the basis for the curriculum is established, the curriculum must be organized for instruction. The process of organizing the curriculum for instruction is called *curriculum development*. There are five steps in the development process: (1) assessment (of curriculum needs), (2) statement of the school's philosophy, (3) statement of curriculum goals, (4) curriculum design, and (5) implementation.

It is necessary to involve others in the curriculum process. The number and type of individuals invited to participate may depend on whether the districtwide or the school site approach to development is used. To be sure, the involvement of faculty is crucial. However, not every teacher wants to be involved at the same level. The curriculum committee is the most commonly used method of generating involvement. The committee may be districtwide, with representatives from the various school buildings and grade levels as members, or school-site, with membership developed from a specific locale. The idea of inviting parents and community members to serve on the committee should be carefully considered. Noneducators can bring additional resources to the development process.

Finally, the end product must be evaluated. Whether the implemented curriculum is a success or a failure, or something in between, should be determined. Any needed modification can result in a thorough product evaluation.

SELECTED BIBLIOGRAPHY

CROUTHAMEL, W. AND S. M. PRETON, "Needs Assessment: User's Manual Resource Guide Needs Assessment; Checklist of Steps (Atlanta: Research and Development Utilization Project, Georgia Department of Education, 1979), Peter Oliva, *Supervision for Today's Schools* (2nd ed.), New York: Longman, 1984.

DUNN, KENNETH AND RITA DUNN, *Teaching Students Through Their Individual Learning Styles: A Practical Approach,* Englewood Cliffs, NJ: Prentice-Hall, Inc., 1979.

ENGLISH F., *Fundamental Curriculum Decisions,* Alexandria, VA: ASCO Yearbook, 1983.

GLICKMAN, C. D., *Supervision of Instruction,* Boston, MA: Allyn and Bacon, Inc., 1985.

GORTON, R. A., *School Administration and Supervision* (2nd ed.), Dubuque, IA: Wm. C. Brown Comp., 1983.

KELLERMAN, BARBARA, ED., *Leadership: Multidisciplinary Perspectives,* Englewood Cliffs, NJ: Prentice-Hall, Inc., 1984.

LORBER, MICHAEL A. AND WALTER D. PIERCE, *Objectives, Methods, and Evaluation for Secondary Teaching* (2nd ed.), Englewood Cliffs, NJ: Prentice-Hall, Inc., 1983.

LOVELL, JOHN T. AND KIMBALL WILES, *Supervision for Better Schools* (5th ed.), Englewood Cliffs, NJ: Prentice-Hall, Inc. 1983.

NEAGLEY, ROSS L. AND N. DEAN EVANS, *Handbook for Effective Supervision of Instruction* (3rd ed.), Englewood Cliffs, NJ: Prentice-Hall, Inc., 1980.

ORNSTEIN, ALLAN C. AND FRANCIS P. HUNKINS, *Curriculum: Foundations, Principles, and Issues,* Englewood Cliffs, NJ: Prentice-Hall, Inc., 1988.

POSNER, G. J. AND A. N. RUDNITSKY, *Course Design: A Guide to Curriculum Development for Teachers* (2nd ed.), New York: Longman, 1982.

PRATT, DAVID, *Curriculum: Design and Development,* San Diego, CA: Harcourt Brace Jovanovich Inc., 1987.

TANNER, D. AND L. TANNER, *Curriculum Development Theory into Practice* (2nd ed.), New York: Macmillan, 1980.

5

The Principal's Relationship with Students

In Chapter 1, we noted that the principal is a key factor in creating a school climate in which enhanced student learning becomes possible. The principal's personal and active involvement in the instructional program is essential if enhanced student learning is to take place. However, the instructional program should not be viewed as limited to the subject-related curriculum. The student activity program of any school can be the major vehicle for the principal in relating to students.

In this chapter, the principal's role in relationships with students will be explored. How the principal can "fit in" for the sake of students will be of primary importance. In addition to the direct involvement in subject-related curricula, the notion of enhancing the instructional program through involvement in the extracurricular program will be examined. Student support areas, such as guidance and counseling and athletics, are viewed as a necessary part of instructional activity.

THE PRINCIPAL'S DIRECT INVOLVEMENT IN THE SUBJECT-RELATED CURRICULUM

The students should witness the principal's active involvement in the academic program. By direct and visible involvement, the principal communicates a message that schoolwork is important and that students are expected to do well. The principal can ensure academic visibility by engaging in a variety of activities, such as the following:

> **Honor roll.** The establishment of, and continuous support for, an academic honor role will convey to students that scholastic achievement will be rewarded. However, the honor-roll system must be designed so that it does not exclude too many students. If the possibility of being on the honor roll is too remote for the average student, the system loses its effect. The principal can preside over an honor-roll assembly at which students receive public recognition for their efforts. The principal could also send personal letters of congratulations to the parents of honor-roll students. The list of students on the honor roll should be posted in some prominent place in the school or even printed in the school newspaper. Local newspapers might even cooperate by publishing the list of student honorees.

> **Visiting classrooms.** A generous part of the principal's day should be spent visiting classes in progress. The principal should not disturb the class's normal routine, however. Teachers can be informed that the principal plans to visit classes as a natural expression of interest and that they should not make a ceremony out of the visits. Likewise, teachers should be reassured that the principal is not visiting to "spy" on them. Of course, even the periodic scheduled evaluation observation can serve the additional purpose of communicating a message of academic interest to students.

Teaching classes. Occasionally the principal might actually teach a class. One approach would be for the principal to serve as a substitute teacher in the regular teacher's absence. The principal might also serve as a guest speaker on academic topics.

Grade reports. The principal can review students' report cards, adding written comments where appropriate. Students who receive report cards that are particularly noteworthy can be invited to the principal's office for a personal visit.

Since principals are not classroom teachers, their opportunities for direct involvement in the academic program are a bit more limited than they are in other areas of school life. The extracurricular programs, on the other hand, provide greater flexibility in allowing for the principal's involvement. Through extracurricular activities, the academic program can be enhanced.

EXTRACURRICULAR ACTIVITIES

The programs referred to in this section have gone by several names over the years. Some use the term *cocurricular,* or *student activities.* What remains the same is the importance of these programs in the overall structure of the school. The wise principal will do well not to take the importance of the programs too lightly. From a school and community relations standpoint, the extracurricular activity program (especially athletics) can be the reason for the school's existence in some communities. In addition, we should note that extracurricular activities do not exist only at the secondary level. Extracurricular programs have been recommended for the elementary school for some time.[1]

Since the athletic program tends to be the largest component of the extracurricular program, it will be treated in a separate section. Extracurricular activities vary from school to school. Figure 5–1 shows some of the more popular types of extracurricular activities.

While athletics tend to be most prominent among the extracurricular activities, the principal must be cautious about allowing athletics to overshadow other activities. Since students must typically "try out" for athletic teams, the program tends to be exclusive. Therefore, sufficient attention must be paid to the interest-oriented activities so as to include as many students as possible in some extracurricular activity. A school should consider offering about twice as many non-

[1] H. C. McKown, *Activities in the Elementary School* (New York: McGraw-Hill, 1938).

STUDENT GOVERNMENT AND PUBLICATIONS	PERFORMANCE GROUPS	CLUBS AND ORGANIZATIONS	INTRAMURALS BOYS' AND GIRLS'	ATHLETICS BOYS' AND GIRLS'
Student council	Dramatics	Chess club	Bowling	Basketball
Student newspaper	Instrumental	Photography club	Golf	Swimming
Student yearbook	Vocal	Literary club	Ping pong	Tennis
Others	Debate	French club	Others	Others
	Others	Others		

FIGURE 5-1. Types of extracurricular activities.

sports activities as sports activities in order to ensure maximum student-body participation.[2]

Purposes and Objectives of the Extracurricular Activity Program

The primary purpose of the extracurricular activity program should be to provide student learning and growth opportunities that cannot be met by the regular academic curriculum. Objectives for each student activity should be written to reflect the purpose as well as the overall philosophy of the school. While each activity will have its own unique set of objectives, certain areas should be reflected in all programs. The following list of objectives could be used as a basis for writing objectives for a variety of student activities. They are basic to a sound set of extracurricular activity objectives.[3]

THE PRINCIPAL'S SUPERVISION OF EXTRACURRICULAR ACTIVITIES

As we noted earlier, extracurricular programs can help the principal to maintain a relationship with the student body. Visibility at sporting events and participation in debates, chess tournaments, and cheerleading contests will help to convey to students that the principal cares.

Beyond just being visible, the principal must organize the activity programs effectively in the first place. A poorly organized activity program will offer more problems than opportunities for the principal.

[2]V. R. Salmon, "Pupil Services" in *The Principalship,* ed. J. Kaiser (Minneapolis: Burgess, 1985) p. 209.
[3]S. Wagner, *Extracurricular Activities Are an Essential Factor in the Student's Self-Concept, Socialization, and Future Success,* An ERIC Report: Ed–119-171.

Students will

1. learn how to use their leisure time more wisely
2. increase and use constructively whatever unique talents and skills they possess
3. develop new avocational and recreationsl interests and skills
4. develop a more positive attitude toward the value of avocational and recreational activities
5. increase their knowledge of and skill in functioning as a leader and/or as a member of a group
6. develop a more realistic and positive attitude toward themselves and others
7. develop a more positive attitude toward school, as a result of participation in the student activities program.

FIGURE 5-2. General objectives for extracurricular activity programs.

The principal might consider organizing programs around twelve key operational elements, as suggested by Wood and colleagues.[4]

1. Student activities should be developed as a result of genuine interest by students.
2. The student activities program should provide for balance between the various kinds of activities.
3. Student activities should have educational values that students can draw upon throughout their lives.
4. The student activities program should reflect democratic values.
5. Student activities should be scheduled so that maximum opportunity is available for participation by all.
6. Procedures should be established which insure that a few students don't monopolize the student activities that are available.
7. Adequate faculty supervision should be provided.
8. Each organized group should submit their charter to the student governing body for approval.
9. Student participation in student activities should not involve excessive cost to the individual or the school.
10. Financial accounting systems for student activities should be established in accordance with good bookkeeping procedures.
11. Careful consideration must be given to the establishment of criteria for membership in each activity.
12. The student activity program should be evaluated periodically.

The principal should consider a supervisory approach that will allow for the monitoring of diverse activities. One possibility is to

---

[4]C. L. Wood, E. W. Nicholson, and D. G. Findley, *The Secondary School Principal* (Boston: Allyn & Bacon, 1979), pp. 218-219.

create an interclub coordinating council which is composed of one or more representatives from each activity. The representatives can report on the business of their activity program while the principal conveys expectations to the council. The council approach is not only a convenient supervisory arrangement, but it also allows students to be involved in discussions about improving their school and enforcing rules.[5]

Gorton has suggested nine organizing principles for extracurricular activity programs.[6]

1. Each activity, as well as the total program, should have well-defined, written objectives.
2. Each activity should be directed by a well-qualified, interested advisor.
3. There should be a written role description for each advisor, as well as a developmental inservice program to upgrade competencies.
4. There should be written role descriptions for the student officers of each activity, and an inservice program should be offered to help them improve their competencies.
5. The various organizational meetings that are held as part of the student activities program should be well planned.
6. A complete written description of the total student activities program should be disseminated to students and other appropriate parties at the beginning of each school year.
7. There should be a director of student activities and a student–teacher advisory council for the total program.
8. The total student activities program and each of the component activities should be periodically evaluated to ascertain effectiveness and to identify areas that are in need of improvement.
9. Each of the student groups in the student activities program should be required to prepare an end-of-the-year summary status report to be disseminated to all appropriate parties.

Regardless of the principal's strategy, the supervision of extracurricular activities has its problems. We will discuss some of these problems next.

PROBLEMS ASSOCIATED WITH EXTRACURRICULAR ACTIVITIES

While the specific problems vary from school to school, the general categories tend to be the same: (1) difficulty in finding advisors, (2) student apathy, and (3) inadequate financial support.[7]

[5]Salmon, p. 209.
[6]R. A. Gorton, *School Administration and Supervision*, 2d ed. (Dubuque, IA: Wm. C. Brown, 1983), pp. 411–415.
[7]*Ibid.*, p. 416.

In a survey conducted by Vornberg and colleagues, principals were asked to respond to questions that identified the problems with extracurricular activities in their schools.[8]

Four issues were identified as major problems:

1. Lack of participation
2. Lack of sponsors
3. Inadequate time allotment for meeting and activities
4. Budget (financial) limitations

The following were identified by at least three schools (in this order of importance):

5. Student apathy
6. Inadequate efforts at fund raising by organizations
7. Excessive time demand on students from jobs and other responsibilities
8. Loss of instructional time
9. Overparticipation by some students
10. Lack of student leadership
11. Lack of supervision
12. Difficulty achieving racial balance
13. Lack of transportation
14. Lack of faculty interest

Vornberg also surveyed students to determine why they might not participate in extracurricular activities. Some interesting results were obtained (see Table 5–1).

A more thorough examination of some of the major problems associated with extracurricular activities is in order. It is clear that lack of student participation and the unavailability of advisors are the top problems.

Lack of Student Participation

For some observers, the lack of student participation seems to be a problem of apathy. However, the recognition that student apathy exists does not explain why students become apathetic. Are students not interested in extracurricular activities because they lack information about the programs? Are the programs offered at a time when the average student has difficulty attending? Perhaps the admissions re-

[8]J. A. Vornberg, J. Zukowski, J. S. Southern, and V. W. Gipson, "Student Activities: What Are the Problems Now?" *Clearing House* 55 (March 1982):322.

TABLE 5-1.

REASON FOR NONPARTICIPATION	PERCENT RESPONDING
Not relevant to needs or interests	76.7
Took up time from school work	47.2
Scheduled during work	38.1
Not elected or selected	27.3
Controlled by social groups	26.1
Not prompted by sponsors	21.0
Involved sponsors who play favorites	15.9
Not advertised	14.8
Costs too much	13.1
Required transportation	11.9
Not "in thing" to do	10.8
Not available to a particular sex	8.0
Dominated by teachers	7.4
Too many membership rules	6.8
Disliked by parents	6.8
Biased or prejudiced	6.3
No voice in activities	4.0

From James A. Vornberg, et. al., "Student Activities: What Are the Problems Now?" *Clearing House,* 55 (March 1982):323

quirements for many of the programs are too restrictive?[9] Of course it is possible that students do not participate because of reasons beyond the control of the principal; such reasons might include the influence of television, after-school jobs, or uninterested parents. While it may be convenient to conclude that one or all of the uncontrollable factors are causing the lack of participation, the principal should always remain "proactive." The principal should concentrate on correcting those factors that can be corrected and should not be defeated by "societal malaise."

While it is not as common as student underparticipation, some schools experience *over*participation. Overparticipation usually occurs in certain "status" activities. In most schools, interschool athletics tend to occupy a high status. However, even the school band can be a status activity, depending on the community. Overinvolvement may be a function of individual student behavior rather than the popularity of a certain activity. The phenomenon of the student "joiner" is present in almost every school. Regardless of the cause of overinvolvement, what should be of concern to the principal are the problems that overinvolvement can produce. For the activities program in general, overinvolvement can cloud the academic purposes of the school or diminish the importance of certain activities that do not have high status, such as

[9]R. E. Gholson, "Research Notes," *Phi Delta Kappan* (September 1979):67.

the chess club or the library club. An additional problem of overinvolvement affects the student directly. The participation of individual students can be negatively affected because of their involvement in too many activities. It is also possible that a few students may capture many of the top leadership offices in the various programs, thus reducing the number of opportunities for leadership growth for other students.

Here are some ways in which the problems of overinvolvement can be reduced:

1. Restrict the number of offices that can be held by any one student.
2. Develop a mechanism for monitoring the potential negative effects of overinvolvement. For example, review grade reports of students who have a tendency to be overinvolved.
3. Keep a centralized record of the number of activities in which each student is participating.
4. Ask advisors to be especially observant of those students who are involved in several activities.

Problems with Advisors

The main problem with faculty advisors is *finding them*. An increase in the demand for advisors, along with a decrease in financial resources to pay for extracurricular activities, complicates the problem. Teachers are unwilling to devote large amounts of time and effort to advising a club if they are not going to be fairly compensated.

In addition, the principal's latitude in simply assigning certain teachers to supervise activities as part of their teaching duties has been limited by the increasing prevalence of collective-bargaining units. Another problem is that advisors are not all paid at an equitable rate. Advisors to special-interest clubs are often paid very little, while the coaching staffs for athletics are paid at much higher rates.

Perhaps the most immediate solution for finding and keeping good advisors is to eliminate the inequities in assigning pay for certain activities. While the school may be facing generally diminishing resources, it is important that each activity bear the burden equally. Inequity among advisors will take a toll on the best of schools. The principal should consider establishing a formal compensation plan, which would establish a pay scale based upon objective criteria such as the amount of time spent advising the activity and the number of student participants.[10]

[10]A.E. Blecke, "Compensating Teachers for Extracurricular Activities," *NASSP Bulletin* (October 1980):78–86.

THE ATHLETIC PROGRAM

In most schools, the athletic program is the largest of the student activities. Because of the many student participants, as well as because of community interest, the athletic program offers the principal unique opportunities to exercise leadership and to further positive school–community relationships. At the same time, the potential for problems is greater in the athletic program than in other student activities. For example, the athletics program might overshadow the academic program. The principal must be on guard to keep athletics in proper perspective. In addition, problems with lack of sportsmanship and girls' sports–boys' sports equality can occur. Ensuring that the athletics program is governed by strong principles and clearly defined goals will assist the principal in the task of leadership.

PRINCIPLES AND GOALS FOR ATHLETICS

Potter and colleagues have suggested four principles for the operation of an athletic program. Several goals are set forth for each principle. Table 5-2 provides a compilation of principles and goals.

The first basic principle of the athletic program should be to maximize the number of playing participants. Second, learning activities should be planned to promote decision making, teamwork, and sportsmanship. Third, the program should be conducted so that the athlete progresses, in physical fitness and physical skills. Coaches must be evaluated to determine their effectiveness in accomplishing the goals of the athletic program.[11]

KEEPING ATHLETICS IN PERSPECTIVE

Athletics can be an important part of the school program. It can both contribute to morale and provide a vehicle for student recognition. If the program is not kept in perspective, however, athletics can have a negative influence on a school. The principal must be careful not to pay more attention to athletics than academics. Not every student in the

[11]Glenn Potter, Thomas Wandzilak and James O'Hanlon, "Making Interscholastic Athletics a Winner," *NASSP Bulletin* (September, 1981):51–55.

TABLE 5-2.   Principles and Goals for the Athletic Program.

PRINCIPLES	GOALS
1. Maximum participation	1. A. Each graduate will have participated in inter-scholastic athletics during at least three semesters.
	B. Each student who expresses interest in a sport will be allowed to complete the season regardless of size or ability.
	C. All participants will have the opportunity for competition against others of their own skill level and ability.
	D. Each squad member will experience actual game or match competition.
2. Cognitive and affective learning	2. A. Athletes on every team will have opportunities to participate in decisions of importance to the team's functioning.
	B. Team members will be engaged in goal-setting in the areas of teamwork, cooperation, and sportsmanship. Feedback will be provided to individuals and the team as a whole on progress toward these goals.
	C. Experiences will be designed so that participants will have an opportunity to practice skills necessary for decision making, teamwork, and sportsmanship.
3. Fitness and skill	3. A. Each athlete shall maintain or increase physical fitness from the beginning to the end of the season.
	B. All students will demonstrate at least the average national levels of physical fitness.
	C. All athletes will progress in ability to perform the skills associated with their sport during the season.
4. Evaluation of the coach	4. A. A formal evaluation of each coach will be conducted each year.
	B. All coaches will do an annual self-evaluation of their work relative to the athletic program goals.
	C. All coaches will establish improvement objectives for their own performance.
	D. Players and their parents should have the opportunity to assess the coach and the program.

From Glenn Potter, Thomas Wandzilak, and James O'Hanlon, "Making Interscholastic Athletics a Winner," *NASSP Bulletin* (September 1981):51–55.

school will participate in athletics, nor are all teachers particularly interested in sports. Overemphasis on athletics can create resentment among nonenthusiasts or even plant the seed for the development of a subculture of "nonjocks."

Keeping athletics in perspective requires that the principal be seen in the classroom as well as at sports events. It means that equal recognition must be given to the nonathletic clubs at student assemblies. The possibility for students to receive awards should be the same for athletic and nonathletic activities. Of course, the principal's perceived attitude toward nonathletic activities may be the most important factor of all. It must not appear as though the principal is grudgingly providing this equity; it must not appear as though balance is being provided because of pity on the "have nots."

Maintaining equality in athletics is not only a sports–nonsports issue. Within the athletic program, a delicate balance between boys' programs and girls' programs must be maintained. Since the early 1970s, Title IX of the Education Amendments has required that principals not discriminate on the basis of sex within any program. Thus, federal law helped female students to gain opportunities in athletics. Because of the long tradition of boys' sports, the principal must guard against the view that girls' athletics are second in importance to boys' sports.

The principal must work toward objective measures of equity as well. For example, the salaries for the coaching staffs for boys' teams and girls' teams should be substantially equivalent. If there are differences in salaries, they should be based on some objective criterion, such as the number of student participants or the length of the season. Coaches' salaries should not be based on perceived importance to the community, on general popularity, or on whether the sport is a boys' sport or a girls' sport.

The principal would be wise to conduct periodic audits of the boys' and girls' athletic programs to determine whether balance is being maintained. The audit might focus on answering the following questions:

1. How many teams are available for girls, as compared with the number of teams for boys?
2. What kinds of uniforms and equipment are girls' teams using, compared with boys' teams?
3. Do girls' teams receive equal and desirable time on the practice field and in the gym?
4. Do girls' teams receive the same kind of publicity as boys' teams?[12]

[12]R. Bornstein, "The Principal's Role in Title IX Compliance," *NASSP Bulletin* (April 1979):40–45.

THE PROBLEM WITH SPORTSMANSHIP

In addition to the difficulties associated with keeping a proper perspective on athletics, the problems associated with sportsmanship should be examined. Poor sportsmanship can manifest itself among spectators as well as players. Poor sportsmanship among players is manifested by arguments with referees. Unfortunately, even fighting with players of the opposing team is not uncommon. Among spectators, poor sportsmanship is manifested when fans boo the officials or throw things onto the playing field. Fighting in the stands among spectators has become commonplace. While the severity of the problem varies from school to school, the potential is there for all schools unless the principal takes an active role in the promotion of sportsmanlike behavior.

Unruly behavior is best handled by promoting positive behavior rather than by imposing more severe punishments and increasing security. The American Association for Health, Physical Education, and Recreation developed a list of five fundamentals for sportsmanship.[13] The principal might consider adopting a sportsmanship code such as the one shown in Figure 5-3.

The athletic program is probably the most successful of all student activities. The principal therefore must devote sufficient attention to both the benefits that it offers and the potential dangers.

STUDENT GOVERNMENT

If it is allowed to function in a meaningful way, student government can be one of the most important methods for teaching good citizenship. It is essential that the student council (the name typically given to the controlling body for student government activities) have the feeling that their ideas contribute to the running of the school.

The following are some objectives that the principal might consider for the student council.

1. To promote the general welfare of the school.
2. To foster, promote, and develop democracy as a way of life.
3. To teach home, school, and community citizenship.
4. To provide school experiences closely related to life experiences.
5. To provide learning opportunities through the solution of problems which are of interest and concern to students.

---

[13]H. Meyer, *Crowd Control for High School Athletics* (Washington, DC: National Council of Secondary School Athletic Directors, 1970), pp. 10–11.

1. *Show respect for the opponent at all times.*
   The opponent should be treated as a guest; greeted cordially on arriving; given the best accommodations; and accorded the tolerance, honesty, and generosity which all human beings deserve. Good sportsmanship is the Golden Rule in action.
2. *Show respect for the officials.*
   The officials should be recognized as impartial arbitrators who are trained to do their job and who can be expected to do it to the best of their ability. Good sportsmanship implies the willingness to accept and abide by the decisions of the officials.
3. *Know, understand, and appreciate the rules of the contest.*
   A familiarity with the current rules of the game and the recognition of their necessity for a fair contest are essential. Good sportsmanship suggests the importance of conforming to the spirit as well as the letter of the rules.
4. *Maintain self-control at all times.*
   A prerequisite of good sportsmanship requires one to understand his own bias or prejudice and to have the ability to recognize that rational behavior is more important than the desire to win. A proper perspective must be maintained if the potential educational values of athletic competition are to be realized. Good sportsmanship is concerned with the behavior of all involved in the game.
5. *Recognize and appreciate skill in performance regardless of affiliation.*
   Applause for an opponent's good performance is a demonstration of generosity and goodwill that should not be looked upon as treason. The ability to recognize quality in performance and the willingness to acknowledge it without regard to team membership is one of the most highly commendable gestures of good sportsmanship. With the fundamentals of sportsmanship as the points of departure, specific responsibilities and expected modes of behavior can be defined.

FIGURE 5-3. Fundamentals of sportsmanship.   Used with permission of the American Association for Health, Physical Education, and Recreation Publications.

6. To provide training and experience in representative democracy.
7. To contribute to the total educational growth of boys and girls.[14]

Providing the student council with meaningful activities can be a challenge for the principal. Principals must keep in mind that the ultimate responsibility for all decisions rests with them. State statutes do not provide authority for students to make administrative decisions. Therefore, the student council can be given authority only to offer recommendations on how the school should be run. In order to prevent misunderstandings, the principal should convey the legal restrictions

[14]Gorton, p. 422.

to the student council advisor. Later, when the student council makes decisions on various school matters, they can do so with the restrictions in mind. The principal can thus reduce the number of decisions that must be denied and therefore not have to continually disappoint the council by sending them a message that their decisions don't count.

If the student council is to provide a meaningful experience for students, the principal must be willing to take a certain amount of risk in letting the council make decisions. As long as the delegation of a particular decision is not in direct violation of a law or board policy, the council can gain valuable lessons by making decisions. This is especially true when the decisions produce a failure in a program or event.

Unfortunately, the council will be limited to activities such as fundraising or promoting school dances. The principal should offer a student council experience that not only gives learning opportunities to students but also improves the educational and social environment of the school. Examples of meaningful activities might include the following

1. Conducting remedial classes in a disadvantaged neighborhood
2. Refurbishing a community center for youth and adults
3. Setting up a city–surburb exchange program
4. Meeting with the principal to recommend new courses for the school's curriculum
5. Arranging for an after-school series of school lectures on "black militancy and white power"
6. Developing a form for evaluating class instruction
7. Organizing a student-led seminar on contemporary issues to be offered in summer school, without grades or credits
8. Setting up a corps of student tutors to help slow learners in the school
9. Developing student-written individualized learning materials
10. Meeting with community leaders to plan for more effective use of community resources
11. Meeting with parents to explore school problems as parents perceive them
12. Making a proposal to the school board for the hiring of teacher aides[15]

The extent to which the principal can allow activities from this list will vary from school to school or even year to year within a school. Regardless of the school or yearly situation, student growth will always be enhanced when the principal respects the role of the student council in the life of the school community.

[15]*Ibid.*, p. 423–424.

GUIDANCE SERVICES

The purpose of guidance services is to assist students in their adjustment to school and society and to help them understand their potential as individuals. While guidance services have traditionally been thought to be a secondary-school phenomenon, the role of guidance services for elementary schools has increased in recent years. As the world becomes more complex, the need for these services seems to increase at all levels.

Guidance services are generally categorized into several areas: orientation, appraisal, pupil data, and counseling. Sometimes psychological and social services come under the guidance area. These two areas will be discussed in Chapter 6.

In larger schools, especially secondary schools, guidance services are carried out by a guidance counselor. A guidance counselor is an education professional who is specifically trained at the graduate level to do the job. In smaller schools, and especially in elementary schools, guidance services may have to be conducted by the principal.

Orientation Service

At the beginning of each school year, students are faced with new challenges. Their books, courses, friends, classmates, teachers, rooms, and even their building may all be new. A principal should not simply open the doors to the school and begin the year. Careful planning for the orientation of new and returning students must take place.

Formal orientation programs for students and parents can be offered during scheduling time. The program should offer the opportunity for students to learn about requirements of the school. Teachers should participate in the orientation so that parents can understand what teachers are going to be expecting from their children. Ensuring that the parents are clear on teachers' expectations will discourage students from playing one side against the other.

The following might be included in an orientation program:

attendance policies
homework
rules of conduct
extracurricular activity participation
food services
disciplinary procedures

Orientation should be held at a convenient time so as to maximize student and parent participation. Figure 5-4 provides some ideas on how the orientation service might take shape.

1. To assist students in selecting and entering school courses and student activities. (STPC) 400 hours.
2. To assist parents in understanding their children's educational program and opportunities available to their children. (STAPEC) 60 hours
3. To develop orientation efforts that will help all students make appropriate choices from the vast number of vocational, special, and academic programs available. (STPC) 40 hours
4. To become knowledgeable concerning school and community resources available to students and parents. (STPAXC) 5 hours
5. To help students gain a greater understanding of the school's guidance services. (STAPHEC) 10 hours
6. To assist with new teachers' orientation. Prepare information and materials to assist new teachers understand the function of guidance. (ATC) 10 hours
7. To assist in credit monitoring throughout the senior year; give feedback to students. (STPC) 150 hours
8. To give special attention to seniors who are in danger of not graduating. (STPAC) 50 hours
9. To orient ninth- through twelfth-grade students to graduation requirements. (STPAC) 25 hours
10. To organize an inservice meeting with junior high counselors to acquaint them with the program of studies. (C) 20 hours
11. To organize a parent clinic dealing with scheduling. (TPAC) 20 hours
12. To orient teachers in faculty meetings as to scheduling and prerequisites for classes. (TAC) 5 hours
13. To provide information on the building, school organization, staff, and community as requested. (STPHEGXC) 5 hours
14. To provide an orientation procedure for the incoming class and for transfer students. (STAPRC) 150 hours
15. To provide information about the guidance services to faculty and especially to new staff members. (TAC) 5 hours
16. To present scheduling information and procedures to students, staff, and junior high counselors. (STAPC) 500 hours
17. To assist in scheduling and making schedule changes within the framework of administrative guidelines. (TAPSC) 1000 hours
18. To revise or establish a procedure for handling new students. (TARC) 12 hours
19. To provide a follow-up conference for each new student to ascertain if satisfactory adjustment is being accomplished. (STC) 12 hours

S– Students (current)	E– Employers
T– Teachers	G– Graduates
A– Administration	R– Registrar
P– Parents	X– Referral agencies
D– Dropouts	C– Counselors
H– Higher education	

FIGURE 5–4. Possible objectives of orientation. Reprinted with permission of Macmillan Publishing Company from Verel R. Salmon, "Pupil Services," in *The Principalship* by J. Kaiser. Copyright © 1985 by Macmillan Publishing Company.

APPRAISAL SERVICE

The appraisal service involves student testing and evaluation. In its broader sense, appraisal includes getting students ready for taking standardized tests as well as educating parents on the meaning of the students' results. The service also includes the principal's evaluation of test results in order to make curriculum or inservice decisions.

Individual tests, such as Rorschach or the Minnesota Multiphasic Personality Inventory (MMPI), will be discussed in the next chapter. As for standardized group testing, the types that are most often used are *ability/aptitude* and *achievement* tests.

Ability/Aptitude Tests

The terms *ability* and *aptitude* have been used interchangeably in recent years. For example, two popular tests that measure mental "ability" have the term *aptitude* in their titles (Differential Aptitude Test and the Multiple Aptitude Test). In our discussion, the term *ability test* will be used.

An ability test is intended to measure students' academic potential. It is not subject-specific. The questions test general knowledge. Therefore, whether a student has studied algebra or English literature before taking the test is not relevant. Of course, the tests are designed to be age-appropriate. The group ability test given to third graders is significantly different from the one given to ninth graders. Verbal ability and qualitative ability subscores for the test are typically given. The ability measure does not change dramatically over the years, and therefore the test need not be given every year. A typical ability-testing program would include grades 3, 5, 7, and 9.

Scores for ability tests are usually reported as an intelligent quotient (IQ). Divulging IQ data can be a very delicate matter. In the wrong hands, the information can be damaging to a student's future. It is important that teachers and parents know how to interpret a group IQ score. This matter will be discussed in greater detail later. For now, it is important for the principal to understand that extreme caution must be used when dealing with IQ scores.

Achievement Testing

A standardized achievement test attempts to provide a relative measure of the extent to which students have mastered particular subject areas. Therefore, the test is subject-specific. The testing company designs the content around what it believes is the typical curriculum for that grade level. The process is called "norming." The test contains several subtests, or "batteries," which are generally given on different days. The test might include sections on reading, mathematics, language arts, social studies, and science.

Achievement test results are usually reported as percentiles or grade equivalents. For example, let us say that the results on the reading subtest for a fifth-grade student are examined. A percentile rank of 62 would mean that the student's reading score was better than the scores of 62 percent of fifth-grade students throughout the nation who took the same test. Along with the percentile score, a grade equivalent of 5.7 could be reported. A 5.7 grade equivalent means that this student's score is equivalent to that of a student who is achieving at the fifth-grade, seventh-month level.

Grade equivalents can help the principal determine whether students are learning at an acceptable rate. In the foregoing example, if the student had taken the test in November, then the baseline grade equivalent would be 5.3 (5 is the year, and .3 is the third month of school—November). Therefore, the student who scores a 5.7 is four months ahead of the average fifth-grade student in that subject area (5.7 minus 5.3 equals 0.4, or four months).

The use of grade equivalents is helpful in identifying possible weaknesses in the curriculum. Since grade equivalents can also be obtained as a mean for an entire grade, the principal can determine the progress of a certain grade in a certain subject.

Getting Ready for Testing

The principal will have to do some planning for the administration of the standardized test. If the school district employs counselors who have testing expertise, it would be wise to include them in the planning and administering of the test. It is common for schools to administer the battery of tests over an entire week. Testing companies usually suggest that schools set aside several hours each day of a particular week, instead of testing all day for a few days.

Several weeks before testing, the principal should begin to prepare students for taking the test. Emphasizing the importance of the test, the principal should encourage students to do their best. Communitywide publicity announcing the upcoming "testing week" might be considered. All faculty members should have a role in the testing program. During the test week, each teacher should have an assignment for administering the standardized test. Teachers can assist in preparing for the test by informing students of certain things they can do to get ready. Some examples might include the following:

1. Get plenty of sleep each night before a testing day.
2. Make sure you have eaten breakfast on the day of testing.
3. Don't schedule a lot of home activities during test week.
4. Look forward to the test, but don't become overanxious.

During testing week, the principal must make a concerted effort to insulate the school from the usual routine so that students can concentrate on taking the test. Interruptions such as end-of-class bells, intercom announcements, and student-delivered messages should be eliminated except for emergencies.

Concerns About "Teaching the Test"

Because of increased pressure on many schools to improve test scores, suspicion about "teaching the test" arises. The concern is that a teacher would actually teach the students the answers to specific questions on the test. This process, of course, would be a form of cheating. However, cheating must not be confused with ensuring test validity. Test validity is met simply by ensuring that test items are related to content that the students were taught in their courses up to the point of their taking the test. Therefore, a math test that asks students to solve linear equations when they have not yet been taught linear equations is an invalid test.

Validity must be considered when choosing a standardized achievement test. The principal must ask whether the questions being asked correspond to the curriculum actually being taught. If the questions are too dissimilar from the school curriculum, perhaps another standardized achievement test should be chosen. If the principal does not have the option of choosing another achievement test, teachers should be directed to ensure that the content covered on the test be included in their lessons plans.

Parent Education

As suggested earlier, schools have come under pressure to show "good" test scores. Indeed parent groups are responsible for much of this pressure—perhaps rightly so. The challenge for the principal is to provide information to parents that will allow them to fairly monitor progress. Much misinformation surrounding the meaning and use of test scores makes a fair assessment of progress difficult.

Using test scores as the only measure of school success can doom many school districts to failure. McPherson has pointed out that there is an overwhelming relationship between achievement and students socioeconomic status. Therefore, in school districts that serve a lower socioeconomic community, test scores may always be below the national norm.[16] However, if the district focuses on periodic increases in scores, or even on maintaining scores, the number of school districts that could show success would dramatically increase.

The use of achievement test scores as the sole determinant of success, particularly if the tests are limited to reading and math, is quite narrow given the many tasks of the modern school. As Erickson notes, "Quite a bit of research evidence suggests that schools which are effective in developing basic skills in mathematics and reading may be lousy schools for developing higher orders of cognitive ability, creative thinking, synthesis, and analysis."[17]

Before schools take full responsibility for the success of education, there should be an awareness that many variables contribute to the education of children. Students experience powerful influences from family, peers, church, and even the media. To suggest that the school should take the entire blame for the way in which students develop is clearly short sighted.

It is helpful for the principal to have objectives in mind when conducting the appraisal service. Figure 5-5 provides some suggestions for appropriate objectives.

[16]R. B. McPherson, R. L. Crowson, and N. J. Pitner, *Managing Uncertainty* (Columbus, OH: Charles E. Merrill, 1986), p. 34.

[17]D. A. Erickson, "The Central Question in Government Regulation of Private Schools Is What Is Plainly Essential for Good Citizenship," *ISACS Magazine* (Autumn 1983):27.

PUPIL DATA

A significant amount of pupil data must be collected and stored by each school. These data include test scores, grades, grade-point averages, attendance, and lists of participants in extracurricular activities. Directory information—pupils' names, addresses, phone numbers, parents' names, and emergency contacts—is also part of pupil data.

In handling student records, the Family Educational Rights and Privacy Act (the Buckley Amendment) must be followed at all times. Some of the main provisions of the act are listed in Figure 5-6.

1. To organize and supervise the testing service for both individual and group testing. (STAC) 200 hours
2. To develop a master schedule of the various tests given throughout the school year, including testing dates. (CTSA) 5 hours
3. To read recent literature on testing data to innovate new methods and materials. (CAT) 10 hours
4. To orient students to the testing program. (CST) 15 hours
5. To order any new tests that will be needed. (C) 5 hours
6. To mail all test that have to be sent out to be scored. (C) 10 hours
7. To observe and check the work of each testing assistant to ensure uniformity and correctness. (C) 5 hours
8. To prepare a simple profile to facilitate the interpretations of test results for administrators, teachers, and students. (STACPE) 25 hours
9. To monitor the GATB* testing program as it develops. (CS) 10 hours
10. To be responsible for college testing. (CTAS) 50 hours
    a. To collect fees when necessary.
    b. To count, store, and return tests.
    c. To obtain proctors when needed.
    d. To ensure appropriate test facility, including microphone.
    e. To consult with custodians to provide adequate building security.
11. To be responsible for district standardized testing. (CTAS) 150 hours
    a. To schedule Lorge Thorndike and TAP.**
    b. To organize orientation meetings with all school personnel who have assignments in the testing program.
    c. To obtain the necessary student runners when administering TAP and Lorge Thorndike tests.
    d. To coordinate the distribution and collection of all test materials.
    e. To see that answer sheets are properly marked and sent to data processing.
12. To coordinate GATB testing. (CS) 24 hours
    a. To order materials.
    b. To administer the battery to selected groups of students.
    c. To interpret results to students.
13. To assist staff in test interpretation and use. (CT) 10 hours

14. To coordinate the individual testing service. (CT) 20 hours
   a. To maintain the test file.
   b. To encourage staff to use the service.
   c. To assist in administering, scoring, and interpretation.
15. To interpret test results to students. (CS) 100 hours

S– Students (current)	E– Employers
T– Teachers	G– Graduates
A– Administration	R– Registrar
P– Parents	X– Referral agencies
D– Dropouts	C– Counselors
H– Higher education	

*GATB (General Aptitude Test Battery)
**TAP (Test of Achievement and Proficiency)

FIGURE 5-5.   Possible objectives for the appraisal service.   Reprinted with permission of Macmillan Publishing Company from Verel R. Salmon, "Pupil Services," in *The Principalship* by J. Kaiser. Copyright © 1985 by Macmillan Publishing Company.

FAMILY RIGHTS AND PRIVACY ACT (BUCKLEY AMENDMENT)
(selected parts) 20 U.S.C.A. § 1232G

§ 1232G. Family educational and privacy rights

Conditions for availability of funds to educational agencies or institutions; inspection and review of education records; specific information to be made available; procedure for access to education records; reasonableness of time for such access; hearings; written explanations by parents; definitions

   (a)(1)(A) No funds shall be made available under any applicable program to any educational agency or institution which has a policy of denying, or which effectively prevents, the parents of students who are or have been in attendance at a school of such agency or at such institution, as the case may be, the right to inspect and review the education records of their children. If any material or document in the education record of a student includes information on more than one student, the parents of one of such students shall have the right to inspect and review only such part of such material or document as relates to such student or to be informed of the specific information contained in such part of such material. Each educational agency or institution shall establish appropriate procedures for the granting of a request by parents for access to the education records of their children within a reasonable period of time, but in no case more than forty-five days after the request has been made. . . .

   (2) No funds shall be made available under any applicable program to any educational agency or institution unless the parents of students who are or have been in attendance at a school of such agency or at such institution are provided an opportunity for a hearing by such agency or institution, in accordance with regulations of the Secretary, to challenge the content of such student's education records, in order to insure that the

records are not inaccurate, misleading, or otherwise in violation of the privacy or other rights of students, and to provide an opportunity for the correction or deletion of any such inaccurate, misleading, or otherwise inappropriate data contained therein and to insert into such records a written explanation of the parents respecting the content of such records. . . .

Release of education records; parental consent requirement; exceptions; compliance with judicial orders and subpoenas; audit and evaluation of Federally supported education programs; record-keeping

(b)(1) No funds shall be made available under any applicable program to any educational agency or institution which has a policy or practice of permitting the release of education records (or personally identifiable information contained therein other than directory information, as defined in paragraph (5) of subsection (a) of this section) of students without the written consent of their parents to any individual, agency, or organization, other than to the following—

(A) other school officials, including teachers within the educational institution or local educational agency who have been determined by such agency or institution to have legitimate educational interests;

(B) officials of other schools or school systems in which the student seeks or intends to enroll, upon condition that the student's parents be notified of the transfer, receive a copy of the record if desired, and have an opportunity for a hearing to challenge the content of the record;

(C) authorized representatives of (i) the Comptroller General of the United States, (ii) the Secretary, (iii) an administrative head of an education agency (as defined in section 1221e−3(c) of this title), or (iv) State educational authorities, under the conditions set forth in paragraph (3) of this subsection;

(D) in connection with a student's application for, or receipt of, financial aid;

(E) State and local officials or authorities to whom such information is specifically required to be reported or disclosed pursuant to State statute adopted prior to November 19, 1974;

(F) organizations conducting studies for, or on behalf of, educational agencies or institutions for the purpose of developing, validating, or administering predictive tests, administering student aid programs, and improving instruction, if such studies are conducted in such a manner as will not permit the personal identification of students and their parents by persons other than representatives of such organizations and such information will be destroyed when no longer needed for the purpose for which it is conducted;

(G) accrediting organizations in order to carry out their accrediting functions;

(H) parents of a dependent student of such parents, as defined in section 152 of Title 26; and

(I) subject to regulations of the Secretary, in connection with an emergency, appropriate persons if the knowledge of such information is necessary to protect the health or safety of the student or other persons.

Nothing in clause (E) of this paragraph shall prevent a State from further limiting the number or type of State or local officials who will continue to have access thereunder.

(2) No funds shall be made available under any applicable program to any educational agency or institution which has a policy or practice of releasing, or providing access to, any personally identifiable information in education records other than directory information, or as is permitted under paragraph (1) of this subsection unless—

(A) there is written consent from the student's parents specifying records to be released, the reasons for such release, and to whom, and with a copy of the records to be released to the student's parents and the student if desired by the parents, or

(B) such information is furnished in compliance with judicial order, or pursuant to any lawfully issued subpoena, upon condition that parents and the students are notified of all such orders or subpoenas in advance of the compliance therewith by the educational institution or agency. . . .

(C) With respect to this subsection, personal information shall only be transferred to a third party on the condition that such party will not permit any other party to have access to such information without the written consent of the parents of the student . . .

Students' rather than parents' permission or consent

(d) For the purposes of this section, whenever a student has attained eighteen years of age, or is attending an institution of post-secondary education the permission or consent required of the the rights accorded to the parents of the student shall thereafter only be required of and accorded to the student. . . .

Pub.L. 90–247, Title IV, § 438, as added Pub.L. 93–380, Title V, § 513(a), Aug. 21, 1974, 88 Stat. 571, and amended Pub.L. 93–568, § 2(a), Dec. 31, 1974, 88 Stat. 1858.

§ 1232h. Protection of pupil rights

Inspection by parents or guardians of instructional material

(a) All instructional material, including teacher's manuals, films, tapes, or other supplementary instructional material which will be used in connection with any research or experimentation program or project shall be available for inspection by the parents or guardians of the children engaged in such program or project. For the purpose of this section "research or experimentation program or project" means any program or project in any applicable program designed to explore or develop new or unproven teaching methods or techniques.

Psychiatric or psychological examinations, testing, or treatment

(b) No student shall be required, as part of any applicable program, to submit to psychiatric examination, testing, or treatment, in which the primary purpose is to reveal information concerning:

(1) political affiliations;

(2) mental and psychological problems potentially embarrassing to the student or his family;

(3) sex behavior and attitudes;

(4) illegal, anti-social, self-incriminating, and demeaning behavior;

(5) critical appraisals of other individuals with whom respondents have close family relationships;

(6) legally recognized privileged and analogous relationships, such as those of lawyers, physicians, and ministers; or

(7) income (other than that required by law to determine eligibility for participation in a program or for receiving financial assistance under such program), without the prior consent of the student (if the student is an adult or emancipated minor), or in the case of unemancipated minor, without the prior written consent of the parent.

(Jan. 2, 1968, P.L. 90–247, Title IV, Part C, Subpart 2, § 439, as added Aug. 21, 1974, P.L. 93–380, Title V, § 514(a), 88 Stat. 574; Nov. 1, 1978, P.L. 95–561, Title XII, Part D, § 1250, 92 Stat. 2355.)

FIGURE 5-6. Selected provisions of the family educational rights and privacy act. Reprinted by permission from *American Public School Law 2/e* by Kern Alexander and M. David Alexander. Copyright © 1985 by West Publishing Company. All rights reserved.

The provisions of the act require some interpretation before they are put into practice. Some of the basic principles of the act should be stated plainly at the outset:

1. All rights regarding a student's records are exercised by that student's parents until the student reaches 18 years of ago. At the age of 18, the student exercises all rights regarding records.
2. A student or his parents have the right to see only that student's records, not the records of any other student.
3. The penalty for any school system that violates the law regarding records is loss of federal funds, after notice and hearing.[18]

Before going further, we should consider the definition of "records" as it applies to the Buckley Amendment. Education records are "those records which are directly related to students, and which are maintained by a school.[19] Essentially the act refers to the cumulative folder that is kept in the school office. The law does not cover teachers' records, which are kept privately by them and are not generally accessible or revealed to any other person except perhaps to a substitute teacher. Therefore, parents do not have any right to inspect a teacher's grade book, diary, or other anecdotal records. It is a common practice for teachers to insert a lot of incidental items in the cumulative folder, such as notes from parents, discipline warnings, and so on. Given the structure of the Buckley Amendment, parents would have access to

[18]T. Flygare, *The Legal Rights of Students* (Bloomington, IN: The Phi Delta Kappa Educational Foundation, 1975), p. 14.

[19]R. J. Shoop and W. E. Sparkman, *Kansas School Law: A Principal's Survival Guide* (Dubuque, IA: Eddie Bowers, 1983), p. 160.

any information held in the cumulative folder. Therefore, teachers should refrain from placing anything in a cumulative folder that they would not want parents or students to see.

Parents have only limited rights to "directory information," a category which includes the following information about the student:

- name
- address
- telephone number
- birthdate
- birthplace
- year in school (grade)
- participation in school activities
- dates of attendance
- awards received
- previous school attended
- weight and height, if member of an athletic team
- other similar data

Unlike official school records, which require parents' permission before they can be distributed, directory information can be given out without first contacting parents. The directory information exception allows the school to provide information to cooperating agencies like the Scouts, Little League, or other agencies interested in contacting students or parents about participation opportunities. Parents can request that their children be excluded from directory information lists. However, parents would have to make this request in writing at the beginning of each school year. Without a specific request, to the contrary, the school can issue directory information at its discretion.

The basic right provided to students and parents with regard to records is the right of access. The right of access to the records takes on several dimensions:

1. Parents have the right to review the education records of their children.
2. The school must establish procedures for granting the request by parents for access to the education records of their children within 45 days of the initial request.
3. Federal funds will be denied to any school that has a policy of denying or effectively preventing parents from having the right to review the education records of their children.
4. Parents have the right to a hearing by the school to challenge the content of the student's education record.
5. Parents have the right to correct or delete any inaccurate, misleading, or inappropriate data contained in the education record.

6. Parents have the right to insert into the records their written explanation respecting the content of such record.

7. Before the release of information contained in any education record, there must be written consent from the student's parent specifying the records to be released, the reasons for such release, and to whom, and with a copy of the records to be released to the student's parent and the student if desired by the parent.

8. Whenever a student has attained the age of 18 or is attending an institution of postsecondary education, the permission or consent required of and the rights accorded the parents of the student shall thereafter only be required of and accorded the student.[20]

Other than the directory information exception, the principal is allowed to release student records to the following without parent permission:

1. To other school officials determined by the school to have a legitimate educational interest in the information.

2. To officials of other schools or school systems in which the student seeks enrollment or intends to enroll provided that the student's parents are notified of the transfer, receive a copy of the records if desired, and have an opportunity for a hearing to challenge the content of the record.

3. To certain authorized representatives of the federal government and state educational authorities in connection with the audit and evaluation of federally sponsored education programs or with the enforcement of the related federal legal requirements. Any and all personally identifiable information must remain confidential to others than the specific official and must be destroyed when no longer needed.

4. In connection with a student's application for, or receipt of, financial aid.

5. To state and local officials to whom such information is specifically required to be reported or disclosed pursuant to state statute adopted prior to November 19, 1974.

6. To organizations conducting studies with certain specific limitations.

7. To accrediting organizations when performing their responsibilities.

8. To parents of a dependent student.

9. In connection with an emergency as specified.

10. States may further limit the number or type of state or local officials who will continue to have access.[21]

In addition to what we have already discussed, the act requires that the school district adopt a specific policy that will enable the law

---

[20]*Ibid.*, pp. 161–162, citing Salvail v. Nashua Bd. of Education, 469 F. Supp. 1269 (O.N.H. 1979).

[21]*Ibid.*, pp. 162–163.

to be implemented in a useful way. This policy must include a provision for parents to have a hearing if they challenge the content of the record. In addition, school districts, must publish the list of parents' rights under the Buckley Amendment. They must publish such a list on a yearly basis, by a method that will provide sufficient exposure, such as a newsletter or an appearance in the local newspaper.

A final note regarding the laws for students' records: The rights of parents are extended to both father and mother, regardless of custody. With the increasing number of single-parent families, it is important for the principal to know that the noncustodial parent has the same rights to the records as the custodial parent does. Although custodial parents often object to their former marriage partners having access to their children's records, the only option for the custodial parent is to obtain a court order directing the school not to grant access to the noncustodial parent.

The following are some suggestions for the pupil data function of the guidance service:

1. To process and maintain accurate records at the school office, including transfer, entry, and dropout records. (RCAP) 450 hours

2. To maintain a college and employer transcript service in accordance with guidelines of the Family Educational Rights and Privacy Act. (RHA) 500 hours

3. To give pertinent information regarding applicants to prospective employers within limits of release forms. (REA) 50 hours

4. To maintain a confidential psychological referral file for counselors and psychologists. (R) 10 hours

5. To keep an accurate record of the enrollment. (RA) 90 hours

6. To work with the school nurse and district pupil services office in the proper operation of the tutoring program. (R) 45 hours

7. To distribute test bulletins and post results. (RA) 35 hours

8. To identify winners of scholastic awards. (R) 10 hours

9. To post grade labels to permanent records. (RAY) 90 hours

10. To work with data processing in all input and output relating to school pupil inventory functions, including grading and attendance. (RY) 100 hours

11. a. To prepare class rank and point average lists for each incoming senior class. (R) 120 hours
    b. To prepare final class ranks and GPA's for graduating seniors. (R) 120 hours

12. To distribute student activity and evaluation sheets to the faculty and to collate results. (STA) 50 hours

13. To perform whatever stenographic duties are requested to meet objectives of the services. (RYAPE) 1050 hours

14. To cooperate with requests of special service departments and agencies (psychological, speech and hearing; welfare department, juvenile court, and mental health services). (RXY) 75 hours

15. To maintain service for students for processing work permits, assignment requests, insurance forms, free or reduced lunch program applications, and general information. (RSTEGY) 600 hours

16. To provide all professional personnel with locater service on students. (RAT) 72 hours

17. To provide visitors such as parents, probation personnel, psychologists, PTA assistants, college representatives, and employers with areas in which to work or to conduct private interviews with students or faculty or both. (RY) 80 hours

18. To keep departmental filing current. (RY) 180 hours

19. To supervise and train senior business students in office procedure. (RY) 30 hours

20. To consult with knowledgeable personnel to gain insight into legalities on matters such as those affecting graduation, grades, credits, employment, and termination of attendance. (RA) 35 hours

21. To provide liaison service to other schools concerning their vocational and special students attending the school. (RA) 25 hours

22. To publish a daily attendance report for schoolwide distribution. (Y) 1116 hours

S – Students (current)	E – Employers
T – Teachers	G – Graduates
A – Administration	R – Registrar
P – Parents	X – Referral agencies
D – Dropouts	Y – Attendance secretary
H – Higher education authorities	

FIGURE 5–7. Possible objectives for the pupil data service. Reprinted with permission of Macmillan Publishing Company from Verel R. Salmon, "Pupil Services," in *The Principalship* by J. Kaiser. Copyright © 1985 by Macmillan Publishing Company.

COUNSELING SERVICE

With the increasing pressures of living in today's society, the school counseling service has become crucial. Students are being faced with a multitude of decisions, many of which seem to come before they are equipped to handle the responsibility. Questions about drugs, sex, and peer relationships often press students to the point of suicide.

Many are philosophically opposed to schools' involving themselves in problems that historically were dealt with within the family or by religious institutions. While there seems to be some increase in participation in religion, this tendency is not matched by increasing closeness in the traditional family unit. The deterioration of the family is probably the single greatest reason that students need outside help with the decisions that growing up requires. While the school counseling service should not replace the family, its availability when family support fails can make a great deal of difference to a student in need.

Larger schools tend to provide counseling services through a certified guidance counselor. Depending upon the severity of the problem, the services of a school psychologist may be required. In smaller schools in which a counselor is not available, the principal or the regular classroom teacher may have to function in the counselor role. Figure 5–8 provides sample objectives for the counseling service.

1. To help each counselee attain an awareness of self, confront threats to self, and thus expand concern for others. (CS) 3040 hours
2. To place a major emphasis on the use of counseling groups in order to increase the number of students reached, to include students who would be categorized as desiring developmental counseling, and to give students a structure in which to share feelings, ideas, values, and concerns with their peers. (CS) 500 hours
3. To perform liaison and referral functions between other school and community resources and to facilitate their use by teachers, students, and families. (CSTPXA) 120 hours
4. To cooperate with the placement service in providing group activities focused toward self-concept, career exploration, post–high school educational planning, and employment seeking. (CST) 40 hours
5. To collect, organize, and write up case studies as a vehicle for improved services. (CTP) 40 hours
6. To promote continued growth among counselors and associates in developing skills to deal effectively with members of the school community. (C) 10 hours
7. To assist faculty members with planning, implementation, and presentation of counseling themes consistent with their subject matter. (CT) 25 hours
8. To assist faculty members with student problems perceived from the vantage point of the classroom. (CTS) 350 hours
9. To assist parents to develop realistic perceptions of their children's development in relations to their potentialities and to assist parents in dealing effectively with their adolescents. (PC) 20 hours
10. To develop and implement a program that increases parent awareness of guidance services available to them and to their children. (PC) 10 hours
11. To assist the orientation service to develop a short-term orientation

group for students entering the school after the first week of school. (CSAP) 4 hours

12. To set up a guidance committee composed of counselors, faculty, parents, students, and business and industry representatives for the purpose of giving their various perspectives on present programs, prospective innovations, and communications. (CPTSEA) 12 hours

13. To plan, administer, and assess a program for incoming students who have the potential for adjustment problems at the school. (CAS) 25 hours

14. To call teacher conferences directed toward sharing techiques successful with particular problem students or developing trial methods through sharing of data and ideas. (CT) 25 hours

15. To assist the orientation service in planning and implementing group presentations to orient students concerning course offerings, scheduling systems and policies, and graduation requirements. (CTS) 6 hours

16. To work with the information service for effective use of brochures, pamphlets, and other printed materials in individual and group counseling. (CEH) 10 hours

17. To cooperative with the feedback service to collect ideas, feelings, and opinions about the school and to set up meetings in which feedback obtained by counselors through student, parent, and staff contacts can be used to improve the program and the school. (CTPDHECX) 6 hours

18. To design and implement in conjunction with the testing service additional specific group and individual techniques for the counseling of students with major concerns about their test performance. (CS) 15 hours

19. To identify, place, and work with underachievers in a program determined beneficial to their development and redirection. (CST) 150 hours

20. To develop a counseling program to assist students with behavioral problems resulting in suspension from classes. (CTSA) 70 hours

S– Students (current)	E– Employers
T– Teachers	G– Graduates
A– Administration	R– Registrar
P– Parents	X– Referral agencies
D– Dropouts	C– Counselors
H– Higher education	

FIGURE 5–8. Possible objectives for the counseling service. Reprinted with permission of Macmillan Publishing Company from Verel R. Salmon, "Pupil Services," in *The Principalship* by J. Kaiser. Copyright © 1985 by Macmillan Publishing Company.

SUMMARY

The principal's relationship with students should be one in which the principal is seen as a staunch supporter of academic success. Each student should feel as though the principal in some way cares about him. The principal must be directly involved in both the subject-related and the extracurricular programs.

The principal can be directly involved in academics by directing an honor roll, visiting classrooms, monitoring grade reports, and even teaching a class from time to time. The principal can be involved in extracurricular programs by making appearances at sporting events and at nonathletic student gatherings. Perhaps the most lasting way in which the principal can be involved in extracurricular activities is to have a good organizational plan from the outset.

Each extracurricular activity should have written objectives. Faculty advisors should have job descriptions that outline their role in the activities they direct. Student officers should also have role descriptions that clearly delineate the limits of their authority. Yearly formal evaluations of each extracurricular activity should be conducted. Through the evaluation process, the principal can detect weaknesses in the program and identify those programs that deserve praise and recognition.

One of the major problems facing extracurricular activities is lack of student participation. It may seem as though it is always the same few students who participate in every activity. The principal can combat student apathy by ensuring that all activities are kept in perspective. Students must not feel that only spectator sports count. Only a small percentage of students can actively participate in football or basketball. Therefore, the principal should attempt to compensate by giving due recognition to activities like chess, debating, drama, and other interest-oriented activities.

For the athletic activities, the principal should encourage not just victory, but sportsmanship. Athletic programs should be monitored to ensure that fair balance is maintained between girls' and boys' activities, as required by Title IX.

The role of guidance services has become increasingly important. The orientation service can help students and parents get off to a good start each school year while ensuring that there are no misunderstandings about expectations between home and school. The appraisal or testing service provides valuable information about students' learning progress. Both achievement and ability tests can help shape curricular goals for the school. The pupil data service can help the principal to better understand students. Student records must be handled in accordance with federal law. Finally, the counseling service can provide the student with help in making difficult life decisions and in coping with the pressures of growing up and getting along with others.

SELECTED BIBLIOGRAPHY

BARUTH, LEROY G. AND EDWARD H. ROBINSON, III, *Introduction to the Counseling Profession, An,* Englewood Cliffs, NJ: Prentice-Hall, Inc. 1987.

BRAMMER, LAWRENCE M., *Helping Relationship, The: Process and Skills* (4th ed.), Englewood Cliffs, NJ: Prentice-Hall, Inc., 1988.

BRAMMER, LAWRENCE M. AND EVERETT L. SHOSTRUM, *Therapeutic Psychology: Fundamentals of Counseling and Psychotherapy* (5th ed.), Englewood Cliffs, NJ: Prentice-Hall, Inc., 1989.

FUOSS, DONALD E. AND ROBERT J. TROPPMAN, *Creative Management Techniques in Interscholastic Athletics,* Melbourne, FL: Krieger, Robert E., Publishing Co., Inc., 1983.

GORTON, R. A., *School Administration and Supervision* (2nd ed.), Dubuque, IA: Wm. C. Brown Company, 1983.

INGELHART, LOUIS E., *Press Law and Press Freedom for High School Publications: Court Cases and Related Decisions Discussing Free Expression Guarantees and Limitations for High School Students and Journalists,* Westport, CT: Greenwood Pr., Inc., 1986.

KUH, GEORGE, *Evaluation in Student Affairs, 1980,* Washington, DC: American Association of Counseling and Development, 1980.

MASON, JAMES G. AND JIM PAUL, *Modern Sports Administration,* Englewood Cliffs, NJ: Prentice-Hall, Inc., 1988.

MCPHERSON, R. B., R. L. CROWSON, AND N. J. PITNER, *Managing Uncertainty,* Columbus, OH: Charles E. Merrill Publishing Co., 1986.

PURKEY, WILLIAM W. AND JOAN J. SCHMIDT, *Inviting Relationship The: An Expanded Perspective for Professional Counseling,* Englewood Cliffs, NJ: Prentice-Hall, Inc., 1987.

SALMON, W., "Pupil Services," J. Kaiser, ed., *The Principalship,* Minneapolis, MN: Burgess Publishing Company, 1985.

SHOOP, R. J. AND W. E. SPARKMAN *Kansas School Law: A Principal's Survival Guide,* Dubuque, IA: Eddie Bowers Publishing Company, 1983.

SYBOUTS, WARD AND WAYNE J. KREPEL. *Student Activities in the Secondary Schools: A Handbook and Guide,* Westport, CT: Greenwood Press, Inc., 1984.

6

The Principal's Relationship with Special Education

Until recently, principals had very little interaction with handicapped students. Handicapped students were placed in special schools or did not attend school at all. In November of 1975, however, Congress passed the Education for All Handicapped Children Act (Public Law 94–142). This federal legislation changed, and continues to change, the way in which public education must deal with the handicapped child. Handicapped children are present in almost every school in the country. The law places the principal in a strategic role regarding special education—a role that requires knowledge, skills, and commitment to the education of the handicapped.

This chapter will explore the ways in which the principal can function effectively in the role of special educator. It is most important that the principal understand special-education law since most special-education activities have their roots in the law. Interaction with special education personnel requires some understanding of the many specialists who are involved in the education of the handicapped. Procedural requisites mean that the principal must understand and participate in the development of each handicapped child's Individual Education Plan (IEP). As special education continues to become part of every school program, the principal must act to facilitate effective relationships between regular and special-education faculty.

UNDERSTANDING SPECIAL EDUCATION LAW

Public Law 94–142 was the law that had the broadest impact on special education, but there were a series of court cases decided in the early 1970s that brought attention to the plight of handicapped children.

EARLY CASES

In 1971 and 1972, two cases were decided that marked the turning point in establishing rights for handicapped children.

Pennsylvania Association for Retarded Children (PARC) v. Commonwealth of Pennsylvania (1971)[1]

In 1971, the laws of Pennsylvania required that children who were certified as "uneducable and untrainable" be excluded from

[1]334 F. Supp. 1257 (E.D. Pa. 1971), 343 F. Supp. 279 (E.D. Pa. 1972).

school. The parents of 17 of these excluded children and the Pennsylvania Association for Retarded Children (PARC) filed suit claiming that the exclusion law violated the equal-protection and due-process clauses of the Fourteenth Amendment to the US Constitution. The court heard expert testimony indicating that all mentally retarded persons are capable of benefitting from a program of education.

As a result of the court's ruling that retarded children could not be excluded from school, the state accepted a consent agreement which provided the following guarantees for retarded children:

1. All mentally retarded children are entitled to a free public education.
2. If the public school does not offer a program suited to the needs of the child, then the state shall provide tuition and maintenance costs at approved institutions.
3. Homebound instruction will be provided where appropriate.
4. Mentally retarded children should be educated with nonhandicapped children (that is, mainstreamed) whenever possible.
5. Periodic reevaluations of each child's progress should be performed.
6. Procedural due-process, notice, and hearing requirements should be developed and implemented.[2]

Mills v. Board of Education of the District of Columbia (1977)[3]

This action was brought on behalf of seven children to enjoin the District of Columbia public schools from excluding them from a public education because of their handicaps. The student plaintiffs alleged that there were 22,000 retarded, emotionally disturbed, blind, deaf, and speech or learning disabled children in the school district. As many as 18,000 were not being furnished with special-education programs. In deciding for the students, the court held that the school district's practice of excluding the majority of handicapped children from school violated the due-process clause of the Fifth Amendment. The school district was required to

1. Admit all children regardless of their handicap.
2. Provide immediate and adequate educational facilities in the public schools or provide for an alternative placement at the school system's expense.
3. Provide an individualized education plan for each child.
4. Provide detailed due-process procedures before placing a child in special education and before altering a child's special-education program.

[2]*Id.*
[3]348 F. Supp. 866 (D.C. 1972).

The PARC case dealt with the rights of mentally retarded children, while the Mills case dealt with the rights of all handicapped children. Taken together, these cases established that handicapped children have constitutional rights and may not be misclassified or excluded from school. They also opened the way for the landmark federal legislation that was to come.

FEDERAL LEGISLATION

The most important federal laws related to the rights of the handicapped child are the Vocational Rehabilitation Act of 1973 (Public Law 93-112) and the Education For All Handicapped Children Act (Public Law 94-142), passed in 1975. While both pieces of legislation offer similar guarantees to the handicapped, there are important differences between them.

Vocational Rehabilitation Act of 1973

This law is commonly referred to as "Section 504," because it is Section 504 of the act that specifically describes the civil rights of the handicapped. According to Section 504:

> No otherwise qualified handicapped individual in the United States . . . shall, solely by reason of his handicap, be excluded from the participation in, be denied the benefits of, or be subjected to discrimination under any program or activity receiving federal financial assistance.[4]

The purpose of Section 504 was to eliminate discrimination on the basis of handicap in any program or activity receiving federal financial assistance. Although Section 504 is primarily directed at discrimination against the handicapped in the areas of housing, employment, higher education, and rehabilitation, it also contains provisions governing educational services to handicapped children. Under the act, an individual is considered handicapped if he:

1. has a physical or mental impairment that substantially limits one or more major life activities.
2. has a record of such an impairment, or
3. is regarded as having such an impairment.

[4]Rehabilitation Act of 1973, Sec. 504, 29 U.S.C.A. Sec. 794.

Six major provisions in Section 504 relate directly to the needs of handicapped children:

1. location and notification
2. free appropriate public education
3. educational setting
4. evaluation and placement
5. procedural safeguards
6. nonacademic services[5]

In general, the recipient of federal financial assistance must attempt to locate and notify qualified handicapped individuals, provide them with a free appropriate public education in the least restrictive environment, and establish adequate procedural safeguards.

The Education For All Handicapped Children Act

In 1975, Congress noted the following:

1. There are more than 8 million handicapped children in the United States today;
2. The special-education needs of such children are not being fully met;
3. More than half of the handicapped children in the United States do not receive appropriate educational services which would enable them to have full equality of opportunity;
4. One million of the handicapped children in the United States are excluded entirely from the public school system and will not go through the educational process with their peers;
5. There are many handicapped students throughout the United States participating in regular school programs whose handicaps prevent them from having a successful educational experience because their handicaps are undetected;
6. Because of the lack of adequate services within the public school system, families are often forced to find services outside the public school system, often at great distance from their residence and at their own expense;
7. Developments in the training of teachers and in diagnostic and instructional procedures and methods have advanced to the point that, given appropriate funding, state and local educational agencies can and will provide effective special education and related services to meet the needs of handicapped children;
8. State and local educational agencies have a responsibility to provide education for all handicapped children, but present financial resources

[5]*Id.*, Sec. 84.32–84.36.

are inadequate to meet the special educational needs of handicapped children; and

9. It is in the national interest that the federal government assist state and local efforts to provide programs to meet the educational needs of handicapped children in order to assure equal protection of the law.[6]

The purpose of this act was to ensure that all handicapped children are given a free and appropriate education. The intent of Congress was to meet the unique needs of handicapped children and to ensure that the rights of these children and their parents are protected. Unlike Section 504, this bill calls for the school to pay the full cost of the special education required for the child. However, school districts can receive federal assistance based on number of handicapped children they serve, up to 12 percent of the school population. Table 6-1 outlines the major provisions of this law.[7]

In addition to the provisions outlined in Table 6-1, the act specifies that a child may be entitled to certain related services if they are necessary for the child to derive maximum benefit from special education. These "related" services might include any of the following:

1. speech pathology
2. audiology
3. psychological services
4. physical and occupational therapy
5. recreation
6. counseling services
7. medical services for diagnostic or evaluation purposes
8. school health services
9. school social work services
10. parent counseling and training[8]

Related services also include free transportation and provisions for early identification and assessment of disabilities. The related services just listed are not all-inclusive; they may include any service that is required for the handicapped child to benefit from special education. As the field of special education grows, the ability to identify children with special needs increases. Schools now serve children with a variety of handicaps. The increase in the number of children with unique needs has led to greater demands upon schools to provide

[6]The Education for All Handicapped Children Act, 20 U.S.C.A. Sec. 1400 (b), (1976).

[7]J. Wiles and J. Bondi, *Supervision: A Guide to Practice,* 2d ed. (Columbus, OH: Chas. E. Merrill, 1986), pp. 89–90.

[8]20 U.S.C.A. Sec. 1401 (17).

TABLE 6-1. Major Provisions of Public Law 94-142.

P.L. 94-142 was enacted by Congress in November, 1975. Its major purpose, as stated in the act, is as follows:

It is the purpose of this Act to assure that all handicapped children have available to them . . . a free, appropriate public education whcih emphasizes special education and related services designed to meet their unique needs, to assure that the rights of handicapped children and their parents or guardians are protected, to assist states and localities to provide for the education of all handicapped children, and to assess and assure the effectiveness of efforts to educate handicapped children. (Sec. 601(c)).

There are six major principles of P.L. 94-142:

1. *Principle of Zero Reject*
   This principle, simply stated, requires that *all* handicapped children be provided with a free, appropriate public education. States are required to provide full educational opportunities to all handicapped children in the age range of 3-18 by September 1, 1978 and to all handicapped children in the age range of 3-21 by September 1, 1980. This principle is implemented by conducting a child find program on an annual basis to locate, identify and evaluate all handicapped children who reside in the jurisdiction of each public agency. If local agencies comply with this principle, they become eligible to receive federal funds based upon the number of handicapped children being served, not to exceed 12% of the school population.
   In addition to providing an educational program to all handicapped children, the public agency must insure that handicapped children have equal opportunities with nonhandicapped children to participate in nonacademic and extracurricular services. In addition, physical education must be provided to every handicapped child.

2. *Principle of Nondiscriminatory Evaluation*
   A handicapped child must receive a full individual evaluation prior to placement in a special education program. A placement decision should be made by a group of persons knowledgeable about the child, the meaning of the evaluation data, and the placement options. The placement recommendation may be suggested by the evaluation team and finalized by a committee who has the responsibility for writing the Individual Educational Plan. All handicapped children must be completely re-evaluated every three years.

3. *Individualized Educational Programs*
   The legislative approach for insuring that educational programs are tailored on an individual basis to the needs of handicapped students is through the requirement of providing individual educational plans for all handicapped students. The IEP must contain the following essentials:
   a. Current level of student's educational performance.
   b. Annual goals.
   c. Short-term objectives.
   d. Documentation of the special education services to be provided.
   e. Time the student will spend in special education and related services.
   f. Time student will spend in regular education.
   g. Dates for initiating service and anticipated duration.
   h. Evaluation procedures and schedules for determining mastery of the objectives.
   Members required to be in attendance at the IEP meeting must include the following:
   a. Representative of the public agency.
   b. The child's teacher.

c. Child's parents.
d. The child, when appropriate.
e. Other individuals at the request of the parents.
f. Individuals who provided the evaluation.

4. *Least Restrictive Environment*
   To the maximum extent appropriate, handicapped children should be educated with children who are not handicapped. The removal of handicapped children to special classes and separate facilities should occur only when the nature or severity of their handicap prevents them from successfully being educated in regular classes with the use of supplementary aids and services.

5. *Due Process*
   Dure process is a procedure which seeks to insure the fairness of educational decisions. It can be viewed as a system of checks and balances concerning the identification, evaluation, and provision of services regarding handicapped students. It may be initiated by the parent or public agency as an impartial forum for presenting complaints regarding the child's identification, evaluation, and placement or for challenging decisions made by another party.

6. *Parent Participation*
   Each of the principles has either the direct or indirect implications for parental participation. At the local level, parents should be permitted to review any educational records on their child which are used by the agency before the meeting to develop the IEP and within a 45-day period after receipt of the request.
   These six principles of P.L. 94–142 provide the basis for the legislative definition of free, appropriate public education.

---

related services. Disagreements between parents and schools about the definition of "related services" continue to be taken to the courts.

When such disagreements are litigated, it is because the service requested by the parents is not specifically defined by law and is therefore subject to interpretation. The most difficult question involves the distinction between medical and school health services. If the proposed related service is considered medical, then the school may not be required to provide the service. The law requires only that the schools provide medical services as they relate to diagnosis and evaluation. Continuing medical service is not required under the law. Medical service is defined in the law as "services provided by a licensed physician." School health–related service is "services provided by a qualified school nurse or other qualified person."[9] Schools must provide related services only when those services are required for the child to benefit from special education.[10]

[9] *Irving Independent School District* v. *Tatro,* 468 U.S. 883, 892 (1984).
[10] *Id.*

Under the Public Law 94-142, handicapped children are defined as children who are

1. deaf,
2. deaf-blind,
3. hard of hearing,
4. mentally retarded,
5. mutlihandicapped,
6. orthopedically impaired,
7. otherwise health impaired,
8. seriously emotionally disturbed,
9. specifically learning disabled,
10. speech impaired, or
11. visually handicapped.[11]

Public Law 94-142 applies regardless of the degree of handicap or the residential status of the child. Initial priority was given to providing services to those children who were not then receiving any services at all, with the secondary goal of upgrading the services of those who were being inadequately served. All schools are required to first determine whether a child has one of the disabilities protected by law and to then further determine whether the child's disability requires special education.

Gifted education is not covered under Public Law 94-142. Therefore, any state wishing to provide services for the gifted must do so at their own expense. Likewise, the rules governing services under 94-142, do not apply to education for gifted students.

Under the law, federal financial assistance is available only if the state develops a comprehensive program to seek to locate and educate all handicapped children within its jurisdiction between the ages of 3 and 21. The state's policy must be reflected in an official plan developed in consultation with the public and submitted to and approved by the secretary of education. The plan must include specific procedural safeguards. If the secretary finds noncompliance with federal guidelines, funding to the offending state may be withheld.

States may develop definitions of "handicaps" that may differ from those listed by Public Law 94-142. The principal is required to follow the state's outline as long as it is not less comprehensive than 94-142. States may always voluntarily provide more benefits or guar-

[11]20 U.S.C.A. Sec. 1401 (17).

antees for their citizens than is required by the federal government. Federal guarantees should be viewed as minimum requirements.

DISCIPLINE OF SPECIAL-EDUCATION STUDENTS

To date, there are no legal restrictions on how the principal may handle the misbehavior of a special-education student, short of suspension or expulsion. However, disciplinary measures should be spelled out in each student's IEP; if they are not, then approaches such as "time out" or "staying after school" could be considered a change in the student's educational program. A teacher or principal may not change a special-education student's program; only the multidisciplinary team that initially developed the child's IEP may change it.

When the misbehavior of a special-education student becomes severe enough that suspension or expulsion is contemplated, the principal must be aware that several restrictions will apply. The following guidelines are compiled from a number of court cases throughout the United States:[12]

1. The school may not suspend or expel a special-education student if the cause of the disruptive behavior was the student's handicapping condition.
2. In order to determine whether there is a relationship between the handicap and the reason for which the student is to be suspended, a trained group of persons (the multidisciplinary team) must be consulted. The principal may not make the determination.

Because removal from school is considered a change in the educational placement of a special-education student, the courts have not allowed a great deal of discretion, even when the multidisciplinary team determines that there is no causal connection between handicap and misbehavior. The Court of Appeals for the Fourth Circuit concluded that a multidisciplinary team had erred when it found no connection between a student's learning disability and his in-shcool behavior as a "drug dealer." The court concluded that the student's learning disability had produced a poor self-image and a susceptibility to peer pressure that led to "pushing drugs."[13]

[12]*S-1* v. *Turlington*, 635 F.2d 342 (5th Cir. 1981); *Doe by Gonzales* v. *Mahen*, 793 F.2d 1470 (9th Cir. 1986); *Schools Bd. of the County of Prince Williams, Virginia*, v. *Malone*, 762 F.2d 1210 (4th Cir. 1985); *Kaelin* v. *Grubbs*, 682 F. 2d 595 (6th Cir. 1982).
[13]School Bd. of the County of Prince William, Virginia, *id.*

PARENTS AND DUE PROCESS

As noted earlier in this chapter, federal law requires that a special-education student's parents be involved in every step of his educational process. Parents have the following basic rights:

1. When the student is first suspected of having a problem requiring special education, parents' permission must be obtained before the student can be assessed (tested).
2. Parents have the right to have the results of the assessment explained to them and to be informed about whether their child could benefit from special education.
3. Parents have the right to participate in the development of an IEP for their child as a result of the assessment.
4. They have a right to receive written notice in advance, and in their native language, of any meeting that will deal with their child's special education program.
5. Parents have the right of access to their child's records; otherwise, confidentiality of the records must be maintained.

In addition to the rights just mentioned, parents have the right to formally disagree with any decision that the school attempts to make regarding their child. If parents disagree with a decision, they must request a due-process hearing. At the hearing, a state-sponsored presiding officer hears both sides of the issue and renders a decision. If the parents are dissatisfied with the decision, they may appeal to the chief state school officer. Parents may take legal action if they are not satisfied with the chief school officer's decision. Parents have the following procedural rights at due-process hearings:

1. the right to be represented by counsel
2. the right to present evidence
3. the right to present witnesses
4. the right to cross-examine the school's witnesses
5. the right to obtain a transcript of the proceedings

Students may not be required to undergo a psychiatric examination for which the primary purpose is to gain information about any of the following:

1. political affiliation;
2. mental and psychological problems potentially embarrassing to the student or his family;

3. sexual behavior and attitudes;
4. illegal, anti-social, self-incriminating, and demeaning behavior;
5. critical appraisals of other individuals with whom respondents have close family relationships;
6. legally recognized privileged and analogous relationships, such as those of lawyers, physicians, and ministers; or
7. income, under certain circumstances.[14]

THE PRINCIPAL AND SPECIAL-EDUCATION PERSONNEL

As the field of special education grows, so does the number of specialized personnel needed to serve the unique needs of the handicapped. In this section, we will discuss the following special-education personnel: school psychologists, school social workers, special-education teachers, speech therapists, and special-education directors.

THE SCHOOL PSYCHOLOGIST

School psychologists are special-education professionals who are trained at the graduate level. They hold at least a master's degree in educational or school psychology and must complete a state-recognized certification program. Many states also require that school psychologists also have a number of years of teaching experience in order to be certified. As the profession becomes more complex, the number of school psychologists holding doctoral degrees is increasing.

The school psychologist serves as the head special-education professional. In many states, no special-education assessment can be complete until the school psychologist confirms that the testing was sufficiently comprehensive. It is also common to have the school psychologist chair each IEP development and followup meeting. The school psychologist is the only special-education professional who may administer psychological tests.

In addition, the school psychologist often provides individual and group therapy for students whose psychological difficulties are impacting on their educational programs. Table 6–2 outlines some of the roles of the school psychologist as suggested by the National Association of School Psychologists.[15]

[14]Family Rights and Privacy Act (Buckley Amendment), 20 U.S.C.A. Sec. 1232 h.
[15]As adapted by R. A. Gorton, *School Administration and Supervision,* 2d ed. (Dubuque, IA: Wm. C. Brown, 1983), p. 393.

TABLE 6-2. The Role of the School Psychologist.

1. Counsels with individual students who are self-referred or referred by teachers, administrators, or community agencies, to help them develop behavior patterns and attitudes which are appropriate to students' environmental and developmental stages.
2. Gathers sufficient information from previous records and through observation and assessment, to determine how a student can best be helped.
3. Assists the school staff to develop criteria and referral procedures for identifying students who need the services of the school psychologist.
4. Assists teachers, administrators, and parents to develop a greater understanding of student behavior, and to create a special climate in the school which maximizes learning and personal growth for the student.
5. Consults with teachers, curriculum specialists, and administrators on possible ways to improve conditions necessary for effective student learning.
6. Encourages teachers and other professional educators to accept responsibility/accountability for (and to help students accept responsibility for) growth toward predetermined goals.
7. Identifies and utilizes remedial/corrective resources available within the school or community.
8. Serves as a liaison between school and community.

SCHOOL SOCIAL WORKER

The school social worker is a trained professional who typically holds a master's degree in social work and has met the state certification requirements. School social workers are usually not required to have teaching experience in order to be certified.

The job of the school social worker, like that of the school psychologist, is multifaceted. The school social worker usually works out of the central office and visits schools based upon referrals. The primary function of the school social worker is to serve as a liaison between the school and the home. The school social worker helps students who are having difficulties in adjusting to the school environment. This professional tends to see students who are having behavioral or emotional problems in school that can be traced back to the family or to neighborhood conditions.

The National Association of Social Workers has outlined some of the functions of the school social worker (Table 6-3).[16]

As society becomes more complex, the problems of living take their toll on both families and students. It is difficult to imagine a school's being able to meet its students' needs without the help of a school social worker.

[16]*Ibid.*, p. 394.

TABLE 6-3. Functions of the School Social Worker.

1. Counsels with parents and students on problems of student adjustment to school.
2. Utilizes community resources in the process of working with children and parents.
3. Consults with staff members concerning community factors which may be affecting problems of student adjustment in school.
4. Collaborates with teachers, administrators, and noninstructional personnel in gathering and sharing information about students, designed to modify or resolve student adjustment problems.
5. Acts as liaison between the school and community agencies.
6. Cooperates with community agencies by providing pertinent information about a student's school adjustment and achievement.

SPECIAL-EDUCATION TEACHERS

There are many types of special-education teachers. They can be classified in two ways: (1) by the type of handicapped students they teach and (2) by the manner in which the students are organized to receive their education. The teaching specialities by handicap type are as varied as the number of categories of handicaps in federal law. There are three methods of delivery: resource, self-contained, and cooperative. Figure 6-1 shows the combinations of handicaps and delivery methods that are most typically found in public education.

Students with learning disabilities (LDs), behavioral disorders (BDs), and speech pathologies are usually educated in mainstream schools. In general, at least one LD teacher is assigned to each building in a school district. Most children with LDs have either an auditory or a visual disability. These LDs are often treated by the resource method. In other words, the LD teacher acts as a resource to the student and to the student's regular classroom teacher. The child will leave the regular classroom several times a week for a specified number of minutes, depending on the severity of the LD. The student thus maintains a primary relationship with regular education while receiv-

FIGURE 6-1. Special-education teaching specialties and typical delivery methods.

SPECIALTY	DELIVERY METHOD
Learning Disability (LD)	LD resource or self-contained LD
Behavioral Disorder (BD)	Self-contained BD or resource
Minor Physical Handicap	Adaptive physical education (Resource)
Low-incidence Handicap (deafness, blindness, or major physical handicap	Special-education cooperative (separate building servicing multiple school districts)

ing special education. Like students with LDs, students with speech problems are usually educated by the resource method.

Children with BDs are not usually served by the resource method. Because BDs have much to do with the environment, the self-contained BD classroom is the most common approach to this speciality. In a self-contained BD class, children with BDs are taught by one teacher for most of the subjects in the curriculum. However, it is common for BD students to take courses such as art, music, or physical education with regular-education students.

Minor physical handicaps include such problems as gross- or fine-motor coordination deficits. Students with these handicaps are usually taught by an adapted physical education (PE) teacher. These children are usually taught in a regular-education building, and their programs do not require equipment beyond that which is included in most school inventories. The adapted PE teacher is usually a certified physical education teacher who has received additional training which allows him to acquire a special-education certificate in the adapted area.

The last special-education teachers to be discussed are those whom the principal may never see. These professionals are the highly specialized teachers of the low-incidence handicapped, so called because relatively few cases of the handicap are usually found in public school districts. The low-incidence handicaps include deafness, blindness, and major physical handicaps. Many school districts are too small to hire their own teacher for deaf students, for example. Therefore, several school districts form a special-education cooperative in which the combined populations include sufficient numbers of students with the same handicaps to warrant the hiring of a specialized teacher.

Although principals may not see these teachers or students on a daily basis, they should be familiar with arrangements for low-incidence handicap education. If the principal has a student in the attendance area with a low-incidence handicap, he will be involved in the IEP staffing and in periodic meetings to discuss the student's progress. The spirit of Public Law 94–142 calls for students with low-incidence handicaps to participate in activities with regular-education students as frequently as possible.

THE SPEECH THERAPIST

Perhaps the greatest number of IEPs are written for speech therapy. Speech therapy is a specialized field usually requiring training at the graduate level. Children with speech problems are served by a resource program, whereby they receive 30 to 60 minutes of one-to-one or small-group therapy each week, depending on the severity of their problems. Students visit the speech therapist in their own school building.

THE SPECIAL-EDUCATION DIRECTOR

The position of special-education director is relatively new in the field of education. It was created because of the increasing complexity of special education. The role of special-education director seems to be in an early state of evolution. As Whitworth and Hatley have noted:

> No clear conceptualization has yet emerged in many states concerning the responsibilities and competencies of special-education administrators. Some local districts elevate a successful teacher to the position, perceiving the role to be largely that of consultant to the classroom teacher. Other districts, viewing the job to be one of management, appoint an experienced general administrator. And yet the actual role of the special-education administrator remains an ambiguous one that has led to a great confusion.[17]

Regardless of the varied backgrounds of special-education directors, there are some common responsibilities that seem to typically fall on their shoulders. In the area of pupil placement, the director sets general policy and monitors day-to-day decisions made at lower levels. In addition, the director often prepares the special-education budget and submits it to the superintendent. The director also participates with the personnel director in recruitment, hiring, and evaluation.

The school principal should be able to work in harmony with the special-education director. The director is typically at the top of the special-education hierarchy in the school district and acts as the superintendent's advisor on matters relating to special education. The director is considered a central-office administrator with status equal to that of an assistant superintendent.

THE PRINCIPAL AND THE SPECIAL-EDUCATION ASSESSMENT PROCESS

The special-education assessment process can be divided into four phases; several steps must be taken at each phase. Figure 6–2 gives a

---

[17] J. E. Whitworth and R. V. Hatley, "The Role of the Special Education Director," *The Journal for Special Educators* 19 (1982):38.

general overview of the special-education assessment process, including development of the IEP.

The IEP is a written commitment of resources necessary to enable a handicapped child to receive special education and related services. The IEP developmental process is designed to provide the best possible educational goals for the handicapped child. In most school districts, the building principal is expected to take responsibility for the referral

FIGURE 6–2. Overview of the special-education assessment process.

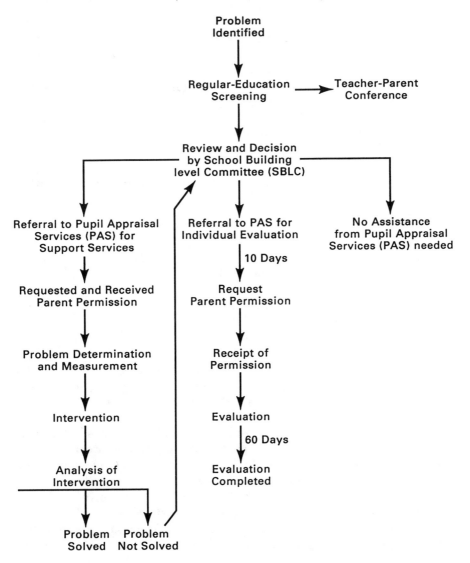

process for children identified as possibly having special-education needs. In some school districts, the principal may be asked to chair all of the meetings, from pre-referral to the final approval of the IEP.

The four phases of the assessment process include referral, evaluation, placement, and reevaluation. The principal should be familiar with the entire assessment process.

THE REFERRAL

The referral process actually starts in the regular-education classroom, when the teacher notices that a child is having a problem. Figure 6–2 indicates that the regular-education staff should first determine whether the child's problem requires immediate intervention or whether a special-education assessment is warranted.

It is recommended that the staff have a conference with the parents to assist in identifying the problem. The following are behaviors that might signal a problem:

- The child is performing poorly on assignments and tests compared with classmates.
- The child is having difficulty completing tasks.
- The child's behavior in class is erratic or disruptive.
- The child is having trouble concentrating; the child's attention span is decreasing.
- The child's peer relationships are deteriorating.

Some schools have pre-referral intervention teams that meet to offer assistance to the regular-education teachers in an effort to meet a student's individual needs.

It should be noted that, although they may not be aware of it, parents have the right to make a referral. The teacher and the principal should be prepared to listen to the parents' description of the problem, with a view toward the possibility that the child might have a special-education need.

If the principal, teacher, and parents are convinced that the child's problem can not be remediated by regular-education approaches, then a referral to the school building–level committee (SBLC), or multidisciplinary team, is appropriate. The SBLC usually includes the following individuals: the special-education director or the school psychologist, one or more special-education teachers, regular-education teachers, the school counselor, the principal, one or more parents or guardians, and the student (if appropriate). A referral form such as the one shown in Figure 6–3 is generally used for initiating contact with special-education personnel.

FIGURE 6–3. Sample referral form for initiating contact with special education.

Teacher Referral to SBL Committee

STUDENT _____ DATE _____

SCHOOL _____ AGE _____ GRADE _____ TEACHER _____

I. Classroom Level   Teacher/Parent Communication Date: _____

A. Concerns–Problems	B. Intervention	C. Results: Carried Out By
1.		
2.		
3.		

II. SBL Committee _____ **Date** _____

SBL MEMBERS

_____   _____
_____   _____
_____   _____
_____   _____
_____   _____

A. Concerns–Problems	B. Intervention	C. Results: Carried Out By
1.		
2.		
3.		
(Continue on St. 12-2 if needed)		

III. SBL Recommendations –

(Problem Resolved_____ Refer for Evaluiation_____ Refer for Support Services_____)

Decision Date: _____

THE REFERRAL CONFERENCE

Once special-education personnel have been contacted, the SBLC must be called together for a referral conference. The parents of the child being referred must be invited to this meeting. Federal guidelines require that the time and place of the conference be set at the parents' convenience.

At the conference, current information on the child should be reviewed, and the next steps to be taken should be determined. Even if the principal has already decided that only special education can help the child, the appropriate intervention is still subject to discussion. The principal must keep an open mind about the possibilities for the child. Special-education personnel may recommend that the child be returned to the regular classroom until additional data are gathered. Alternatively, the SBLC may determine that the child's problem does not call for special education. Most of the time, however, the referral conference determines that there is sufficient evidence to warrant special-education assessment in order to develop a specific diagnosis. When evaluation is needed, the parents' permission must be obtained.

Evaluation

The child's problem is diagnosed through a comprehensive assessment, which involves the administration of appropriate tests. Particular care must be taken to select the right tests. The details of the evaluation are determined by the following federal guidelines:

1. Tests and other evaluation materials are provided and administered in the child's native language or other mode of communication.
2. Tests have been validated for the specific purpose for which they are used.
3. Trained personnel shall administer tests and conform to the instructions for administration provided by the test developer.
4. A test shall be selected and administered so that it accurately reflects the child's aptitude or achievement rather than reflecting the child's impaired sensory, manual, or speaking skills, except where those skills are the factors that the test purposes to measure.
5. No single procedure is used as the sole criterion for the determination of an appropriate educational program for the child.
6. The child is assessed in all areas related to the suspected disability.
7. Tests selected should not be racially or culturally biased.
8. Tests should be administered in the child's primary language.

9. Test procedures should be organized so that the evaluation is made by a multidisciplinary team that includes a teacher or other specialist with knowledge in the suspected area of disability.[18]

The principal should note that parents are entitled to schedule an independent evaluation. According to Public Law 94–142, the independent evaluation must be made by a qualified examiner not employed by the public agency (the school district) responsible for educating a child. A qualified person is one who has met certification, licensing, registration, or other such state requirements. When parents request an independent evaluation, it is often because they disagree with the test results.

Placement

Once the evaluation has been completed, the SBLC meets for a placement conference. At this conference, the student's IEP is developed. Most states provide an IEP form that the SBLC can use to facilitate the placement conference (see Figure 6–4).

The IEP form should contain the following information:

1. determination of the child's primary and secondary handicap
2. statement of the goals of the educational program
3. statement about the extent to which the child will participate in regular-education activities
4. date on which the services will begin and the anticipated duration of those services
5. frequency of progress reports being sent home
6. identification of the school personnel participating in the conference and of those responsible for the implementation of the IEP.

One of the major themes of Public Law 94–142 is the placement of the child in the "least restrictive environment." There should be some acknowledgement at the placement conference that the child will be receive as much mainstream instruction as his handicap will allow.

Reevaluation

After the IEP has been developed and the program has begun, the child's progress must be periodically reevaluated. Federal law requires

[18]J. S. Kaiser, ed., *The Principalship* (Minneapolis: Burgess, 1985), p. 114.

INDIVIDUALIZED EDUCATION PROGRAM
DEPARTMENT OF EDUCATION

Placement/Services _____

System _____
Meeting Date(s). _____

Student Name _____
DOB _____ ID # _____

INDIVIDUAL
EVALUATION DATE _____
HOMEBASED SCHOOL _____

PRIMARY
EXCEPTIONALITY _____
OTHER SCHOOL _____ Grade _____

SECONDARY
EXCEPTIONALITY(ies) _____
TYPE IEP: _____ Interim _____ Initial _____ Review _____ Transitional

Position _____ Describe type of categorical or generic class setting.

IEP PARTICIPANTS: Signatures | Signatures

Parent _____ Representative of System _____
Teacher(s) _____ Eval. Rep. _____
_____ Other(s) _____
Student _____

DATE TO _____
BEGIN _____

EXPECTED TIME:
___ Less than one year
___ One Year

SPECIAL EDUCATIONAL PROGRAM (check one)
Specially Designed Regular Instruction
  (Minimum Standards)
* Alternative to Regular Placement
  (Separate Minimum Standards)
* Combination of the above (Describe)

LONG-TERM EDUCATIONAL GOALS (check one)
___ High School Diploma
___ High School Equivalency Diploma
___ Certificate of Achievement

ADAPTED PHYSICAL EDUCATION:___ Yes ___ No
(If YES, give frequency/amount)

REGULAR CLASSES AND ACTIVITIES (with non-exceptional students)
___ Spelling ___ Soc. Studies ___ Vocational
___ Reading ___ Science ___ Art/Music
___ Writing ___ Phys. Ed. ___ Lunch
___ English ___ Electives ___ Recess ___ Assemblies

MODIFICATIONS NEEDED IN REGULAR CLASS

Min/day in Regular Class

Min/days in Special Class

☐ None

PLACEMENT/LRE ASSURANCE: Check placement below. Justify why less restrictive place-
ment(s) is not appropriate and why the placement selected is appropriate.

_____ Regular Class with Adapted P.E. only
_____ Regular Class with Speech Therapy only
_____ Regular Class with Supplemental Aids and Services
_____ Regular Class with Resource
_____ Self-Contained Class with Regular
_____ Self-Contained Class
_____ Special School
_____ Hospital/Homebound
_____ Regular Class with Center for the Gifted Students
_____ Regular Class with Center for the Talented Students

Copy of "Educational Rights of Exceptional
Children" given to parent.

Signature _____
Date _____

LENGTH OF INSTRUCTIONAL PROGRAM:
___ 180 days ___ In excess of 180 days
  (describe)

RELATED SERVICES	Date to Begin	Sessions/ Week	Time/ Session	Indiv/ Group	Dura- tion	Comments

Special ___ Yes (describe)
Transportation ___ No

COMMENTS:

Person(s)/Agency(ies) Responsible
for Overall Implementation
System Administrator _____
Other (describe) _____

I agree to ensure that the program and services described in this IEP are provided. REPORTS ON THE
STUDENT'S PROGRESS WILL BE SENT HOME EVERY _____ WEEKS.

After discussing my child's special education needs, I approve this proposed IEP/Placement. I realize that
I may revoke this permission at any time.

DATE _____ Supervisor/Designee Signature _____

DATE _____ Parent/Guardian/Surrogate Parent Signature _____

COMPLETE THE FOLLOWING ONLY IF THE EDUCATIONAL PROGRAM CHOSEN ABOVE IS AN ALTERNATIVE OR A COMBINATION PROGRAM:

*The implications of placement in an alternative or combination program have been explained to me and I
realize that my child will not participate in all aspects of the Competency Based Education Program and
may not receive a high school diploma as a result of this program decision.

DATE _____ Parent/Guardian/Surrogate Parent Signature _____

FIGURE 6–4. Sample IEP form.

that the IEP be reviewed at least once a year, and that another comprehensive reevaluation be completed at least every three years.

After the child's IEP has been reviewed, adjustments should be made. If the child has made progress as planned, then new goals are set for the following year. The new placement may be in a less restrictive environment than that of the year before. The idea is to continue to progress toward a complete return to the regular-education program.

SPECIAL EDUCATION–REGULAR EDUCATION RELATIONSHIPS

The job of the regular-education teacher and the principal is not over once a student has been placed in special education. In fact, the job of regular education has just begun. In most instances, the student will continue to spend a majority of time in the regular classroom. The fact that one or more special-education students in the regular classroom will be leaving at various intervals throughout the week to visit a special-education teacher can pose a number of problems for both the teacher and principal.

The results of a study conducted by Davis showed that most principals (1) receive very little exposure to special education as part of their training program in educational administration; (2) consider formal training in special education for principals to be extremely important; and (3) believe that their time involvement with special-education issues has been substantially increased as a result of federal special-education legislation.[19]

In a study by Bonds and Lindsey, regular-education teachers perceived the principal as adequately performing in the role of instructional leader for special-education matters. However, those same teachers believed that principals should better acquaint them with Public Law 94–142 regulations, should conduct more classroom observations, and should more closely monitor scheduling of regular-education and special-education activities.[20]

Principals must strive to increase their knowledge of special

[19]W. E. Davis, "An Analysis of Principals' Formal Training in Special Education," *Education* 101 (1980):89–94.

[20]C. W. Bonds and J. Lindsey, "The Principal in Special Education: The Teachers' Perspective," *Education* 102 (1982):407–410.

education and to facilitate a good working relationship between regular and special education.

INCREASING COMMUNICATION

Increasing communication about special education can be an effective vehicle for promoting education for handicapped children. The principal should target two groups: (1) the parents and the community and (2) regular-education teachers.

Formal newsletters, bulletins, and personal appearances are good avenues for communicating with parents and with the community. However, writing a separate bulletin for special education might serve to promote the idea that special education is not an integral part of the school. It would be far wiser for the principal to keep the special-education program in mind when writing general school bulletins. References to special-education activities throughout such bulletins promote a sense of program unity with regular education.

When communicating with regular-education teachers, the principal must make an effort to include special-education teachers as part of the group. For example, special-education teachers should be present at all faculty meetings. Faculty input on regular-education program development should come from special-education teachers as well as from regular-education teachers.

Staffing Arrangements

The principal can promote closer relationships between regular-education and special-education teachers by arranging faculty work groups. Every school building has a number of teacher committees that plan curriculum, discipline, the school calendar, and even social activities. The principal should make sure that each committee includes a number of special-education teachers. Every opportunity that regular-education and special-education teachers have to work and "play" together increases the likelihood that they will come to understand each other.

SUMMARY

Since the passage of Public Law 94–142, special education has become part of every school program in the United States. Consequently, the role of the principal as it relates to special education and regular education has changed. The principal must become familiar with the laws that shape special education.

The Education For All Handicapped Children Act (Public Law 94–142) requires that handicapped children

- be provided with a free and appropriate education
- be educated in the least restrictive environment appropriate to their needs
- be evaluated in a language that they and their parents can understand
- be given an IEP
- have their parents participate in all decisions regarding their education program
- be provided with due process in the event that they (or their parents) do not agree with school authorities' decisions regarding their education program

The principal should be familiar with the jobs done by various school-education personnel. Most principals work with a school psychologist, a school social worker, speech therapists, a variety of special-education teachers, and a director of special education.

The development of an individualized special-education program includes the following steps: (1) identification of a potential problem, (2) diagnosis of the problem, (3) development of the IEP, and (4) placement in the appropriate program. Each child's program must be re-evaluated annually.

The principal should promote a close working relationship between regular and special education. This can be accomplished by increasing communication between the two groups and by including both regular- and special-education teachers on committees.

SELECTED BIBLIOGRAPHY

BAINE, DAVID, *Instructional Design for Special Education,* Englewood Cliffs, NJ: Educational Technical Publications, Inc., 1982.

BARBACOUI, DON R. AND RICHARD W. CLELLAND, *Public Law 94–142: Special Education in Transition,* Arlington, VA: American Assn. of School Administrators, 1978.

BRENNAN, WILFRED K., *Curriculum for Special Needs,* New York: Taylor & Francis, Inc., 1984.

BUDOFF, MILTON AND ALAN ORENSTEIN, *Due Process in Special Education: On Going to a Hearing,* Cambridge, MA: Brookline Books, 1984.

CREMINS, JAMES J., *Political Issues in Special Education,* Springfield, IL: Charles C. Thomas Pub., 1981.

DUNN, KENNETH AND RITA DUNN, *Teaching Students Through Their Individual Learning Styles: A Practical Approach,* Englewood Cliffs, NJ: Prentice-Hall, Inc., 1979.

GOLDBERG, STEVEN S., *Special Education Law: A Guide for Parents, Advocates, and Educators*, New York: Plenum Publishing Corp., 1982.

HOWELL, KENNETH W. AND MODA K. MOREHEAD, *Curriculum Based Evaluation in Special and Remedial Education*, Columbus, OH: Merrill Publishing Co., 1987.

KNEEDLER, REBECCA D. ET AL., *Special Education for Today*, Englewood Cliffs, NJ: Prentice-Hall, Inc., 1984.

MAHER, CHARLES A. AND RANDY E. BENNETT, *Planning and Evaluating Special Education Services*, Englewood Cliffs, NJ: Prentice-Hall, Inc., 1984.

MAYER, C. LAMAR, *Educational Administration and Special Education: A Handbook for School Administrators*, Needham Heights, MA: Allyn & Bacon, Inc., 1981.

MORRIS, RICHARD J. AND BURTON BLATT, EDS., *Special Education: Research and Trends*, Elmsford, NY: Pergamon Bks., Inc., 1986.

PODEMSKI, RICHARD S. ET AL., *Comprehensive Administration of Special Education*, Rockville, MD: Aspen Pubs., Inc., 1984.

REAMS, BERNARD D. JR., ED., *Education of the Handicapped: Laws, Legislative Histories and Administrative Documents, Vol. 55*, Buffalo, NY: William S. Hein and Co., Inc., 1982.

SAGE, DANIEL D. AND LEONARD C. BURRELLO, *Policy and Management in Special Education*, Englewood Cliffs, NJ: Prentice-Hall, Inc., 1986.

SOCITY, JONATHAN AND SHIRLEY BULL, *Special Needs: Bridging the Curriculum Gap*, New York: Taylor and Francis, Inc., 1987.

TURNER, DONALD G., *Issues in Education of the Handicapped*, Bloomington, IN: Phi Delta Kappa, Educational Foundation, 1983.

WILES, J. AND J. BONDI, *Supervision: A Guide to Practice (2nd ed.)*, Columbus, OH: Charles E. Merrill, 1986.

ZIGMOND, NAOMI AND ADA VALLECOLSA, *Assessment for Instructional Planning in Special Education*, Englewood Cliffs, NJ: Prentice-Hall, Inc., 1983.

7

The Principal
and the Law

The effective principal should be thoroughly competent in school law. The practice of the principalship is shaped by the law. School law provides the parameters within which the principal must operate.

The principal may review the law in either a positive or negative light. Lack of knowledge concerning the law can breed the negative view, and the law thus becomes an obstacle to the practice of the principalship. However, if the principal takes the time to become familiar with the foundations of school law, this knowledge can provide a source of strength. By staying abreast of current legal developments, the principal can make the law his ally. What might have been the basis of inconvenience for the principal now becomes the much-needed firm ground upon which to make decisions.

Increased judicial involvement in schools is clear. The potential for the principal to violate a teacher's or student's rights is sufficient reason for having some knowledge of school law. Not every principal has access to advice from a school attorney. Where access is available, the time it takes to obtain that advice may make it too late to be useful. Often the principal's need for advice is immediate. This chapter will examine two aspects of the interaction between the principal and the law. First, the need for the principal to know and apply school law to practice will be considered as an aspect of developing "legal literacy"and conducting a legal audit within the school. Second, the substantive areas of teacher and student rights will be outlined, and the way in which they have shaped the principal's behavior will be examined.

LEGAL LITERACY

The term *legal literacy,* as used here, describes the extent to which the principal has become educationally founded in school law. It also includes those steps that the principal takes to provide for continuing education in matters of school law.

THE NEED FOR LEGAL LITERACY

Research indicates that teachers and school administrators have an inadequate knowledge of even the most obvious court decisions affecting education. In 1978, Zirkel, as chairman of Phi Delta Kappa's Commission on the Impact of Court Decisions on Education, conducted a survey to determine the extent to which school leaders could recognize the Supreme Court decisions currently affecting school operations. The results showed that the average score on a twenty-item test was 10.7, only slightly above 50 percent.[1] Zirkel concluded:

> In my opinion, the overall results constitute a failing grade for school leaders. I say this not only because of the importance of the Supreme Court's decisions (that failed to be recognized) but because of the nature of the items and characteristics of the respondents. The items merely call for recognition, not recall or higher-order cognitive skills.[2]

More recently, Menacker and Pascarella tested teachers and administrators in city and suburban public schools in the Chicago metropolitan area. A ten-item questionnaire attempted to measure knowledge of education-related Supreme Court rulings.[3] The total group of 299 respondents scored an average of 64.4 percent correct. While administrators scored higher than teachers (74 percent correct compared to 63 percent correct for the adjusted mean) the administrators' results were still disappointing. The authors expressed concern about the findings:

> [O]ur findings reveal an ineffective and haphazard communication network for transmitting important Supreme Court decisions. . . . The dispensing of information on school law should begin in teacher preparation programs, should continue in programs preparing school administrators, and should become a regular part of inservice programming for educators at all levels and in all locations.[4]

ESTABLISHING LITERACY

Most graduate-level programs for school principals include some preparation in school law. For principals who find a formal course lacking in their own education, school-board or school-administrator workshops can help to compensate for the absence of the rudiments. Professional-association workshops and seminars can also be part of a continuing legal education package that principals establish for themselves. Continuing education can be advanced by membership in school-law organizations such as the National Organization on Legal

[1] P. A. Zirkel, "A Test on Supreme Court Decisions Affecting Education," *Phi Delta Kappan* 59 (1978):521–555.

[2] *Ibid.*, p. 522.

[3] J. Menacker and E. Pascarella, "How Aware Are Educators of Supreme Court Decisions that Affect Them," *Phi Delta Kappan* 64 (1983):424–426.

[4] *Ibid.*, p. 426.

Problems of Education (NOLPE). Such organizations provide a continuing source of current school-law information.

The purpose of any continuing-education course in school law should not be to make an attorney out of the school principal. Rather, the intent should be to acquaint principals with some of the legal fundamentals affecting their positions and the profession. Those who fish and hunt must know the game laws. Those who operate automobiles must know the traffic laws. As citizens and members of society, we must know right from wrong, morally but also legally.[5]

The principal's legal education should have a specific focus. The principal must have enough knowledge about the law to know initially what questions to ask when confronted with a potential problem. Principals must be able to know when legal issues are being implicated in the day-to-day problems faced in practice. In addition, they must know when to ask for advice from the school attorney. At that point, the principal must have sufficient knowledge to be able to evaluate the quality of the advice. The principal must keep in mind that the attorney is not a professional educator. It is the principal, not the attorney, who will be responsible for the effects that legal advice may have on the educational program. Weighing the attorney's advice, rather than being contemptuous of it, should be considered a sign of wisdom on the part of the principal. Also, the evaluation of advice will be important for understanding it sufficiently to be able to communicate about the matter to teachers, students, or parents.

EVALUATION OF LEGAL ADVICE

The principal may wish to consider four factors in the evaluation of legal advice: (1) the source of the advice, (2) facts comparison and statutory analysis, (3) legal jurisdiction, and (4) the school attorney's opinions.

Source of Advice

The principal should ask the attorney to supply the legal source from which the advice is derived. If the principal ultimately decides to use the advice as part of an administrative decision, he may be called upon to "back up" his position. Having case names, statute, or regulation citations available can provide powerful support to a decision.

[5]W. H. Roe and T. L. Drake, *The Principalship* (New York: Macmillan, 1980).

Facts Comparison and Statutory Analysis

The principal should ask the attorney to supply the facts of the case that is being suggested as controlling. The principal can then compare the facts of the case with the facts surrounding the immediate school problem. Are the facts similar? If not, the legal principle enunciated in the case will not apply in the situation in question. If the source of the legal advice is a state or federal statute (law made by a legislative body) or an administrative regulation, the principal must be sure that he understands the language of the law before assuming that it does or does not apply. The attorney should translate the statute or regulation into plain language. Often the language of statutes must balance a line between being understandable and being legally correct. For example, insurance policies are notorious for their incomprehensibility. However, insurance policies are generally not written to be understandable. Rather, they are written to be legally "tight"—that is, to contain all of the legal language provisions necessary, no matter how abstruse, in order to protect the interests of the parties in the event of litigation.

A key element in analyzing a statute is the form of the predicate used in the phrasing. The predicate *shall* means one thing and *may* quite another. For example, the Kansas Statutes Annotated at 72-9003 reads:

> Every board *shall* [emphasis added] adopt a written policy of personnel evaluation procedure in accordance with this act and file the same with the state board.[6]

The predicate *shall* requires full compliance with the provisions of the statute. In the example, the board would have no option in the matter of the establishment of evaluation policy for professional personnel. The board could not decide that it doesn't want to commit itself in writing to a specific policy but would rather keep it as an understanding with the teacher group. The statute expressly points to a written policy. On the other hand, if the operational predicate in the statute is *may,* then this is a cue for a school authority option. In the present example, a *may* replacing a *shall* would mean that the board could look upon the establishment of a written policy for evaluation as a matter of their discretion. In other words, the statute provides the school authorities with a choice. If it is to school officials' benefit to accept and use

[6]Kan. Stat. Anno., Ch. 72, Sec. 9003.

the provisions of the statute, they can do so. At the least, the local education authority can ignore the statute. State statutes are filled with a myriad of optionlike statutes that are used or not used by school authorities as they deem appropriate. All the statutes in this category can be recognized by the predicate *may*. These statutes should not be confused with those using the predicate *shall*. The "shall statutes" require strict compliance. The general confusion comes in simply recognizing the existence of the "may statutes." It is common to find the school administrator believing that all statutes are compliance requirements. The recognition of the difference can provide a new-found source of freedom in the practice of the principalship.

Legal Jurisdiction

The principal must know the jurisdiction in which the law applies. For example, a state court decision from Kansas will not control in New York. On the other hand, a decision of the Supreme Court of the United States would apply to every school in the country. In analyzing the jurisdiction, two aspects must be considered. First, if the law applies in a particular jurisdiction, then it is controlling and must be followed. If it is discovered that the law under consideration does not control, it does not automatically mean that the law may be dismissed. A law that is controlling in one jurisdiction may be "persuasive" in another district. In other words, it may be that no case has yet been brought in that jurisdiction concerning a certain legal issue. When confronted with the matter for the first time, a court, although not required to do so, may look to another jurisdiction for precedent. The extent to which the principal complies with law that is found to be merely "persuasive" will depend on how conservative he wishes to be in practice. A cautious principal might feel more comfortable complying with persuasive law. A principal more prone to enjoying the freedom of a less restrictive environment might feel better complying with only those laws that are controlling. Whichever path is chosen, it is essential to know at the outset whether the law is controlling or persuasive.

Laws enacted by one's own state legislature (statutes) are considered to be controlling. Those state statutes that have been construed— that is, judicially interpreted—by the court are of somewhat more value than those not yet construed. Once more, those statutes that have been the subject of challenge by a state court are more stable than those that have not. Those statutes that have not yet withstood the test of a court challenge always stand the chance of being found unconstitutional at some later point. As with state statutes, cases decided within the state court system are controlling.

Figure 7-1 describes the typical levels within a state court system. Most states have a three-tiered judicial structure, which includes a district court, a court of appeals, and a supreme court. The lowest level, the district court, is the court of general jurisdiction. This is where a state case is *tried;* hence it is the state's trial court. In large metropolitan areas, the district or trial court is sometimes called a *circuit* court. These courts are usually organized on a county basis and are therefore sometimes referred to as the *county* court. The judge or magistrate is not required to render a written opinion but may do so at the request of the district attorney or attorney general if the outcome of the case appears to have some significance. The party who loses at the district-court level may appeal to the second level, which is the state court of appeal. Depending upon the outcome, either party may approach the state's court of last resort, which is the state supreme court. In some areas of the country, this court is known as *superior court.*[7]

Federal statutes (those laws enacted by Congress) are controlling in all jurisdictions of the United States. Federal case law is controlling only in a specific district or circuit unless the case was decided by the US Supreme Court. Figure 7-2 describes that segment of the federal

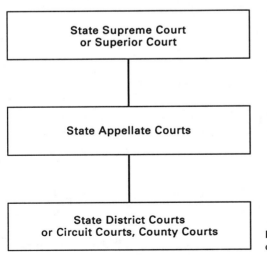

FIGURE 7-1. Three-level state court system.

[7]T. J. Sergiovanni, M. Burlingame, F. M. Coombs, and P. Thurston, *Educational Governance and Administration* (Englewood Cliffs, NJ: Prentice-Hall, 1980).

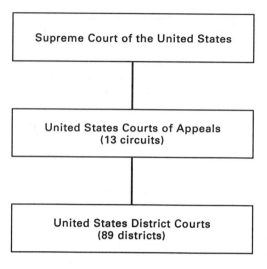

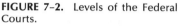

FIGURE 7–2. Levels of the Federal Courts.

court system of interest to education. The lowest level of trial level is the US District Court. These courts are disbursed throughout the United States and US territories in 87 districts. A particular state may have several US district courts depending on its size and population density. A decision of a federal district court from a court representing a district is controlling, but only in that part of the state. Therefore, federal district court decisions are of limited impact since they control such small areas.

Appeals from the district courts are made to the circuit courts of appeal. At this level, the potential for impact is far greater than at the district level. The jurisdictional territory for a federal appeals court decision is determined by the boundaries depicted in Figure 7–3. The United States is divided into thirteen circuits. A decision handed down from the federal appeals court representing one state would be controlling in that state as well as in all other states within the circuit.

School Attorney's Opinions

In the final analysis, the principal must always evaluate legal advice against the backdrop of his own knowledge. Legal advice should rarely be taken "as is." The principal must remember that the school attorney's advice will tend to be conservative. By advising the conservative "don't-do-it" approach, attorneys may believe that they are acting in the principal's best interest. This avenue will stand the best chance of keeping the principal out of court which is, of course, a duty of the attorney. However, the play-it-safe approach tends to have a

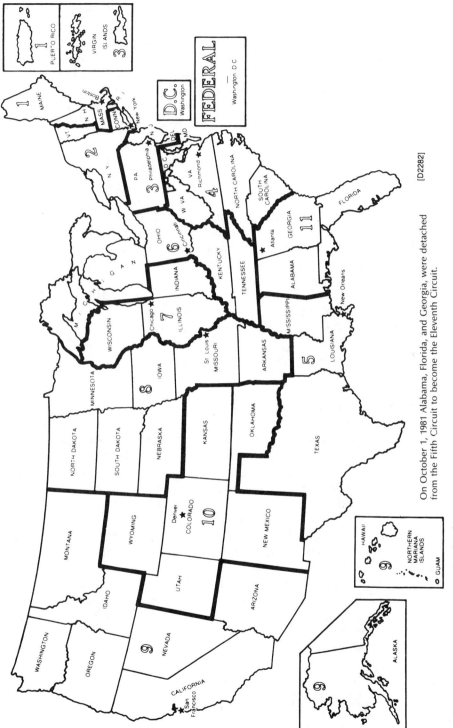

FIGURE 7–3. The thirteen federal judicial circuits.

On October 1, 1981 Alabama, Florida, and Georgia, were detached from the Fifth Circuit to become the Eleventh Circuit.

[D2282]

193

dampening effect on the creative aspects of the instructional program. The principal should not feel restricted from using leadership skills because of the law. Perhaps the greatest benefit derived from legal literacy is the freedom to be creative. Knowledge of the law should and can provide the stimulus for the worry-free exercise of leadership skills so necessary in the practice of the principalship.

TEACHERS' RIGHTS

The subject of teachers' rights can be looked upon as a balancing of competing interests. On the one side there exists the teachers' freedom to exercise personal rights. On the other side there exists governmental authority to restrict these rights for the welfare of the schools.[8] The tension between these two interests have produced a plethora of case law flanked by a substantial volume of state and federal legislation. Much of teachers' rights involve an understanding of three areas: (1) the rights of teachers with the US Constitution as a source, (2) teachers' protection against employer discrimination, and (3) teachers' rights when being dismissed.

CONSTITUTIONAL RIGHTS OF TEACHERS

Many teachers' constitutional rights have been recognized as a result of deprivation of the exercise of free speech and expression. Generally, a teacher may not be dismissed, demoted, or transferred because of the exercise of free speech. The leading case on this matter is *Pickering* v. *Board of Education.*[9] Prior to *Pickering,* the courts viewed teacher employment as a privilege. This *privilege doctrine* was used by the courts to sustain the dismissal of teachers for whatever reason the board of education may have had. In 1968, when the US Supreme Court decided *Pickering,* a new judicial view was forwarded concerning the constitutional rights of teachers. The Court believed that the interest of the government to impose restrictions on teachers must be weighed against the interests of the teachers. Neither the government's interest nor the teachers' is absolute.[10]

---

[8]For a thorough explication of teachers' rights, see M. McCarthy and N. Cambron, *Public School Law* (Boston: Allyn & Bacon, 1981).

[9]391 U.S. 563 (1968).

[10]K. Alexander and M. Alexander, *The Law of Schools, Students, and Teachers* (St. Paul: West, 1984).

In the case itself, Marvin Pickering, a public school teacher in Will County, Illinois, was terminated some time after he wrote a letter to the local newspaper criticizing the board of education. Specifically, Mr. Pickering disagreed with the board's disparate expenditure of funds between the educational and athletic programs. The board claimed that the letter contained false statements damaging the reputations of the board members and school administrators. In using the "balancing-of-interests" approach in analyzing the case, the Court asked: (1) Was the substance of the letter a matter of public concern? and (2) Did the letter actually produce disruption in the school system?[11] The Court concluded that the letter was a matter of public concern. Also, the record revealed that the letter did not precipitate any disruption in the system. In determining the lack of disruption, the Court noted that the letter was not directed at anyone with whom Pickering would have daily contact in the work environment.[12]

Given their analysis, the Court concluded that "absent proof of false statements, knowingly or recklessly made, a teacher's views on public issues cannot form the basis for dismissal."[13] Later cases continued to apply the *Pickering* standards to a variety of situations. In 1972, the Federal Appeals Court for the Second Circuit held that a teacher's dismissal for wearing a black armband in protest of the Vietnam War was in violation of freedom of expression.[14] Still later, the Federal Appeals Court for the Seventh Circuit concluded that a teacher had been impermissibly transferred for having made public comments in favor of collective bargaining.[15] It is interesting to note that the courts have viewed *some* disruption of the school operation as insufficient basis for teacher transfer. It appears as though other conditions would have to be met by the board before a transfer or termination would be sustained when free speech issues are involved. School authorities were successful in terminating a teacher for encouraging students to oppose the ROTC's visiting their school. The court found (1) that the teacher's speech was unrelated to his class subject matter (algebra) and (2) that it actually interfered with the operation of the school.

An additional dimension was added to the *Pickering* criteria in 1977 when the US Supreme Court decided *Mt. Healthy City School District* v. *Doyle.*[16] In *Mt. Healthy,* a nontenured teacher telephoned a radio station to criticize a dress code for teachers. The teacher, Doyle,

---

[11]*Pickering* at 570.
[12]*Id.* at 572–573.
[13]*Id.* at 574.
[14]*James* v. *Bd. of Education of Central S.D. No. 1, Addison,* (2d Cir. 1972).
[15]*McGill* v. *Board of Education at Pekin Ele. S.D. No. 108,* 602 F. 2d 774 (7th Cir. 1979).
[16]429 U.S. 274.

had previously been involved in altercations of a reprimanding nature. However, Doyle challenged his dismissal as an impermissible curtailment of his right to free speech. In addition to 1968 precedents, the Court asked whether the teacher could show that his free speech was a substantial factor in the board's decision to terminate. A positive answer then triggers the need for the authorities to show by preponderance of evidence that the board would have reached the same decision to terminate absent the free-speech exercise. Finding for Doyle, the Court concluded that the exercise of protected speech should place an employee in no better or worse position with regard to continued employment.[17] The Court found that the board would not have reached the same conclusion if it were not for Doyle's phone call to the radio station.

The principal should note that whether teachers choose to exercise their free speech in public or in private will not change the protection provided teachers by the First Amendment. This standard was announced by the Supreme Court in *Givhan* v. *Western Line Consolidated School District.*[18] Bessie Givhan, a junior high English teacher, met privately with her principal in order that she might criticize school policies on racial discrimination. The principal alleged that Givhan was insulting, loud, hostile, and arrogant in manner during their meeting, and she was therefore terminated for insubordination. In holding for the teacher, the Court refused to recognize a lesser degree of protection for free speech because the communication was in private.

To summarize the discussion on free-speech rights for teachers, the principal should remember the following points: (1) A teacher may not be punished (dismissed, transferred, or demoted) for engaging in free speech. (2) The principal can assume that the teacher is protected unless there exists some conditions that cancel the teacher's protection. A teacher may not be protected if the speech is purely personal in nature and produces an interference with the smooth running of the school.

EMPLOYMENT DISCRIMINATION

Social and political movements of the 1980s and 1970s produced a number of federal acts which resulted in an increase in teacher protection, not only by degree but in kind. The Civil Rights Act of 1964, the

[17]*Id.* at 285–286.
[18]439 U.S. 410.

Equal Pay Act, the Age Discrimination in Employment Act, the Pregnancy Discrimination Act, and the Rehabilitation Act all stand in safeguard of discrimination based on race, sex, age, religion, or handicap. In addition to these federal acts, most states have enacted companion legislation that gives protection equal to, or in some cases greater than, that provided by federal law. The school principal must be aware that local board policies and collective-bargaining contracts may also be a source of legal protection for teachers. The principal will benefit from an understanding of the federal discrimination laws that follow. Through the federal laws, the principal can become acquainted with those areas that are likely to be sensitive when dealing with teacher employment issues. Protections against discrimination in employment cover race, sex, religion, and age.

Race Discrimination

The primary source of protection in the area of race discrimination comes from Title VII of the Civil Rights Act of 1964. Title VII prohibits employers with fifteen or more employees from discriminating on the basis of race and covers hiring, promotion, compensation packages, and most conditions of employment.[19] When attempting to show racial discrimination, teachers or other school employees have two avenues open. They may try to show that the employment practice has an *adverse impact* on the minority group of which they are part, so that they should receive the protection of Title VII. Another approach is to allege that the employment practice resulted in their receiving *disparate treatment* because of their race.

Adverse impact has been defined as

employment practices that are facially neutral in their treatment of different groups but that in fact fall more harshly on one group than another. Proof of discriminatory motive . . . is not required.[20]

In order to establish a case of *adverse impact,* the employee must show a causal connection between the facially neutral employment practice and the disproportionate exclusion of the protected group from that portion of the workforce under scrutiny.[21] The disproportionate exclusion is shown through the use of statistics. If the school employee is successful in showing disparate statistics, the burden of proof shifts to the employer, who must prove that the policy or practice is justified

[19]42 U.S.C. Sec. 2000 et seq.
[20]*International Brotherhood of Teamsters* v. *U.S.,* 431 U.S. 324, 335.
[21]*Dothard* v. *Rawlinson,* 433 U.S. 321.

by a valid job necessity. For example, in 1981 a school district successfully defended a race discrimination challenge based on their use of teachers' test scores. In *Newman* v. *Crews,*[22] the school district based teachers' salaries on scores from the National Teachers Examination. This practice resulted in the denial of pay raises to a much larger proportion of black than white teachers. However, the court found no fault with the practice since it was justified by the need to attract well-qualified teachers and to encourage self-improvement.

To establish a case of *disparate treatment,* a much greater burden of proof rests with the employee. The employee must show that the school district *intended* to treat individuals differently because of their race. Three specific methods are available for the school district employee to prove disparate treatment. First, the teacher may present evidence that the employer has made statements that point to a discriminatory motive.

Second, the teacher can try to establish that he was treated differently than persons with whom he was "similarly situated."[23] In other words, the rejected teacher can attempt to prove that the employer kept the position open after he was rejected and continued to seek applicants with his qualifications. For cases of alleged discrimination involving conditions of employment, such as vacation or termination, the application of the standard "similarly situated" becomes important. The school district is not expected to apply the terms of employment evenly to all employees. For example, teacher who are classified as head teachers or master teachers may conceivably be treated differently than regular classroom teachers. If the district were to decide that it must eliminate a teaching position because of financial needs, it could eliminate the only minority teacher in the district provided that previously established objective criteria, such as teacher evaluation scores and seniority, were used. If the choice became one of terminating a black teacher or a white teacher, the black teacher might be terminated legitimately if that teacher's evaluation scores were lower than the white teacher's, even if both had the same seniority and teacher status. In one such case, the two teachers were not similarly situated (different evaluation scores) and therefore could not provide the basis for proof by comparative evidence.[24]

The third method of proving disparate treatment involves the use of statistics. The validity of the use of statistics as evidence lies in the assumption that an employer who does not discriminate will have a

---

[22]651 F. 2d 222 (4th Cir. 1981).

[23]*McDonnell Douglas* v. *Green,* 411 U.S. 792 (1973).

[24]*EEOC Compliance Manual,* Vol. 2, Sec. 604, Office of Compliance, Decisions Division, Bureau of National Affairs, Inc.

workforce that mirrors the racial and ethnic composition of the area from which the workforce is drawn.[25] An inference of disparate treatment through the use of statistics might be drawn if, for example, minority teachers have been confined primarily to a few schools with predominantly minority pupils.

Once the teacher claiming discrimination establishes the case, the school district can attempt to rebut the charge by articulating a nondiscriminatory reason for the action. Then the burden of proof remains with the teacher to show by a preponderance of evidence that the legitimate reasons offered are a pretext for racial discrimination.

School districts seem to have won their cases when the courts have found that the reasons for differential treatment were based on quality of performance or other considerations unrelated to race.[26] Employers are not required to accord preference to minorities if non-minority applicants are considered better or even merely equally qualified for available positions. The principal should not confuse this standard with those employer actions taken for the sake of affirmative action. A school district may elect to participate in improving the racial balance in the teaching force and therefore give preference to a minority teacher.

If the school district is under a court order to remedy past practices of discrimination, then it is possible that the differential treatment of minority teachers would preclude the employers' allowed discretion under Title VII. A teacher who is successful in a Title VII discrimination suit may be awarded back pay accruing from two years prior to the filing of the charge.[27] In addition, the court may order that the victim be hired, promoted, or reinstated in the next available position. The court may also grant retroactive seniority. However, seniority systems that are not maintained with the intent to discriminate may not be eliminated by the court even though the system perpetuates the effects of past discrimination.[28]

Sex Discrimination

As is the case with racial discrimination claims, a major source of protection in sex discrimination is Title VII of the Civil Rights Act of 1964. The conditions necessary for the teacher to successfully receive a judgment, as well as those conditions necessary for a school employer to defend, are essentially the same when filing for sex discrimination

---

[25] *Coble* v. *Hot Springs School Dist.,* 682 F. 2d 721 (8th Cir. 1982).
[26] *Lewis* v. *Central Piedmont Community College,* 689 F. 2d 1207.
[27] *U.S.* v. *Lee Way Motor Freight, Inc.* 20 (BNA) F.E.P. Cases 1345 (10th Cir. 1979).
[28] *American Tobacco Co.* v. *Patterson,* 102 S. Ct. 1534 (1982).

under Title VII. Since 1982, however, sex discrimination claims have also been brought under Title IX of the Education Amendments of 1972.

While school employees, as individuals, have a right to sue under Title IX, the act does not allow for personal remedies, such as a reinstatement or back pay, as are provided by Title VII. The sanction for a Title IX violation is the cutoff of federal funds to the program in the school district where the violation is found. The threat of the interruption of federal funds is a powerful incentive for a school district to amend its program and thus provide the employee with the opportunity previously barred.

Title IX applies to any public or private educational institution, whether a preschool or an elementary, secondary, vocational, professional, or postsecondary school. However, an institution is excluded from the act if it is controlled by a religious organization to the extent that the enforcement of Title IX would conflict with a religious precept of that organization.[29] Title IX violations are proven and defended in the same way that they are under Title VII. As was discussed earlier, the decision of whether to use Title VII or Title IX is based upon what the alleged victim wishes to accomplish. Most cases that are filed with the hope of a change in institutional policy might be brought under Title IX. If individual employee damages are sought, Title VII is the common vehicle. The context from which sex discrimination is claimed often results from pregnancy-related policies or sexual harassment.

Since pregnancy affects only women, any employment disadvantage befalling women because of pregnancy can result in a claim of sex discrimination. An employer is prohibited from excluding pregnancy benefits in comprehensive medical insurance plans.[30] Maternity-leave provisions are also prescribed under Title VII. Pregnancy must be treated as an illness would be. Just as employees are permitted to decide when they are too sick to work, the school district cannot decide for the pregnant employee when she must terminate work. The courts have also decided that Title VII requires that a school district policy must allow teachers to use accumulated sick leave for pregnancy-related illness.

In addition to sick leave, employees often take unpaid leave if additional time off is needed to recover from giving birth. The Supreme Court held that Title VII requires school districts to recognize accumulated seniority upon the return from maternity leave.[31] The courts

[29]20 U.S.C. Sec. 1681 (a) (3) and (4).
[30]42 U.S.C.A. 2000 e (k) (1978).
[31]*Nashville Gas Co.* v. *Salty,* 434 V.S. 136 (1977).

have also required that districts not exclude maternity leave while including other leaves in computing a teacher's probationary period toward tenure.[32]

Teachers who are unwed parents are also protected by Title VII. School districts' claims that unwed parenthood constitutes immorality or that the employment of unwed parents in schools contributes to the problem of pregnancies among high school girls have repeatedly been rejected by the courts.[33]

Title VII is the primary source of protection against sexual harassment. Sexual harassment has been defined as "repeated and unwelcomed advances, derogatory statements based on . . . sex, or sexually demeaning gestures or acts."[34] Claims are filed when the victim has experienced adverse employment consequences, such as termination, demotion, or a bar to benefits, in connection with the sexual harassment. The school district has an affirmative obligation under Title VII to investigate teachers' complaints of sexual harassment by supervisors. Failure to investigate complaints can lead to a judgment against the school district.[35]

In order to victims to find success in the charge, they need not prove that the harassment actually resulted in the loss of tangible job benefits, according to the federal Court of Appeals.[36] The Equal Employment Opportunity Commission (EEOC) has issued guidelines concerning sexual harassment in the workplace. The EEOC would inquire if sexual harassment is

1. an explicit or implicit term on condition of employment
2. used as a basis for employment decisions
3. has the effect of unreasonably interfering with individuals' work performance
4. creates an intimidating, hostile, or offensive working environment[37]

School district employers are directly responsible only for sexual harassment of employees by supervisors. Harassment occurring among workers at the same level is beyond the purview of the EEOC guidelines. An exception takes place when the employer knew of or should have known of harassment among employees and failed to take corrective measures.

[32]*Schwabenbauer* v. *Bd. of Education,* 498 F. Supp. 119 (W.D. N.Y. 1980).

[33]*Andrews* v. *Drew Municipal Separate S.D.,* 507 F. 2d 611 (5th Cir. 1975).

[34]N. Doyle, "Sexual Harassment in Public and Private Employment," *Education Law Reporter* 3 (1982):227.

[35]*Miller* v. *Bank of America,* 600 F. 2d 211 (9th Cir. 1979).

[36]*Bundy* v. *Jackson,* 641 F. 2d 934 (D.C. Cir. 1981).

[37]29 C.F.R. Sec. 1604. 11 (a) (1980).

Religious Discrimination

As is the case with racial and sex discrimination, Title VII of the Civil Rights Act of 1964 also protects employees from religious discrimination. The free-exercise clause of the First Amendment would require that employers not force teachers to relinquish their religious beliefs as a condition of employment. Teachers also have the right to abstain from certain school activities that they claim would conflict with their religious beliefs.

At the same time, there is a limit to teachers' free-exercise rights. For example, teachers abstaining from school activities can be disallowed if the absence would disrupt the operation of the school or impede the instructional program in some way. In addition, teachers cannot use the free-exercise protection to refuse to teach a portion of a state-required curriculum because it is claimed to conflict with their religious views.

Many of the claims filed in the religious-discrimination area surround the school districts' failure to "accommodate" teachers with certain religious beliefs. Section 701 (j) of Title VII places an affirmative duty upon the employer to accommodate employees' religious beliefs so long as that can be done without "undue hardships on the conduct of the employer's business." What is undue hardship? The term was defined by the Supreme Court in the case of *Trans World Airlines* v. *Hardison*.[38] The case concerned the employer's efforts to rearrange the schedule of a member of the Worldwide Church of God who could not work from sundown Friday until sundown Saturday each week and on certain other special religious holidays. The employer met with the employee on several occasions in an effort to arrive at a satisfactory arrangement. The employer did accommodate the observance of the special holidays and authorized the union steward to find an employee who would swap shifts. However, no one was willing to trade. The Court noted that the employee performed a duty critical to the continuous seven-day operation of the airline, and that the failure to get that work done would disrupt the operation. The Court ruled that the employer had done all that was required of it to avoid a violation of Title VII. The employer would be required to bear no more than a *de minimis* cost and could not be required to discriminate against other employees by requiring them to fill in for someone else in order to effect accommodation.

In sum, a school district must make an effort to accommodate the religious beliefs of its employees to the extent that work activities do

[38]432 U.S. 63 (1977).

not force the employees to do something contrary to their religion. The employer may be expected to use a variety of methods to accommodate, such as accepting voluntary substitutes, permitting work-shift exchanges, using flexible scheduling, and changing job assignments. However, the employer is not required to place undue hardship on the school district in total deference to the need to accommodate. Indeed, school districts cannot confer specific benefits on employees for religious reasons, such as paid leave available only for sectarian observances. In addition, a certain amount of impairment of the teachers' religious beliefs may be required in order to protect vulnerable public school children from religious inculcation.

Age Discrimination

Persons who have reached the age of 40 but are less than 70 years of age are protected against age discrimination by the Age Discrimination in Employment Act (ADEA). Passed by Congress in 1967, the act prohibits all forms of adverse employment conditions resulting from employer discrimination because of an employee's age.

A claim results when an employee younger than those within the protected age group is in some way preferred over the older employee and that preference is based solely on age. The US Department of Labor and certain federal courts have interpreted ADEA to also include a prohibition in age discrimination among employees *within* the protected age group. Therefore, a school district could not give preferential treatment to someone who is 42 over someone who is 61.[39]

Within the definition of "employer," the ADEA indicates a qualification of at least twenty employees. Therefore, school districts with under twenty employees would be outside the protection of the act.[40]

In order for an employee to move an ADEA violation, most courts require that the disparate treatment standard of review be used. (We mentioned this theory earlier when we discussed racial discrimination.) Thus, the teacher would need to show that the school district *intentionally* discriminated based upon age. The burden of proof rests with the teacher, and the requirement to show intentional disparate treatment on account of age is particularly difficult.

Aging is an unavoidable condition that all persons will experience, regardless of their race, creed, or sex. The aging process and its concomitant effect on certain physical abilities and mental faculties gives rise to a natural turnover in the workforce. Older people leave

[39]29 C.F.R. Sec. 860. 91 (a); *Loeb* v. *Texton, Inc.,* 600 F. 2d 1003 (1st Cir. 1979); *Polstorff* v. *Fletcher,* 452 F. Supp. 17 (N.D. Ala. 1978).
[40]29 U.S.C. Sec. 630 (b).

and younger people enter. Therefore, the replacement of an older employee by a younger one does not give rise to the same inference of discrimination as the replacement of a black employee by a white employee.[41]

More recently, however, both a federal court of appeals and a Missouri federal district court have ruled that an employee could establish a violation of ADEA, regardless of motive, by establishing that employment practices have a disparate impact on older employees.[42] The appeals case dealt with a school board policy that required the personnel office to give preference in hiring to those teachers with less than five years of experience. The district defended itself by claiming that the policy was needed for financial reasons. Teachers with less experience could be paid less than their more experienced associates. The victims were able to produce evidence that showed that over 92 percent of the state's teachers over 40 years old had at least five years of experience. Only 62 percent of teachers under 40 had the same level of experience. The court concluded that these statistics proved that the board policy had a disparate impact on teachers over 40.

The school district has several avenues of defense in a ADEA case. The first is an affirmative defense based on ADEA's permitting age discrimination if age is a bona fide occupational qualification (BFOQ) necessary for the operation of the business. In order to be successful with this defense, the school district must establish that there is a factual basis for believing that nearly all persons of a certain age group are incapable of performing the work safely and efficiently and that the foundation of the operation of the school district would be in peril if persons of that age were employed.[43] The only leading US Supreme Court case on age discrimination used an affirmative defense. In 1976, the Court reviewed a constitutional challenge to the Massachusetts law that required police officers to retire at the age of 50. The Court found that the retirement of police officers at 50 has a rational relationship to the objective of protecting the public by ensuring a physically competent police force.[44]

The school district might also attempt to establish that the age-discriminatory action was taken on the basis of reasonable factors

[41]J. A. Rapp, ed., *Education Law* (New York: Matthew Bender, 1984).

[42]*Geller* v. *Mackham,* 635 F. 2d 1027 (2d Cir. 1980); *Leftwich* v. *Harris-Stowe State College,* 540 F. Supp. 37 (E.D. Mo. 1982).

[43]*Usery* v. *Tamiami Trail Tours, Inc.,* 531 F. 2d 224 (5th Cir. 1976).

[44]*Massachusetts Bd. of Retirement* v. *Murgia,* 427 U.S. 307 (1976).

other than age or for good cause.[45] This defense attempts to defend by rebuttal—that is, to establish that the action was taken for a legitimate nondiscriminatory reason. An action for "good cause" is viewed as being motivated by the teacher's failure to perform the job at a minimally acceptable level of competence or by the failure to comply with reasonable school district regulations. The "reasonable-factors-other-than-age" defense will pertain to a situation not arising from the teacher's work performance.

Finally, the school district can successfully defend itself by establishing that it was taking actions that were in compliance with a bona fide seniority system or bona fide employment benefits plan, except that the system or plan can neither require nor permit compulsory retirement before the age of 70. Generally, a bona fide seniority system or benefits plan is one which was established for reasons unrelated to age.[46]

School districts have been successful in defending age discrimination based on a bona fide occupational qualifications for school bus drivers. As with a statute that would permit police officers' forced retirement at 50, a school board's concern for the highest level of safety in the transportation of children has been regarded as a legitimate objective which would permit the retirement of bus drivers before age 70.

In all jurisdictions except the Third Circuit Court of Appeals (Delaware, New Jersey, and Pennsylvania), school districts have been unsuccessful in implementing the forced retirement of teachers *before* age 70. In the third circuit, however, a retirement of teachers at age 65 was allowed. The court reasoned that since all "similarly situated" teachers were treated similarly under the law, the plan did not constitute age discrimination.[47]

A number of states have enacted companion statutes that protect against age discrimination in employment at the state level. Principals should check the status of any age discrimination statutes in their state, since the state can provide even more protection than is afforded at the federal level. In matters related to the rights of citizens, the states can always provide protections where none may exist at the federal level. More often, the states will extend those rights that are only minimums by federal law.

---

[45]29 U.S.C. Secs. 623 (f) (1) and (3).
[46]Rapp, *Education Law,* Sec. 6.04[3] [g].
[47]*Kuhar* v. *Greensburg-Salem S.D.,* 616 F. 2d 676 (3d Cir. 1980).

TEACHER DISMISSAL

The term *dismissal* must be distinguished from terms that seem similar, but are actually quite different. *Dismissal* is the termination of a tenured teacher at any point, or the termination of a probationary teacher's employment at the end of the contract period by board option not to renew. A *nonrenewal* is the termination of a probationary teacher's employment at the end of the contract period by board option not to renew.[48] Therefore, the term *termination* is general and simply means the separation of teachers from their jobs. It isn't sufficiently specific to be used in a legal framework. Certainly the term *fired* is not used in the school setting, as this term suggests activities more typical in private industry.

The distinctions between *dismissal* and *nonrenewal* are important, since one or the other calls for a different level of due process that must be afforded the teacher prior to the action taken.

What is *due process?* The concept of due process stems from the Fourteenth Amendment to the US Constitution:

> No state shall make or enforce any law which shall abridge the privileges or immunities of citizens of the United States nor shall any State deprive any person of life, liberty, or property without due process of law, nor deny to any person within its jurisdiction the equal protection of the laws.

While very difficult to define precisely, due process can be discussed broadly as meaning that an individual has both liberty and property interests. These rights cannot be taken without notice and an opportunity for a hearing. Beyond these minimums, the level of due process that must be given depends generally on the status of the teacher (tenured or probationary) and on whether a liberty interest is involved in the termination.

Teachers' property interest is simply their right to do a job. This right is created by the employment contract in the case of probationary teachers, and usually by the states' tenure laws for those teachers on tenure. A liberty interest is an interest in one's good name. Liberty interest may be implicated if the reason for dismissal involved damage to the teacher's potential for future employment.[49] The determination of potential damage to future employment should be anticipated by school authorities, especially if the dismissal might create a stigma or might damage an individual's reputation. Failure to provide due pro-

[48]McCarthy, *Public School Law,* p. 107.
[49]*Bd. of Regents* v. *Roth,* 408 U.S. 564 (1972).

cess to a teacher whose liberty interest is involved can result in the nullification of the school authorities' action.

If eligible, full procedural due-process rights would include the following:

1. notice of charges
2. impartial hearing
3. representation by counsel
4. presentation of witnesses on the teacher's behalf
5. cross-examination of adverse witnesses and challenge of incriminating evidence
6. opportunity to appeal to higher legal authority, including access to courts.[50]

Dismissal of Nontenured Teachers

The level of due process required for the nonrenewal of a probationary teacher's contract is determined by state law. Generally, however, nontenured teachers' contracts may be nonrenewed at the end of any probationary year. This may be done without providing a hearing. Depending on whether the nonrenewal comes at the end of the first, second, or third year of probation, the board may not even be required to provide reasons for the nonrenewal. The number of years that a teacher must remain on probation varies from state to state, although the principal would not find much variation in the one-to-three-year standard. In most states, only the minimal procedural guarantee of a timely notice is required for the dismissal of a nontenured teacher. Thus, states recognize some property rights for nontenured teachers, but these rights are far less than those offered the tenured teacher.

A dismissal that might involve a teacher's liberty interest is an exception to the minimum procedural due process. If a liberty interest is involved, the teacher would then be eligible for full procedural due-process rights. It should be noted that a teacher must do more than simply claim a liberty interest. The possibility of damage to the teacher's good name must be proved. Once more, the mere fact that the teacher was dismissed is not in itself sufficient proof that damage to good name took place. The Court in *Board of Regents* v. *Roth* said that "it stretches the concept too far to suggest that a person is deprived of 'liberty' when he simply is not rehired in one job but remains as free as before to seek another."[51]

An additional exception to minimum procedural due process oc-

[50]W. Valente, *Law in the Schools* (Columbus, OH: Chas. E. Merrill, 1980).
[51]408 U.S. 564, 575 (1972).

curs when the nontenured teacher is dismissed prior to the expiration of the contract year. The contract itself establishes a property right. Therefore, full due-process procedures must be given to those who are dismissed during the term of the contract.

Dismissal of Tenured Teachers

Before tenured teachers can be dismissed, the full procedural due-process rights outlined by state law must be provided. Once more, school authorities cannot dismiss the tenured teacher unless they have "cause." As is the case with tenure laws generally, the definition of the word *cause* will vary from state to state. The range of specificity in definition is great. In 1977, Floyd Delon compiled a nationwide listing of tenure statutes that attempt to define *cause* as used for the grounds for dismissal of tenured teachers.[52] Table 7–1 shows that California provides the highest number of specific causes for dismissal (eight) while states such as Maine, Kansas, and New Mexico list only one cause as a statutory definition. In those states, *cause* has no real definition other than a qualifying adjective or two (good cause, just cause, or sufficient cause). The lack of statutory specificity allows school authorities to exercise wide discretion in identifying reasons for the dismissal of tenured teachers. Regardless of which "cause" is used, however, substantial evidence must document the grounds asserted.

The most common "causes" listed by statute for the dismissal of tenured teachers are incompetency, insubordination, and immorality. Regardless of which cause is used, the board of education must have evidence that the teacher did in fact perform, or fail to perform, in certain ways that must result in dismissal. The board may not simply allege that the teacher is incompetent, insubordinate, or immoral without evidence. It is at this point that the board must rely heavily on the administration to supply the evidence. It is typically the building principal who has gathered the necessary documentation which provides the support for the dismissal.

The principal should be aware of the basic legal standards that have emerged pertaining to the nature of evidence for dismissal of tenured teachers. Neill and Curtis provided a list of six guidelines pertaining to evidence:

1. It must be substantial.
2. It must be relevant to establish the alleged facts.

---

[52]F. Delon, *Legal Controls on Teacher Conduct: Teacher Discipline* (Topeka, KS: NOLPE, 1977).

	Incompetency	Unfitness for Service	Negligence, Neglect of Duty	Failure to Provide Designated Instruction	Failure to Attend Required Institutes	Inefficiency	Incapacity	Insubordination	Refusal to Obey School Board Regulations	Noncompliance with School Laws	Disloyalty, Subversive Activity	Contract Violation, Cancellation, Annulment, Breach	Conviction of Specified Crime	Immorality	Untruthfulness, Dishonesty, Falsification of Application, Records	Drunkenness, Intemperance	Addiction to Drugs and/or Selling Drugs	Cruelty	Conduct Unbecoming a Teacher, Misconduct in Office	Unprofessional Conduct	Violation of Code of Ethics	Revocation of Certificate	Cause (Good, Just, Sufficient)	Failure to Obey State Laws	Other
Alabama	X		X		X			X						X									X		
Alaska	X								X			X		X						X					
Arizona																									X
Arkansas												X													
California	X	X	X	X					X	X	X		X	X	X	X				X		X		X	X
Colorado	X		X	X				X					X	X									X		
Connecticut	X					X		X						X									X		
Delaware	X		X					X			X		X	X					X						
Florida	X		X					X					X	X		X	X		X						
Georgia	X							X						X									X		X
Hawaii								X	X					X									X		X
Idaho									X				X	X					X				X		X
Illinois	X		X											X				X					X		
Indiana	X		X					X	X		X			X									X		
Iowa	X		X											X									X		
Kansas																									
Kentucky	X		X		X			X						X					X						
Louisiana	X		X												X										X
Maine																									
Maryland	X		X					X						X					X				X		
Massachusetts								X	X	X	X		X						X				X		
Michigan			X						X							X							X		
Minnesota			X					X	X		X		X	X					X				X		
Mississippi	X		X										X	X		X		X							X
Missouri	X		X		X			X	X				X	X											X
Montana	X	X	X		X			X						X										X	X
Nebraska	X		X		X			X		X			X	X	X										
Nevada		X	X		X			X					X	X	X					X		X			
New Hampshire	X													X		X									
New Jersey								X	X										X				X		X
New Mexico																							X		
New York	X		X		X			X						X					X		X				
North Carolina	X		X		X	X			X		X		X	X			X						X		
North Dakota					X	X			X			X	X	X					X				X		
Ohio					X				X					X									X		
Oklahoma	X		X								X			X			X								
Oregon			X		X			X	X				X	X							X				X
Pennsylvania	X		X						X		X			X			X	X							X
Rhode Island									X					X	X	X	X						X		
South Carolina	X		X						X		X		X	X	X								X		
South Dakota	X		X						X				X	X	X	X						X			
Tennessee	X		X	X	X			X	X		X		X	X			X	X	X		X				
Texas			X						X		X		X	X				X							
Utah																									
Vermont	X		X						X			X							X				X		
Virginia	X		X					X	X	X				X									X		
Washington																									
West Virginia	X		X						X				X	X		X	X	X					X		
Wisconsin							X							X									X		
Wyoming	X		X	X				X						X									X		

Reprinted from NOLPE Monograph, F. Delon, *Legal Controls on Teacher Conduct: Teacher Discipline* 12 (rev. ERIC/CEM–NOLPE Monograph, 1977).

From Floyd Delon, *Legal Controls on Teacher Conduct: Teacher Discipline* (Topeka, KS: NOLPE 1977). Used with permission of National Association on Legal Problems (NOLPE).

3. It must be developed in a constitutionally approved way (no illegal wire taps, for example).
4. It must be documented, which, in its simplest form, means recording the time, date, and place, with witnesses listed, if any.
5. Evidence presented at the hearing should be limited to charges made.
6. The rules of evidence applicable in court proceedings do not apply in a strict sense to dismissal hearings.[53]

There is no question that the principal's written evaluations play a significant role in the accumulation of substantial evidence. It should be noted that only one unsatisfactory rating of a tenured teacher unsupported by specific instances showing unfitness may be a sufficient basis for dismissal.[54] In another instance, it appears that three unsatisfactory ratings along with two years' worth of conferences with the principal were sufficient in Pennsylvania to sustain the test of proof for proper grounds for dismissal.[55]

The written evaluation is often used in connection with dismissal for incompetency. *Incompetency* has been broadly defined by the courts. However, the term can be used to connote a lack of some requisite ability. Among the three most widely asserted grounds for dismissal, incompetency is the most difficult to prove and requires the most documentation. In addition, some states, such as Illinois, require that a distinction be made between those causes that are remediable and those that are not. If the teacher has been found to be incompetent and is consequently dismissed, the court will look to see whether the incompetency was remediable. If it is found to be remediable, the school must show that attempts were made to remediate the teacher's incompetency.

School authorities' use of immorality as a cause for dismissal has come under closer scrutiny by the courts in recent years. Generally, the courts will require that there be proof of a relationship between the immoral conduct and unfitness to teach. The exception seems to be in the area of sexual conduct between teacher and student. The courts have consistently held that sexually related conduct between a teacher and student is sufficient cause for dismissal. There is a presumption of unfitness to teach when teacher–student sexual conduct is found.

Insubordination, the willful disregard for or refusal to obey school regulations and official orders,[56] is the easiest to prove among the

---

[53]S. Neill and J. Curtis, *Staff Dismissals: Problems and Solution* (Sacramento, CA: American Association of School Administrators, 1978).
[54]*Steffen* v. *Bd. of Directors,* 32 Pa, Commw. 187, 377 A. 2d 1381 (1977).
[55]*Hoffman* v. *West Chester Area School Bd.,* 40 Pa Commw. 374, 397 A. 2d 482 (1979).
[56]Delon, *Legal Controls,* p. 36.

three causes for dismissal most often used. Since conduct is measured against the existence of a rule or policy, insubordination is more readily documented by school authorities and is thus more supportable than other causes.

A dismissal based upon insubordination is likely to be upheld by the court if it finds that the teacher acted willfully, deliberately, fraudulently, evasively, defiantly, or contemptuously with respect to a policy, rule, or order from a superior.[57] However, a dismissal may be held unjustifiable if the order that the teacher disobeyed was unreasonable. Teachers dismissed improperly on insubordination grounds have been reinstated by courts for various reasons: insufficient evidence to prove the misconduct had occurred; insufficient showing of the existence of the alleged rule violated; lack of authority for issuance of the rule or order by the board; bias or discrimination against the teacher in the enforcement of the rule; or a violation of the teacher's First Amendment academic freedom or freedom of speech.[58]

Constitutional Restrictions in Teacher Dismissals

Teachers do not relinquish their First Amendment rights by choosing to teach in the public schools.[59] Therefore, school authorities may not dismiss a teacher for the exercise of a First Amendment right. The rights of the teacher in the context of the First Amendment include the freedom to speak out on matters of public concern, the freedom to speak symbolically on political matters, academic freedom, and the freedom to express oneself through association.

If a teacher believes that she has been dismissed because of conduct that is constitutionally protected, she has the burden to prove that her exercise of these rights was a substantial or motivating factor in the board's decision. If she meets that burden, the board must then respond by a preponderance of the evidence to show that it would have arrived at the same decision without having considered the protected conduct. The teacher must be placed in no worse a position than she would be in if she had not engaged in the protected conduct.

Assuming that the dismissal was ordered as a punishment for the exercise of First Amendment rights, the analysis moves to another level. The First Amendment does not give the teacher absolute protection. Rather, the court will consider the school's need to promote an efficient public service in balance with the teacher's rights. Since

[57] Rapp, *Education Law,* Sec. 6.12 [8] [b].
[58] *Ibid.,* Sec. 6.12 [8] [c].
[59] *Tinker* v. *Des Moines Independent School Dist.,* 393 U.S. 503, 506 (1969).

community standards and state interests vary, a case-by-case approach to the balancing test is used.

Academic Freedom as a Bar to Teacher Dismissal

Academic freedom is difficult to define. However, a specific "interest" that has commonly been included under academic freedom is the freedom to teach subject matter without fear of administrative reprisals. For the principal, the questions become: Does academic freedom guarantee the teacher complete freedom in expressing personal ideas and philosophies to students in the classroom? What topics or issues can the teacher discuss in a course? Can the principal limit the type of material used by the teacher because it may be controversial?

The concept of academic freedom has more often been associated with higher education. College professors have enjoyed the notion that they should be given the widest range of discretion in controlling their own courses and research.[60] However, it is not only college professors that have the protection of academic freedom. The courts began addressing the issue of academic freedom for classroom teachers beginning in the late 1960s. The Supreme Court has not yet decided enough cases to provide definitive answers to the extent of academic freedom for classroom teachers. Nonetheless, the number of lower-court rulings are sufficient to support some general guidelines.

As with other constitutional rights for teachers, the courts have used the "balancing of interests" approach in analyzing academic freedom cases. It is the need to balance the teachers' interest in academic freedom against the school's interest in providing proper instruction. Perhaps the teacher is least protected when expressing personal opinions to students when those opinions are unrelated to the course or to the general school objectives. A teacher who announced to the class his personal opinions on political candidates was successfully dismissed by school authorities as a reason for dismissal. More difficulty arises, however, when the teacher decides to use classroom material that school authorities or the community considers controversial.

Controversy can develop when the teacher selects classroom material that is viewed as obscene or sexual in nature. In 1969, the case of *Keefe* v. *Geanakos*[61] found for a teacher being dismissed for using *Atlantic Monthly* in her senior English class. The article contained the word *bastard* in several places. When parents complained, the teacher was terminated. The First Circuit Court of Appeals found that the

---

[60]R. Fuchs, "Academic Freedom: Its Basic Philosophy, Function, and History," *Law and Contemporary Problems* 10 (1968): 431–446.
[61]418 F. 2d 359 (1st Cir. 1969).

article was scholarly rather than obscene. The court noted that "the sensibilities of parents are not the full measure of what is proper education."[62] In a similar case in 1970, an Alabama teacher was warned by school authorities to stop using Kurt Vonnegut stories in her junior English class. After considering the warning, the teacher determined that she had a professional duty to continue to use the material. The federal district court analyzed that the materials would not be protected if they were inappropriate for the age or maturity of the students and if they created a substantial threat of disruption. Since the court found neither of these exceptions to protection present, the teacher was reinstated.

Anticipating Dismissal

When a teacher appears to be inadequate for the job, the principal should begin a frank but helpful dialogue with the teacher. The notice of dismissal, if and when it comes, should never be a surprise to the teacher. It isn't unusual for a court to look for prenotice conferences with the principal as a factor in determining the justification of a teacher dismissal. A New York case involved a teacher who was dismissed for violating a written rule. The court found for the teacher, however, since school authorities could not show that they had given ample warnings through conferences with the principal.[63]

In a Massachusetts case,[64] a male teacher was reinstated after being dismissed for wearing a beard. The court stated that the dismissal was invalid because the school authorities had never warned the teacher that he might be dismissed for violating the teacher dress code. The principal should keep the legal standard of "fair warning" in mind throughout the staff supervision process.

Board members should not become involved in counseling teachers who are being considered for dismissal. Nor should board members participate in the evidence-gathering process for the dismissal. The reason for this prohibition stems from the principle of separating the "adjudicatory and prosecutorial functions." In other words, those who will be judges must not be the same as those who are the prosecutors. It is expected that when board members dispose themselves for a teacher dismissal hearing, they will be unbiased in their decision. There is a presumption of bias when "the judges" are involved in the evidence-gathering process.

Before the superintendent approaches the board of education to

---

[62]*Id.* at 363.
[63]*In re Appeal of Lillian Brin,* 7 Educ. Dept. Rptr. 10 (N.Y. 1967).
[64]*Lucia* v. *Duggan,* 303 F. Supp. 112 (D. Mass. 1969).

recommend a teacher dismissal, conferences with the teacher's principal are essential. The principal should brief the superintendent regarding evaluations and records of the teacher's behavior. After the superintendent receives the necessary evidence from the principal, statutes, board policies, and collective-bargaining agreements should be checked.

In the final analysis, dismissing a teacher requires careful, predesigned planning and should never be undertaken as a quick reaction to an isolated event.

Summary of Teacher Dismissal

Dismissing a teacher, whether tenured or probationary, must not be considered lightly by school authorities. It should be undertaken only as a last resort to unsuccessful efforts at working with the teacher toward improvement. The school principal has the chief role in teacher-dismissal decisions. It is the principal who must assemble the necessary evidence in order for the superintendent to move forward with a recommendation to the school board. The following list of generalizations provided by McCarthy and Cambron-McCabe are helpful by way of summarizing teacher dismissals.

1. A teacher is entitled to procedural due process if dismissal action impairs a property or liberty interest.
2. Due process requires, at a minimum, that a teacher be notified of charges and provided with an opportunity for a hearing.
3. Full procedural rights in a dismissal hearing include representation by counsel, examination and cross-examination of witnesses, and a record of the proceedings; however, formal trial procedures are not required.
4. An adequate notice of dismissal must adhere to statutory deadlines, follow designated form, allow the teacher time to prepare for a hearing, and specify charges.
5. Lack of proper notice can result in reinstatement of the teacher.
6. The school board is considered an impartial hearing tribunal unless bias of its members can be clearly established.
7. The burden of proof is placed on the school board to introduce sufficient evidence to support a teacher's dismissal.
8. Courts generally have held that probationary employment does not involve a property interest, except within the contract period.
9. A probationary teacher may establish a liberty interest, and thus entitlement to a hearing, if nonrenewal imposes a stigma or forecloses opportunities for future employment.
10. Tenure status, defined by state law, confers upon teachers a property interest in continued employment, and tenured teachers can be dismissed only for cause.

11. Cause for dismissal varies extensively among the states, but may include such grounds as incompetency, neglect of duty, immorality, insubordination, unprofessional conduct, and other good and just cause.

12. Incompetency is generally defined in relation to classroom performance — classroom management, teaching methods, grading, pupil–teacher relationships, and general attitude.

13. Immoral conduct can result in dismissal when a relationship is established between the conduct and the teacher's effectiveness in the school system.

14. Dismissal for insubordination is based on the refusal to follow school regulations and policies.

15. Declining enrollment and financial exigencies constitute adequate cause for dismissal of tenured teachers.

16. An improper dismissal can result in an award of damages, reinstatement, and/or attorney's fees.[65]

STUDENTS' RIGHTS

Beginning in the late 1960s, the role of the school principal with respect to students' rights began to change. In fact, before the US Supreme Court decision in *Tinker* v. *Des Moines Independent Community School District,*[66] in which students were considered "persons" under the Constitution, it could be said that students had little or no rights. Principals had been able to suspend or expel students without being questioned by the courts. The *in loco parentis* (in place of parents) concept allowed the principal wide latitude in controlling student conduct. However, the concept of *in loco parentis* has given way to a stricter judicial approach in student affairs. As Phay points out:

> Over time, the *in loco parentis* doctrine was substantially modified . . . and the courts became more willing to examine school actions and to overturn those found arbitrary or unreasonable.[67]

In order for the principal to be successful in student control and discipline, a grasp of student rights is essential. Student rights can be understood by inquiry into the following areas: (1) What are the rights of students when being suspended or expelled? (2) What are students' rights to privacy in school? and (3) What are students' First Amendment rights? Each of these areas will be examined in the following sections.

[65]McCarthy, *Public School Law,* p. 136.
[66]393 U.S. 503 (1969).
[67]R. E. Phay, *The Law of Suspension and Exclusion: An Examination of the Substantive Issues in Controlling Student Conduct* (Topeka, KS: NOLPE, 1975).

STUDENT RIGHTS IN SUSPENSION AND EXPULSION

When being faced with suspension or expulsion, students have both procedural and substantive due-process protections. As expulsion is typically a greater deprivation than suspension, the level of due process is greater. This exemplifies the fact that due process is a matter of degree. The greater the student's punishment, the more care must be afforded the student in providing due process.

Procedural Due Process

Among the most widely used disciplinary tools, suspensions are used to punish students for violating school rules. A suspension is generally considered a temporary separation of the student from school or activity. More recently, the "in-school suspension" has been used, whereby students stay on school premises but are removed from the routine they would normally have been following if not suspended. As of 1975, when the US Supreme Court decided *Goss* v. *Lopez*,[68] all students have the right to procedural due process even for short-term suspensions. The Court defined short-term suspensions as those of ten days' duration or less. As a result of the *Goss* decision, many states and school boards around the country enacted procedural safeguards for students being suspended.

The principal must always use the procedures from the authority source that affords the greatest degree of due process for the student. For example, if the state statutes outline the four steps to be followed but the school district not only outlines the four steps of the state but adds three more of its own, the principal must use all of the procedures. A school district would not be legally permitted to afford fewer procedural safeguards than the state provides. Once more, a state may not require less than was outlined by the Supreme Court in *Goss*. The principle is that a lower level of legal authority may always provide more procedural due process in addition to that provided by a higher level. At a minimum, *Goss* provided that students be afforded

1. oral or written notice of charges;
2. an explanation of the evidence if the student denies the charges; and
3. some kind of hearing that includes an opportunity to present the student's view of the incident.

The *Goss* Court went on to point out that there need be no delay in time between the notice and the subsequent hearing. Once more, the

[68]P. A. Zirkel, ed., *A Digest of Supreme Court Decisions Affecting Education* (Bloomington, IN: Phi Delta Kappa, 1978).

Court recognized the need for "emergency" suspensions. If a student's presence poses a threat to persons, property, or the academic program, removal may take place immediately, without notice or hearing. However, the notice and hearing must follow within a reasonable time.

When it comes to expulsion, there is no Supreme Court decision that outlines the minimum procedural requisites as is the case for suspension. However, the judiciary, in its varied jurisdictions, provided a list of six considerations:

1. Written notice of charges, the intention to expel, and the place, time, and circumstances of the hearing, with sufficient time for a defense to be prepared
2. a full and fair hearing before an impartial adjudicator
3. the right to legal counsel or some other adult representation
4. the opportunity to present witnesses or evidence
5. the opportunity to cross-examine opposing witnesses
6. some type of written record demonstrating that the decision was based on the evidence presented at the hearing[69]

Since no Supreme Court decision exists, the lower-court decisions, and especially state law and board policies, govern the procedures for suspension. Generally, an expulsion is for a period of time in excess of ten days. A student usually will not be allowed to be separated from school for a period to exceed the remainder of the current academic year. It is also generally true that a principal may initiate expulsion proceedings, but only the school board, with the recommendation of the superintendent, can expel the student.

Substantive Due Process

The legal requirements of due process should be not be understood as simply ensuring that certain procedures are followed. Regardless of how carefully the principal or school board follows procedural due-process guidelines, the suspension or expulsion could be challenged for violating substantive due process.[70]

Substantive due process is difficult to define. It can be understood by comparison to procedural due process. Briefly, procedural due process requires that orderly steps be taken to ensure that a student is treated fairly before some right or interest is terminated. Because

[69]McCarthy, *Public School Law*, p. 288.

[70]L. F. Rossow, "The Relationship Between the Level of Recognition of Substantive Due Process Rights in Student Suspensions and Administrative Practices, School Board Policies and Other Selected Variables in Illinois Public High Schools" (EdD dissertation, Loyola University of Chicago, January, 1983).

procedural due process involves a reference to specific guidelines, it is far easier to determine when there has been a violation of procedural due process as compared to substantive due process. For procedural due process, either the guidelines have been followed by the principal or they have not.[71]

Substantive due process, on the other hand, has to do with the extent to which the standards of *fundamental fairness and fair warning* are met. These standards assist with judging whether the student received fair treatment at the hands of the principal. In his 1983 doctoral dissertation, Rossow defined fundamental fairness as a

> ... standard as applied to student suspension/expulsion that requires that the punishment imposed be in proportion to the offense committed. Further, fundamental fairness requires that suspension not be imposed for a minor infraction of the rules or for the kind of conduct for which other students in the past have received only mild punishment.[72]

In the first instance, fundamental fairness requires that "rules" exist. The school rules for behavior must be written so as to describe those offenses that lead to suspension or expulsion.[73] Once more, the rules must be reasonable. As far back as 1966, the court in *Burnside* v. *Byars*[74] laid down the principle of reasonableness for school rules of behavior. In *Burnside,* a group of black students at a Mississippi public high school wore "freedom buttons" to school. The principal directed the students to remove the buttons. When the students failed to obey, the principal suspended the thirty-five students.

The students later filed suit, alleging that their rights under the First and Fourteenth Amendments had been violated. The court found for the students and held:

> We conclude after carefully examining all the evidence presented that the regulation forbidding the wearing of "freedom buttons" on school grounds is arbitrary and unreasonable . . .[75]

While the court was not willing to admit that jurists should sit in judgment over the wisdom of school rules, they did say that they would

---

[71]L. F. Rossow, "Administrative Discretion and Student Suspension: A Lion in Waiting," *Journal of Law and Education* 13 (1984):419.

[72]Rossow, *The Relationship Between the Level of Recognition of Substantive Due Process Rights in Student Suspensions and Administrative Practices* (EdD dissertation, Loyola University of Chicago, 1983) pp. 17–18.

[73]*Ibid.,* p. 20.

[74]363 F. 2d 744 (5th Cir. 1966).

[75]*Id.* at 748.

decide "whether they [rules] are a reasonable exercise of the power and discretion of the school authorities."[76]

The standard of fair warning must also be considered by the principal when attempting to provide for substantive due process. Fair warning has been defined as follows:

> The Constitutional standard which requires that a student has known or should have known he/she was violating a rule which could result in suspension before the suspension penalty be imposed.[77]

The right of fair warning in suspension cases continues to be recognized today. In 1979, a Texas appeals court heard the case of *Galveston Independent School District* v. *Boothe.*[78] David Boothe, a public high school student, was caught just off school grounds with a small amount of marijuana. Following a hearing, David was expelled by the board of education for one quarter of the school year. The court decided for the student and ordered that he be reinstated. In so doing, the court held: "Rules and regulations upon which the expulsion was based were not specific enough to apprise the student of the nature of conduct prescribed."[79]

The record showed that the student's possession of marijuana was not on the school property, but was in a car parked on an adjacent street. David was verbally warned not to bring marijuana onto the campus, but it was not shown that possessing marijuana in a car parked on an adjacent street is "on campus." The administrative regulations indicated that the place where possession of marijuana was prohibited was "in our schools." The administration did not intend that the phrase should indicate a place of prohibition; rather it was intended to be more general. Nevertheless, because the court considered the interpretation of the rule to be possibly unclear to the student, the expulsion was set aside. They said: "Before a student can be punished by expulsion for violation of a school rule, regulation, or policy, must fairly apprise him of the type of prohibited conduct by which he may be expelled."[80]

It would seem that, beyond being legally required, the need to establish clearly written rules for student behavior is an aid to school administrators. In her study of high school behavior codes, Lines pointed out: "A published code at least gives a student fair warning

---

[76]*Id.*

[77]Rossow, *The Relationship Between,* p. 18.

[78]*Galveston Independent School District* v. *Boothe,* 590 S.W. 2d 553 (1979).

[79]*Id.* at 553.

[80]*Id.* at 557.

and is easier to challenge in the courts. Thus, even such a code can help prevent teachers and principals from imposing arbitrary rules."[81]

Student Rights of Privacy

The issue of pupil searches is perhaps the most litigated in the area of student privacy. The Fourth Amendment to the US Constitution protects against *unreasonable* searches and seizures by the state. Therefore, a search of student possessions in and of itself is not illegal. It is the *unreasonable* search that is unconstitutional.

Until recently no definitive guidelines existed on a national basis that the school principal could apply to student searches. In January of 1985, however, the Supreme Court handed down *New Jersey* v. *T. L. O.*[82] For the first time in 193 years, the myriad of lower-court rulings, which differed slightly in each jurisdiction, could be set aside or confirmed. The case arose out of a Piscataway high school where T. L. O. (the label given to the defendant in this case to protect the student's identity) was a 14-year-old girl who had been sent to the administrative office for smoking in the bathroom. She denied that she had been smoking, so the assistant principal, Theodore Chaplick, asked for her purse. Upon opening the purse, Chaplick found a package of cigarettes.

On further examination, the assistant principal found a substance resembling marijuana. T. L. O. was taken to the police station, where she admitted selling marijuana in school. She was suspended for ten days, and a delinquency petition was filed against her in juvenile court. The New Jersey Supreme Court held that the search was unreasonable and that the results of the search were inadmissible as evidence at the juvenile proceeding.

The US Supreme Court reversed, holding that while the Fourth Amendment prohibition of unreasonable searches applies in the school setting, the school administrator needs only "reasonable suspicion" in order to conduct a legal search. The Court rejected arguments that school administrators must have a warrant before searching and that they must meet the same standard of "probable cause" as police officials.

While the Court showed that the test for student searches need be only reasonable suspicion, they warned that the search must be "reasonably related to the objectives of the search and not [be] excessively

---

[81]P. M. Lines, "Codes for High School Students," *Inequality in Education* 8 (1981):25.
[82]105 S. Ct. 733.

intrusive in light of the age and sex of the student and the nature of the infraction."[83]

The Court ruling leaves intact most of the prior judicial recommendations for conducting searches. In addition to the *T. L. O.* decision, it is wise for the school principal to be aware of these ancillary conditions and observations:

1. All students have a reasonable "expectation of privacy" for certain possessions kept in certain places. For example, possessions in pockets or purses have been considered within a reasonable expectation of privacy. Possessions that have been considered not within a reasonable expectation of privacy are anything in the hallway, in the parking lot, or *in plain view*. Students' lockers have also been considered beyond students' expectation of privacy when the school forewarns students that lockers are not the exclusive domain of students and that routine locker searches will be conducted. A search is an intrusion into the student's reasonable expectation of privacy.

2. A search is an intrusion into the student's reasonable expectation of privacy. Before the school principal intrudes upon the student's expectation of privacy, "reasonable suspicion" must exist that the student is breaking some rule or law. For example, if the principal enters a student locker, no caution need be taken. Entering a student locker is not a search, since a student has no reasonable expectation of privacy with regard to the locker. If the principal enters a student's purse, however, the *T. L. O.* guidelines must be followed. The difference here is that the student has a reasonable expectation of privacy with regard to the purse.

3. Once the principal decides to intrude upon the student's reasonable expectation of privacy, the way in which the court will analyze the behavior if the case is litigated should be understood. The court will "balance" the degree of intrusion upon the student against the degree of the school's need to maintain order. For example, principals have not been successful in court when the degree of intrusion went as far as a "strip search." The courts have considered the strip search too great an intrusion upon students' privacy, and the need to preserve that privacy outweighs the school's need to maintain discipline. The closer the principal's search gets "to the body," the more difficult it will be for the court to sustain the action.

First Amendment Rights of Students

Students' First Amendment freedoms were first recognized in 1943, with *West Virginia Board of Education* v. *Barnette*.[84] The Court

[83]T. J. Flygare, "High Court Approves Searches of Students but Ducks Many Tough Issues," *Phi Delta Kappan* 66 (1985):504–505.
[84]319 U.S. 624 (1943).

declared that First Amendment guarantees must receive "scrupulous protection" in schools "if we are not to strangle the free mind at its source and teach youth to discount important principles of our government as mere platitudes."[85] Most of the litigation in the First Amendment area involves issues of freedom of speech and, more recently, freedom of religion. This section will focus on these two areas.

Freedom of Speech and Expression

The landmark case of *Tinker v. Des Moines Independent School District*[86] in 1969 brought considerable attention to freedom of speech for students. In *Tinker,* a group of public school pupils wore black arm bands to class in order to protest the Vietnam War. The students were suspended from school. The Court held that the wearing of the arm bands was symbolic expression which could not be punished unless the principal could show that the student behavior would materially and substantially interfere with the operation of the school and the rights of other students to learn. Mere apprehension of disturbance is not a sufficient basis for such action on the part of school authorities.[87]

The rule of law developed in *Tinker* remains valid today. An administration has the authority to punish students for misbehavior. When the misbehavior involves freedom of speech, however, the administrator must consider students' constitutional rights as they exert their control.

The law is clear in allowing students to be punished *after the fact* if their behavior interferes with the educational process, but the issuance of *prior restraints* on expression places a burden of justification on school administrators. It is the punishment of students' behavior for exercising freedom of speech prior to any actual disruption that is constitutionally problematic.

However, courts have considered certain speech to fall beyond the protection of the First Amendment. Speech intended to elicit immediate disruptive action (called "fighting words" by the courts) can be prohibited. This should not be confused with students' criticism of school regulations or of an administrator's decisions, which is generally considered protected speech.

Also, expression that threatens or encourages violence, such as boycotts, sit-ins, or excessive noise, can be curtailed. Administrators must ensure that the school rules that punish one of the speech-related behaviors are very specific. Overbroad school rules in this area can

[85]*Id.* at 637.
[86]393 U.S. 503 (1969).
[87]Zirkel, *Digest of Supreme Court,* p. 38.

result in a judgment against school officials.[88] The material and substantial disruption that, if present, would allow punishment does not include school administrators' disruption. In *Gebert* v. *Hoffman*,[89] the court held that the school administrators' assertion that a demonstration hampered their performing regular duties was an inadequate basis for disciplining students involved in a peaceful protest.

Freedom of Religion

The right of students to participate in religious activities within the confines of the public school is limited by the Establishment Clause of the First Amendment. The phrase "Congress shall make no law respecting an establishment of religion"[90] has been used by the courts to disallow a variety of student religious activities. Some of these prohibited activities include praying, participating in ceremonies that may have a religious component, using religious symbols, bible reading (except for literary purposes), and use of school facilities by religiously oriented student clubs. In sum, freedom of religion for students in public school has been almost a contradiction in terms.

In the mid-1980s, however, students were given the right to assemble for religious purposes under federal law. On August 11, 1984, President Reagan signed H.R. 1310 into law. The law effectively overturned previous federal court decisions that either prohibited or allowed local policies prohibiting the use of school facilities for the religious activities of students. PL 98-377, otherwise known as the "Equal Access Act," requires that high school students wishing to meet for religious purposes must be given the same opportunities as the school gives to other high school student groups.[91]

More specifically, the act outlines two areas of obligation for public high schools who receive federal funds. First, the act demands that schools that allow student noncurricular groups to use school facilities provide a "fair opportunity" to all noncurricular student groups to use those facilities, regardless of the religious, political, or philosophical nature of the group. Schools are deemed to have offered a fair opportunity when they provide that student-initiated groups (1) meet voluntarily, (2) before or after school, (3) without sponsorship by the school, (4) are not attended or controlled by outsiders, and (5) do not interfere with other school activities. The second obligation demands

---

[88]*Rasche* v. *Bd. of Trustees of U. of Ill.*, 353 F. Supp. 973 (N.D. Ill. 1972).
[89]336 F. Supp. 694 (E.D. Pa. 1972).
[90]U.S. Constitution, Amendment I.
[91]L. F. Rossow, "Coping with the 'Equal Access Act,'" *Kansas School Board Journal* 23 (1984):4.

that the school not discriminate against religious, political, or philosophical student groups based on the content of the groups' activities.[92]

Until this federal law is challenged in court, it appears that students will have freedom of religion in terms of extracurricular meeting activities. This one area stands as a rare exception to the nearly nonexistent freedom of religion in the school setting.

PREVENTIVE SCHOOL LAW

Preventive school law is like preventive medicine. It is based on the premise that "an ounce of prevention is worth a pound of cure." The theory of preventive school law can best be understood by contrast to the typical dispute-centered law. Brown and Dauer provide a good description:

> Dispute-centered (school law) focuses largely if not exclusively on things that have already happened. Preventive (school law) is concerned largely if not exclusively with things that might happen in the future.[93]

Thus, one of the outstanding characteristics of preventive school law is that it is future-oriented. It is focused on planning. It is offensive as opposed to reactive to impending legal problems. In a sense, preventive school law attempts to create facts that will exist in the future so that the principal can control legal events rather than allowing those events to control him.

If the principal is not satisfied with the legal result that would flow from one set of facts, he can draft school rules and administrative directives in such a way as to yield an entirely different set of facts when a point of legal dispute is eventually reached. This approach to anticipating through "fact-simulation scenarios" can be applied to principals' decisions regarding student discipline, library books, religious holidays, or any other area that might involve a legal issue.[94]

The use of preventive school law assumes that the principal has some basic knowledge of school law. It is the principal who, in addition,

[92]L. F. Rossow, "Can the 'Equal Access Act' Survive the Three-Part Test? or Vice Versa!" *NOLPE Notes* 18 (1985):1.

[93]L. Brown and F. Dauer, "A Synopsis of the Theory and Practice of Preventive Law, Part I," *Preventive Law Reporter* 1 (1982):7.

[94]W. C. Nednar, "Preventive School Law," in *School Law Update: Preventive School Law*, ed. Thomas Jones (Topeka, KS: NOLPE, 1983):1–14.

must participate in the separate technique of the "legal audit." Again, Brown and Dauer provide a most apt analogy:

> Most people can recognize but few can monitor their serum triglycerides and many don't even know that they should. It is therefore the professions obligation to suggest, to make available, and to analyze the lab work on some periodic basis. A checkup [or audit] is a regular part of preventive professional care; the utility of professional service is not limited to treating the client who arrives, fortuitously, with a broken arm.[95]

The principal's role in participating in a legal audit will be discussed in the next chapter. Within the general framework of preventive school law, however, certain questions should always be asked before initiating new educational programs or activities:

1. Will the new program cause injury?
2. Who might be injured?
3. How might someone be injured?
4. Will the injury be educational, psychological, or occupational?
5. Will the new program negatively affect minority groups?

Once there are answers to these questions, the new program can be evaluated from the legal standpoint to ensure that it provides the foundation of good preventive school law practice.[96]

There are a number of good reasons for practicing preventive school law. Perhaps the best rationale is the one that comes closest to addressing an ever-pressing problem in today's public schools—limited resources. Preventive school law practices can save the high cost of litigation. While some time and resources must be spent in the short run to develop good preventive practices, the money saved by avoiding having to defend oneself in a lengthy court action is well worth the effort.

SUMMARY

The need for the modern school principal to become legally literate is paramount. The school district attorney cannot be available for every decision that the principal must make involving school law.

[95]L. Brown and F. Dauer, "A Synopsis of the Theory and Practice of Preventive Law, Part II." *Preventive Law Reporter* 3 (1982):5.

[96]M. S. McClung, "Preventive Law and Public Education: A Proposal," *Journal of Law and Education* 10 (1981):37.

Principals should have a working knowledge of the rights of teachers. Teacher's rights extend to almost every area of the work environment. Charges of employment discrimination by teachers can be directed at principals for discriminatory decisions based on race, sex, religion, or age. Federal legislation specifies the nature of the protection that teachers are provided. Many states have their own employment discrimination statutes which go beyond the protections developed by federal acts.

Teachers receive a substantial degree of protection when they are being considered for termination. Teacher tenure laws provide the primary basis for this protection. In addition, depending upon the reason for the termination, teachers may be able to invoke their federal constitutional rights.

Students have rights under the Constitution. In addition, states have provided students with certain procedural and substantive guarantees in the event that they undergo serious punishment. The principal must be aware of the legally prescribed steps to be taken when suspending students from school. Once more, the elements of fundamental fairness and fair warning must be followed during the disciplinary proceedings.

In the final analysis, the principal can avoid many legal problems by practicing preventive school law. By examining school rules and teacher personnel policies with an eye toward prevention, the principal can avoid having to react to a legal problem after it has already occurred.

SELECTED BIBLIOGRAPHY

ALEXANDER, KERN AND DAVID ALEXANDER, *American Public School Law, (2nd ed.)*, St. Paul, MN: West Publishing Company, 1985.

ALEXANDER, K. AND M. ALEXANDER, *The Law of Schools, Students, and Teachers*, St. Paul, MN: West, 1984.

BARR, MARGARET, ed., *Student Affairs and the Law;* San Francisco, CA: Jossey-Bass, 1983.

COBB, JOSEPH J., *An Introduction to Educational Law: For Administrators and Teachers*, Springfield, IL: Charles C. Thomas, Pub., 1981.

CONNERS, EUGENE T., *Educational Tort Liability and Malpractice*, Bloomington, IN: Phi Delta Kappa, 1981.

FISCHER, LOUIS, DAVID SCHIMMEL, AND CYNTHIA KELLY, *Teachers and the Law, (2nd ed.)*, New York: Longman, 1987.

LAMORTE, MICHAEL W., *School Law: Cases and Concepts, (2nd ed.)*, Englewood Cliffs, NJ: Prentice-Hall, Inc., 1987.

LANZAROME, MICHAEL R., *Education Law: The Rights of Students and Teachers*, New York: McGraw-Hill, Inc., 1988.

McCarthy, M. and N. Cambron, *Public School Law* (2nd ed.), Boston: Allyn and Bacon, 1987.

Menacker, Julius, *School Law: Theoretical and Case Perspectives,* Englewood Cliffs, NJ: Prentice-Hall, Inc., 1987.

Monks, Robert L. and Ernest I. Proulx, *Legal Basics for Teachers,* Bloomington, IN: Phi Delta Kappa, 1986.

Munro, Robert J., *Grievance Arbitration Procedure: Legal and Policy Guidelines for Public Schools,* Milwood, NY: Associated Faculty Press, 1982.

Nednar, W. C., "Preventive School Law," *School Law Update . . . Preventive School Law,* ed. Thomas, Jones, Topeka, KS: National Organization on Legal Problems in Education, 1983.

Rapp, J. A., ed., *Education Law,* New York: Matthew Bender, 1984.

Rossow, Lawrence F., *Search and Seizure in the Public Schools,* Topeka, KS: National Organization on Legal Problems of Education, 1987.

Rossow, Lawrence F., *The Law of Student Expulsions and Suspensions,* Topeka, KS: National Organization on Legal Problems of Education, 1989.

Valente, William, *Education Law Public and Private,* St. Paul, MN: West, 1985.

8

Legal Aspects of the Instructional Program

The United States has become a litigious society. When parents disagree with schools, it is no longer uncommon for the disagreement to be decided by a court. One of the frequent areas for disagreement concerns *what* children are taught. Do parents have the right to demand that the school curriculum be shaped in a manner consistent with their own philosophies? The answer to this and related questions about the control of the instructional program will be explored in this chapter. Specifically, the following legal issues will be addressed: legal authority for the curriculum, legal parameters for curricular content, censorship, and copyright.

LEGAL AUTHORITY FOR THE CURRICULUM

When considering who and what is the legal authority for the school curriculum, several key areas should be examined: (1) the source and extent of legal authority vested in the schools; (2) legal issues related to the local instructional program; (3) the legal status of homework, and (4) the law surrounding minimum competency testing.

Source of Legal Authority for the Curriculum

One of the best summaries of state laws on curriculum appeared in a report of a National Institute for Education study in 1974:

> In all states the local district must offer a curriculum that the state prescribes. The degree of control exercised by the education agency differs from state to state. In about half the states the local district must offer the curriculum prescribed by the state. . . . Even in those states where districts retain some discretion, course offerings must still be chosen within state guidelines. . . . For example, all schools must offer courses in American history and government. The statutes of nearly all states contain such requirements. In addition, the choice of the district is often limited by state board guidelines regulating the number, content or quality of the courses. Some states provide that a district must offer a specified number of courses. Some also enforce the dictates . . . by making the district's choice of curriculum a requirement for accreditation. Sanctions for noncompliance would include . . . loss of state aid. . . . The local district selects its curriculum offerings on the basis of the extent of authority delegated by the State.[1]

[1]National Institute for Education, *Study of State Legal Standards for the Provision of Public Education,* (1974), p. 28.

The source of authority for the curriculum follows the same path as that for the general authority for schools. The highest authority is the state constitution, followed by the state legislature, the state board of education, and, finally, the local school board. Except for Louisiana, Oklahoma, and Utah, the state constitutions are silent about curriculum.[2] State constitutions typically give "plenary" (total) power to the legislature to determine the curriculum. However, most legislatures create statutes that provide very broad parameters for curriculum. Take for example, this excerpt from the school laws of the state of Kansas:

> Every accredited elementary school shall teach reading, writing, arithmetic, geography, spelling, English grammar and composition, history of the United States and of the state of Kansas, civil government and the duties of citizenship, health and hygiene, together with such other subjects as the state board may determine. The state board shall be responsible for the selection of subject matter within the several fields of instruction and for its organization into courses of study and instruction for the guidance of teachers, principals and superintendents.[3]

Beyond the stipulation of the broad areas of study, additional details are left to the state boards of education. The state boards may then determine how much of each area the student will study. This is usually accomplished by regulating the number of units of study required for graduation. A state board might also decide to expand on the broad parameters set by state statute. The state statutes for curriculum may be regarded as minimums. The local board of education is generally given the authority to decide which textbooks and materials to use to teach the curriculum. There are a few states that require standardization of textbooks throughout the state. This is accomplished by establishing a state textbook commission or other similar statewide organization. Another approach is for the state board of education to develop an "approved" list of textbooks from which the local board can choose. The approved-list approach provides some local discretion while allowing the state board to maintain its share of control. In about half the states, local school boards can adopt courses

---

[2]In Louisiana, the state Constitution requires that students be taught about the constitutional system of the state and national government and about the citizenship duties. Oklahoma requires that agriculture, horticulture, stock raising, and domestic science be taught. In Utah, the constitution requires the teaching of the metric system.

[3]Kan. Stat. Ann. 72-1101 (1985).

of instruction, but they usually require approval from the state board. Few states give complete control for textbook selection to the local board.

It is important for the principal to know the source of authority for the curriculum that is being used in the school. Parents or even teachers may complain about the inclusion of certain courses. The possibility for curriculum changes will be a function of the source of authority.

Legal Issues Related to the Local Instructional Program

Legal issues affecting the instructional program often include the following areas: eliminating courses and activities, grade and course placement, and promotion and graduation.

Eliminating Courses and Activities.   Once the state statute and the state board requirements have been met, the school district enters into the nebulous area of the elective curriculum. Conflicts with parents have arisen when the elective curriculum expands into areas formerly reserved to for family control. The question becomes, what rights do parents have to exclude or include their children where school board–developed courses are concerned? *Primary parental initiative* is one legal theory. With this theory, parents are seen as the parties who should have the opportunity to make selections from the prescribed courses for their children. The parent's right to choose is seen as superior to that of the school authorities. While this theory might be well received in many modern communities, it was originally voiced at the turn of the century and was associated with a pioneering view of the United States.[4]

The prevailing legal theory is that the school has the discretion to add or eliminate courses or activities not mandated by the state. Over parents' objections, courts have found that neither parents' nor students' rights are violated when a school does not offer the same courses available in other school districts.[5] This objection arises when, for example, certain school districts offer advanced courses in mathematics or the sciences while others do not, or when, due to budget limita-

[4]*School Board Dist. N. 18* v. *Thompson,* 103 p. 578 (Okla. 1909).
[5]*Bd. of Education of Okay Independent School Dist.* v. *Carroll,* 513 p. 2d 872 (Okla. 1973).

tions, school districts reduce or eliminate music and art courses. Reductions in services are not overruled by the courts unless the reductions were made for arbitrary or capricious reasons.[6] Acceptable reasons generally include declining enrollment and financial exigency.

Grade and Course Placement.   Almost all state laws give authority to the local school boards to establish standards for grade placement and promotion. For example, courts have upheld the authority of school officials over parents' objections when the school refused to admit a child to a particular grade because of an age requirement, even though the parents produce evidence of the child's advanced achievements.[7]

While the courts generally defer to the judgment of the school in these matters, it has not upheld the application of dual standards. For example, an Illinois school district had a policy of admitting first-time students to grade 1 on the basis of their having reached the age of 6. However, students currently enrolled in a kindergarten were required to pass an achievement test before being promoted to first grade. The Illinois court ruled that the practice was discriminatory.[8] This case should put the principal on alert where the issue of promotion from kindergarten to first grade is concerned. In states in which kindergarten is offered but is not a requirement, parents have the right to keep their children at home until the children reach the compulsory age of 6. At this time, the child becomes eligible for first grade regardless of whether the child has attended kindergarten or not. To have it otherwise would be to penalize the parents for simply complying with the state compulsory educational law instead of opting for starting the child early in the optional-kindergarten program. This aspect of the law makes the practice of "flunking" kindergarten legally suspect. Once the child enters first grade, the school can retain the child in that grade for as long as the school deems necessary.

Promotion and Graduation.   In recent years, state legislatures have moved toward requiring some form of exit test before students can be promoted or graduated. This minimum competency testing approach will be discussed in detail in a moment. For now, it can be noted that

---

[6]*Borough* v. *Governing Bd. of El Segundo Unified Sch. Dist.,* 173 Cal. Rrtr. 729 (1981).

[7]*Frost* v. *Yerozunis,* 385 N.Y.S. 2d 181 (1976).

[8]*Morgan* v. *Bd. of Education,* 317 N.E. 2d 393 (Ill. 1974).

the courts have consistently held that school administrators have the authority to set academic standards and grant promotion and eventual graduation based on those standards—as long as the standards themselves are neither discriminatory nor applied in a discriminatory way.[9]

The principal should note, however, that withholding promotion or graduation is considered by the courts to be a most severe punishment. For many years, courts have upheld the school's authority to deny promotion and graduation only when the student has failed for purely academic reasons. When schools have withheld promotion for reasons other than academic (such as cheating or failure to pay fees), the courts have held these misbehaviors to be insufficient to warrant the punishment of not being promoted.[10] The general principle is that once the student has "earned" promotion, it must be granted. Misbehavior should be punished in ways other than withholding promotion.

However, denial of participation in graduation ceremonies is another matter. The courts view participation in the graduation ceremony as a privilege. School authorities have discretionary power in this area and may use the denial of graduation-ceremony participation to maintain discipline. For example, a North Carolina court upheld the exclusion of a student from a graduation ceremony because he refused to wear a cap and gown.[11]

MINIMUM COMPETENCY TESTING

In 1982, thirty-eight states had statutes or state board regulations requiring minimum competency testing (MCT) before a diploma could be awarded.[12] The practice of MCT has provoked litigation. Students and parents objecting to MCT have raised issues in the following areas: (1) sufficient notice that the test will be required, (2) adequacy of preparation for the test, (3) applicability of the test to special-education students, and (4) opportunities for remediation.

[9]For example, *Johnson* v. *Sullivan*, 571 p. 2d 798 (Mont. 1977).
[10]For example, *State* v. *Wilson*, 297 S.W. 419 (Mo. App. 1927); *Ryan* v. *Bd. of Education*, 257 p. 945 (Kan. 1927).
[11]*Fowler* v. *Williamson*, 251 S.E. 2d 889 (N. Car. 1979).
[12]*Education Week*, "Changing Course—A Fifty State Survey of Reform Measures," February 6, 1985, pp. 11–30.

Proper Notice

Since education is a property right, students must be given due process before that right is taken away. The Fourteenth Amendment is the source of this right; it is the application of the Fourteenth Amendment that requires the principal to provide due process before suspending a student. If a student might not receive a diploma because of failing the MCT, the student must be forewarned so that he can take proper steps to prepare for the test.

How much notice is required? The amount of time varies depending upon the intended use of the MCT. More notice is required when the MCT is to be used to determine whether a student receives a terminal diploma than when it is to be used for promotion from grade to grade.

The Court of Appeals for the Fifth Circuit held that a thirteen-month notice for imposition of a statewide MCT in order ιο receive a diploma was *insufficient* time to prepare for the test.[13] When courts have held that the amount of time given for MCT preparation was sufficient, it has been for a two- to four-year notice.[14] When using a MCT for grade promotion, the courts tend to defer to the school to set whatever test standards they deem appropriate. Students do not have the same degree of property right in the case of promotion from grade to grade as they do in the case of a terminal diploma. However, if a school uses an end-of-year MCT as the sole basis for promotion, then students may have a greater degree of property right. In this case, the school might be required to give two years' notice before starting the MCT program.

Adequacy of Preparation

One of the first states to use widespread MCT was Florida. In 1981, Florida's test was challenged as being invalid. In other words, it was contended that students who were required to take the test had not been adequately taught the subject matter that would appear. The Court of Appeals for the Fifth Circuit required the state of Florida to prove that the test covered material that had actually been taught to students.[15] While the state was ultimately successful in demonstrating

[13]*Debra P.* v. *Turlington,* 644 F. 2d 397 (5th Cir. 1981).
[14]*Johnson* v. *Sikes,* 730 F. 2d 644 (11th Cir. 1984). *Anderson* v. *Banks,* 540 F. Supp. 761 (S. D. Ga. 1982).
[15]*Debra P., id.* at 406.

the test's validity, the lesson for school authorities is that the area of test validity is subject to challenge. The principal should be prepared to offer evidence that the MCT being used is fundamentally fair.

MCT for Special Education

Handicapped students can be required to take and pass the same MCT as nonhandicapped students.[16] However, handicapped students must be given the necessary opportunity to satisfy the requirements for graduation or promotion—that is, the opportunity to successfully pass the MCT. The difficulty is in determining whether the typical educational program for handicapped children provides realistic preparation for the MCT. It would seem outrageous to suggest that a student who is deaf or blind must pass the same test as a regular-education student. For that matter, any number of emotional or learning handicaps would seem to preclude any reasonable chance of passing the MCT.

Some states realize the mismatch between handicapped students and MCT programs. As a solution, handicapped students may be awarded a certificate of completion instead of a regular diploma.[17] This approach may seem unfair on the face of it. After all, why should handicapped students receive what seems to be a second-class diploma just because they are handicapped? However, judicial thinking does not always seem fair. If handicapped students were given the same diplomas as nonhandicapped students even though they had not passed the test, this might be in violation of the Fourteenth Amendment. What would be the status of a nonhandicapped student who failed the MCT and was not given a diploma as a result? Part of the idea behind the use of the MCT is to guarantee to the public and to potential employers that the holders of the diploma have mastered certain standards. While it is unfortunate that certain handicapped students could never pass the MCT, the school district cannot legally "hide" the fact that such students did not pass the MCT by awarding them the same diploma as that awarded to nonhandicapped students.

Opportunities for Remediation

As a general rule, the school must give students who fail the MCT an opportunity to retake the test. In addition, the school has some responsibility to provide remedial instruction for such students in

---

[16]*Brookhart* v. *Illinois State Bd. of Education,* 697 F. 2d 179 (7th Cir. 1983).
[17]M. McCarthy, "The Application of Competency Testing Mandates to Handicapped Children," *Harvard Educational Review* 53 (1983): 148–150.

order to increase their chances of passing the second time around. The school should be able to identify failing students' deficiencies as part of the MCT process, and these deficiencies can become the target of the remedial instruction.[18]

THE LEGAL STATUS OF HOMEWORK

Over the years, the courts have been supportive of the school's authority to require homework and to punish students who do not comply.[19] The theory is that the school has the authority to reasonably extend itself beyond the school day. When this extension has not been reasonable, the courts have held for the objecting parents. For example, when a Mississippi school imposed a daily home study period from 7:00 P.M. to 9:00 P.M., the court ruled that the home study period was an invasion of the parents' right to control their children.[20]

Parents of a student athlete in Texas challenged a league rule that forbade students' attendance at "summer athletic camps." The student's parents claimed that the rule violated the "family-choice doctrine." They further argued that there is a "private realm of family life which the state cannot enter." The appellate court rejected the parents' claims, holding that "parental authority falls short of being constitutionally absolute." In deciding for the school, the court upheld the validity of the summer-camp rule.[21]

THE CURRICULUM AND FREEDOM OF RELIGION

The First Amendment of the US Constitution states that "Congress shall make no law respecting an establishment of religion or prohibiting the free exercise thereof." Therefore, the federal and state governments can neither promote nor prohibit religion. The public schools are agents of the state and are therefore part of government. The restrictions embodied in the religion clause apply directly to the public schools.

For purposes of analysis, the religion clause can be separated into two parts: the establishment clause and the free-exercise clause.

[18]M. McCarthy, *Public School Law*, 2d ed. (Boston, MA: Allyn and Bacon, Inc., 1987, p. 88).

[19]*Mangum* v. *Keith*, 95 S.E. 1 (Ga. 1918); *Balding* v. *State*, 4 S.W. 579 (Tex. 1887).

[20]*Hobbs* v. *Germany*, 49 So. 515 (Miss. 1909).

[21]*Kite* v. *Marshall*, 661 F. 2d 1027 (1981).

The Free-Exercise Clause

The free-exercise provision means that schools cannot do anything to prohibit students from practicing their religion. In other words, schools cannot force students to believe or not believe something that is contrary to their religion. State law or school-district policy to the contrary, the principal is not required to grant an automatic exemption to those who claim religious objection. If parents were to take the matter to court, they would have to show two things to win the case: (1) *coercion*—that is, that a school requirement (to read certain books, for example, or to participate in certain activities) forces the student to do something that is contrary to his religion; (2) *compelling state interest*—that is, that the school does not have a compelling interest in forcing all students to participate.

The Establishment Clause

The establishment clause requires that schools do nothing to promote religion. Generally, the courts have disallowed activities such as praying, bible reading, and religious discussion in the classroom. Since 1970, the courts have used what is known as the *tripart test* for determining whether an activity is in violation of the establishment clause: (1) Does the activity have a secular (public) purpose? (2) Does the activity avoid having the primary effect of advancing religion? (3) Does the activity avoid excessive government entanglement with religion? If the school activity passes all three prongs, then there is no violation. Failure on any one of the prongs means that the activity is unconstitutional.[22]

Course Requirements and Religious Objections

Parents and students of various faiths have objected to the inclusion of certain courses or activities in the curriculum. In *Davis* v. *Page*,[23] parents who were Apostolic Lutherans objected to exposure of their children to any audiovisual material. The parents claimed that is was a sin to watch images produced by electronic equipment. Ruling against the parents, the court reasoned that audiovisual materials are an accepted educational tool that did not interfere with the children's religious practices.

---

[22]*Lemon* v. *Kurtzman*, 403 U. S. 602 (1971).
[23]385 F. Supp. 395 (D.N.H. 1974).

In *Grove* v. *Mead School District No. 354*,[24] parents objected to the classroom use of a sophomore-level English book called *The Learning Tree*. The book has as its theme the life surrounding racism from the perspective of a teenage boy in a working-class black family. The court noted that although the book contains some reference to religion, it is minor. Nevertheless, the parents, who were fundamentalist Christians, claimed that requiring their child to read the book had the effect of inhibiting their religious beliefs. The court found no validity to the parents' free-exercise claim. It reasoned as follows:

> The state interest in providing well-rounded public education would be critically impeded by accommodation of Grove's wishes.
>
> If we are to eliminate everything that is objectionable to any of [the religious bodies existing in the United States] or inconsistent with any of their doctrines, we will leave public education in shreds.[25]

The leading case, *Mozert* v. *Hawkins County Board of Education* was recently decided by the Court of Appeals for the Sixth Circuit. A Tennessee family claimed religious interference because their elementary-school children used the Holt Reading Series. The parents called themselves "born-again Christians," and the mother testified that "the word of God as found in the Christian Bible is the totality of my beliefs."[26]

The children's father had found "objectionable passages in the readers that dealt with magic, role reversal, or role elimination, particularly biographical material about women who have been recognized for achievements outside their homes, and emphasis on one world or a planetary society."[27]

Both parents testified under cross-examination. They objected "to passages that expose their children to other forms of religion and to the feelings, attitudes, and values of other students that contradict the plaintiffs' religious views without a statement that the other views are incorrect and that the plaintiffs' views are the correct ones."[28]

In deciding for the school district, the court reasoned as follows:

> [A]ctions that merely offend or cast doubt on religious beliefs do not on that account violate free exercise. An actual burden on the profession or exercise of religion is required.

[24]753 F. 2d 1528 (1985).
[25]*Id.* at 1533.
[26]*Mozert* v. *Hawkins County Bd. of Education*, 827 F. 2d 1058, 1061 (1987).
[27]*Id.* at 1062.
[28]*Id.*

In short, distinctions must be drawn between those governmental actions that actually interfere with the exercise of religion, and those that merely require or result in exposure to attitudes and outlooks at odds with perspectives prompted by religion.[29]

By now it should be clear that students or parents must do more than claim a religious objection if a student is to be excused from an activity. One commentator summarized the issues of parents' religious objections as follows:

While the free-exercise clause may permit students to manifest their religious beliefs in the school setting, their claims must be religious in origin and based on an aversion to an activity that goes to the heart of the basic tenets of an organized and historically established faith. . . . Courts also have expressed concern that these personal attitudes and values not be allowed to stifle the free exchange of ideas in classrooms so necessary for the education of citizens.[30]

CENSORSHIP

We have discussed the role of students and parents in shaping the curriculum through their religious objections. This activity operates as one of the major forms of censorship on the school program. However, school authorities themselves exercise censorship whenever they decide not to include some kind of information or activity in the curriculum because it might be controversial. School boards, school administrators, and even legislatures at times will control the curriculum by a reference to their own view of the world.

To what extent does censorship of the school program by school authorities represent an unconstitutional infringement on students' right to be informed? To what extent may the principal censor the use of classroom materials, student newspapers, or library books? The parameters of the principal's authority to deal with these areas will be discussed in the following sections.

Censorship of Classroom Materials

One of the cases that best illustrates the powers of school officials to censor classroom material is *Zykan* v. *Warsaw Community School.*[31] A group of students at Warsaw High School in Indiana sued the school

[29]*Id.* at 1068.
[30]Bruce Beezer, "The Right of Students to be Informed," *The Educational Forum* 45, no. 4 (May 1981): 443–444.
[31]637 F. 2d 1300.

board for ordering the removal and destruction of the textbook *Values Clarification* from the English curriculum. In addition, the students alleged that the board carried on "a policy prohibiting the use of reading materials that 'might be objectionable.' They further allege that the board took these actions because particular words in the books offended their social, political, and moral tastes and not because the books, taken as a whole, were lacking in educational value."[32]

The students claimed that the standards of academic freedom and their "right to be informed" disallowed school officials from imposing their own personal beliefs on students. In deciding for the school board, the Court of Appeals for the Seventh Circuit noted that high school students *do not* enjoy the same degree of academic freedom that is permitted at the college level, where the concept was originally applied. They reasoned:

> A high school student's lack of the intellectual skills necessary for taking full advantage of the marketplace of ideas engenders a correspondingly greater need for direction and guidance from those better equipped by experience and reflection [that is, school authorities] to make critical educational choices . . . As a result, the community has a legitimate, even a vital and compelling interest in the choice [of] and adherence to a suitable curriculum for the benefit of our young citizens.[33]

While the court endorsed the school authorities as having broad discretionary powers to censor the curriculum, it did point out several school board behaviors that would be unconstitutional: (1) insisting upon instruction in a religiously-inspired dogma to the exclusion of all other points of view (for example, teaching that creationism is the only true interpretation for the beginning of humankind), (2) placing a flat prohibition on the mention of certain relevant topics in the classroom, or (3) forbidding students to take an interest in subjects not directly covered by the regular curriculum.[34]

In cases in which the classroom teacher has been punished for using materials that school administrators believed to be inappropriate, they were required to show that the use of the offensive material substantially disrupted the educational environment. In two illustrative cases in which teachers were dismissed for using offensive material, the administration was unable to show substantial disruption. The teachers were reinstated with back pay.[35]

[32]*Id.* at 1302.
[33]*Id.* at 1304.
[34]*Id.* at 1305–1306.
[35]*Parducci* v. *Rutland,* 316 F. Supp. 352, *Dean* v. *Timpson Ind. S.D.,* 486 F. Supp. 302.

Censorship in the School Library

In the 1970s, the courts tended to view the school's authority to censor library books and to develop curriculum as equally broad. In 1982, however, the US Supreme Court threw new light on this issue when it decided the case of *Board of Education, Island Trees Union Free School District* v. *Pico*.[36] In this New York case, a group of high school students sued the school board for removing from the library shelves ten books that it considered offensive. The students claimed that the board had removed the books because particular passages offended their social, political, and moral tastes and not because the books, taken as a whole, were lacking in educational value. The board responded by explaining that the books were removed because they were "anti-American, anti-Christian, anti-Semitic, and just plain filthy," and contained "obscenities, blasphemies, brutality, and perversion beyond description."

In a five-to-four decision, the Court affirmed the order of the appellate court to require the federal district court to hold a trial to determine the motivations of the board in removing the books. After the Supreme Court's decision was handed down, the Island Trees School Board voted to return the books to the library.

While this case can be viewed as a victory for students' rights, the Court cautioned about overgeneralizing the decision into related areas. This case did not involve the curriculum, textbooks, or required reading. It did not concern the acquisition of library books. It involved only the *removal* of library books once they had been absorbed by the school library.

Writing for the majority, Justice Brennan reasoned as follows:

> First Amendment rights of students may be directly and sharply implicated by the removal of books from the shelves of a school library . . . because the Constitution protects the right to receive information as a corollary of the right of free expression . . . access to ideas prepares students for active and effective participation in the pluralistic, often contentious society in which they will soon be members.[37]

Brennan went on to point out that school boards should not exercise their power to remove books from the library when they are motivated by partisan or political ideas and when they intend to deny students access to ideas with which they personally disagree. However,

[36]457 U.S. 853 (1982).
[37]D. Schimmel, "The Limits on School Board Discretion: *Board of Education* v. *Pico*," *Education Law Reporter* (1983): VI 285.

it would be permissible for the board to remove books that were pervasively vulgar or educationally unsuitable.

Censorship of the School Newspaper

Much of what is known today about students' rights was decided by the judiciary during the 1970s. The authority of school administration to censor the activities of the school newspaper was primarily limited to material that was obscene.[38] In 1988, however, the US Supreme Court decided a censorship issue which has vastly broadened the scope of school authority regarding school newspapers.

The case of *Hazelwood School District* v. *Kuhlmeier*[39] had its origin in St. Louis County, Missouri. Three journalism students at Hazelwood East High School sued, declaring that their First Amendment rights had been violated. The students had written separate articles on two controversial topics—teenage pregnancy and the impact of divorce.

The journalism students, as part of their research for the articles, interviewed several pregnant students. They also interviewed students of divorced parents, one of whom offered his opinion about his father's behavior.

Prior to publication of the articles, the school principal ordered two pages to be deleted. The principal reasoned that the parts of the pregnancy article concerning sexual activity and contraception would be inappropriate for younger students at the school. He found parts of the divorce article inappropriate since it contained quotes from a student condemning his father when the father had not been given any opportunity to respond to the material.

In deciding for the principal, the Court found no constitutional violation in the censoring decision. It saw the principal's decision as reasonable. The principal could reasonably have concluded that the students who wrote and edited the articles had not sufficiently mastered the portions of the journalism curriculum pertaining to the treatment of controversial issues, personal attacks, possible invasions of privacy, and the legal, moral, and ethical restrictions imposed upon journalists within a school community that includes adolescent subjects and readers.[40]

The Court reasoned further that educators indeed have authority

[38]See, for example, *Fujishima* v. *Bd. of Education,* 460 F. 2d 1355 (7th Cir. 1972).
[39]108 S. Ct. 562 (1988).
[40]D. McFall, "US Supreme Court Restricts Scholastic Free-Speech Rights," *NOLPE Notes* 23 (January 1988):1.

over school-sponsored publications and other expressive activity of students. The school's permitting the newspaper activity does not create an open forum wherein students' views may be aired freely. In the instant case, the board provided a school-sponsored publication within an adopted curriculum. There was no intent to open the pages of the student newspaper to indiscriminate use by student reporters and editors. Instead, the clear intent was to reserve a forum for a supervised learning experience for journalism students.[41]

COPYRIGHT LAW IN EDUCATION

Copyright laws have existed since the turn of the century. However, it was not until 1978, when major revisions to the Copyright Act[42] took place, that schools began to pay attention to copyright laws.

The primary purpose of the Copyright Act is to promote the creation and dissemination of knowledge and ideas, not simply to protect the economic interests of authors.[43] All original works of authorship are covered under the copyright law. The law establishes statutory copyright protection from the time of the actual creation of a work of authorship. Creation occurs at the time the work is fixed in writing or record, and extends for 50 years after the author's death.[44] Although copyrights can be registered with the federal government, formal registration is not required under the law. Protection begins with the work's creation. Protected works include pieces of writing, paintings, sculpture, photographs, movies, sound recordings, videos, and computer programs.[45]

The owner of the copyright has the legal authority to reproduce the work, to distribute copies, and to display the work in public. Copyrighted material is not to be used by others unless the owner of the copyright gives permission. Herein lies the problem for teachers. Teachers would be under great hardship if they were required to obtain permission every time they used copyrighted material. Perhaps

---

[41]*School Law Reporter* 29 (March 1988):2.

[42]P.L. 94–553, 90 Stat. 2541 et. seq., 17 U.S.C. Sec. 101 et. seq.

[43]V. M. Helm, *What Educators Should Know About Copyright,* Fastback 233 (Bloomington, IN: Phi Delta Kappa, 1986), p. 9.

[44]R. J. Shoop and W. E. Sparkman, *Kansas School Law: A Principal's Survival Guide* (Dubuque, IA: Eddie Bowers, 1983), p. 164.

[45]M. Clay Smith, "Classroom Use of Copyrighted Materials," *West's Education Law Reporter* 43 (February 4, 1988): 1.

predicting such a problem, exceptions were recognized when the Copyright Act was passed by Congress for certain uses of copyrighted material. The exceptions pertinent to teachers fall under the fair-use doctrine.

Fair use has been defined as "the privilege in others than the owner of the copyright to use the copyrighted material in a reasonable manner without his consent, notwithstanding the monopoly granted to the owner. . . ."[46] Because of the fair-use doctrine, teachers and librarians are able to use copyrighted material *within limits*. We will explore the boundaries of the fair-use doctrine in the rest of the chapter.

Fair Use in the Classroom

Copying materials for classroom use is either a copyright infringement (which is against the law) or an exemption under fair use (which is within the law). Therefore, the goal of every teacher should be to ensure that the activity comes within the fair-use exemption.

The Copyright Act stipulated four factors which determine fair use:[47]

1. *Purpose and character.* The purpose of copying the material should be strictly related to education. The purpose should not be for the copier to make a profit.
2. *Nature.* The nature of work being copied is important. For example, copying a newspaper article (which is an informational work) is more likely to be considered fair use than copying a poem or story out of a book (which is creative work). Copying pages from a workbook created for school use is usually considered an infringement because copying a workbook deprives the copyright holder of the opportunity to make a profit.
3. *Amount.* The number of pages copied relative to the number of pages in the entire work should be small. Copying an entire work can be considered beyond fair use. Copying more than 50 percent of a work approaches infringement.
4. *Potential market.* The copying must not reduce the potential market and sales of the work. This would cut into the profits of the copyright holder and would therefore probably not be considered fair use.

[46]M. M. McCarthy and N. H. Cambron-McCabe, *Public School Law,* 2d ed. (Boston: Allyn & Bacon, 1987), p. 257, citing *Marcus* v. *Rowley,* 695 F. 2d 1171, 1174 (9th Cir. 1983).

[47]17 U.S.C. Sec. 107.

The four factors just outlined can be applied to any copying activity within or outside of education. Because Congress anticipated the great amount of copying that goes on in schools, it commissioned a group of authors, publishers, and teachers to develop guidelines for copying in educational institutions. While the guidelines do not have the force of law, they are widely used by the courts in determining whether a specific challenged copying activity constitutes fair use.

Guidelines for Classroom Copying in
Not-For-Profit Educational Institutions

I. *Single Copying for Teachers*

   A single copy may be made of any of the following by or for a teacher at his or her individual request for scholarly research or for use in teaching or preparation to teach a class:

A. A chapter from a book;

B. An article from a periodical or newspaper;

C. A short story, short essay, or short poem, whether or not from a collective work;

D. A chart, graph, diagram, drawing, cartoon, or picture from a book, periodical, or newspaper;

II. *Multiple Copies for Classroom Use*

   Multiple copies (not to exceed in any event more than one copy per pupil in a course) may be made by or for the teacher giving the course for classroom use or discussion, *provided* that:

A. The copying meets the tests of brevity and spontaneity as defined below; *and,*

B. Meets the cumulative effect test as defined below; *and,*

C. Each copy includes a notice of copyright.

Definitions

   Brevity

   (i) Poetry: (a) A complete poem if less than 250 words and if printed on not more than two pages or (b) from a longer poem, an excerpt of not more than 250 words.

   (ii) Prose: (a) Either a complete article, story, or essay of less than 2,500 words, or (b) an excerpt from any prose work of not more than 1,000 words or 10% of the work, whichever is less, but in any event a minimum of 500 words.

   (iii) Illustration: One chart, graph, diagram, drawing, cartoon, or picture per book or per periodical issue.

   (iv) "Special" works: Certain works in poetry, prose, or in "poetic prose" which often combine language with illustrations and which are intended sometimes for children and at other times for a more general audience fall short of 2,500 words in their entirety. Paragraph "ii" above notwithstanding, such "special works" may not be reproduced in their entirety; however, an excerpt comprising not more than two of the published pages of such special work, and containing not more than 10% of the words found in the text thereof, may be reproduced.

Spontaneity

(i) The copying is at the instance and inspiration of the individual teacher, and

(ii) The inspiration and decision to use the work and the moment of its use for maximum teaching effectiveness are so close in time that it would be unreasonable to expect a timely reply to a request for permission.

Cumulative Effect

(i) The copying of the material is for only one course in the school in which the copies are made.

(ii) Not more than one short poem, article, story, essay, or two excerpts may be copied from the same author, nor more than three from the same collective work or periodical volume during one class term.

(iii) There shall not be more than nine instances of such multiple copying for one course during one class term.

(The limitations stated in "ii" and "iii" above shall not apply to current news periodicals and newspapers and current news sections of other periodicals.)

III. *Prohibitions as to I and II Above*

Notwithstanding any of the above, the following shall be prohibited:

A. Copying shall not be used to create or to replace or substitute for anthologies, compilations, or collective works. Such replacement or substitution may occur whether copies of various works or excerpts therefrom are accumulated or reproduced and used separately.

B. There shall be no copying of or from works intended to be "consumable" in the course of study or of teaching. These include workbooks, exercises, standardized tests, and test booklets and answer sheets and like consumable material.

C. Copying shall not:

(a) substitute for the purchase of books, publishers' reprints, or periodicals;

(b) be directed by higher authorities;

(c) be repeated with respect to the same item by the same teacher from term to term.

D. No charge shall be made to the student beyond the actual cost of the photocopying.[48]

---

[48]Copyright Law Revision, H.R. Rep. No. 1476, 94th Cong., 2d Sess. 68.

COPYING MUSIC

Congress also provided quidelines for the copying of music to be used for educational purposes. Many of the same principles that guide the written word also guide music.[49]

Guidelines for Educational Use of Music

A. Permissible Uses
  1. Emergency copying to replace purchased copies which for any reason are not available for an imminent performance provided purchased replacement copies shall be substituted in due course.
  2. (a) For academic purposes other than performance, multiple copies of excerpts of works may be made, provided that the excerpts do not comprise a part of the whole which would constitute a performable unit such as a section, movement, or aria, but in no case more than 10% of the whole work. The number of copies shall not exceed one copy per pupil.
     (b) For academic purposes other than performance, a single copy of an entire performable unit (section, movement, aria, etc.) that is (1) confirmed by the copyright proprietor to be out of print or (2) unavailable except in a larger work may be made by or for a teacher solely for the purpose of his or her scholarly research or in preparation to teach a class.
  3. Printed copies which have been purchased may be edited or simplified provided that the fundamental character of the work is not distorted or the lyrics, if any, altered or lyrics added if none exists.
  4. A single copy of recordings of performances by students may be made for evaluation or rehersal purposes and may be retained by the educational institution or individual teacher.
  5. A single copy of a sound recording (such as a tape, disc, or cassette) of copyrighted music may be made from sound recordings owned by an educational institution or an individual teacher for the purpose of constructing aural exercises or examinations and may be retained by the educational institution or individual teacher. (This pertains only to the copyright of the music itself and not to any copyright which may exist in the sound recording.)

B. *Prohibitions*
  1. Copying to create or replace or substitute for anthologies, compilations, or collective works.
  2. Copying of or from works intended to be "consumable" in the course of study or of teaching such as workbooks, exercises, standardized tests, and answer sheets and like material.
  3. Copying for the purpose of performance, except as in A(1) above.
  4. Copying for the purpose of substituting for the purchase of music except as in A(1) and A(2) above.

---

[49]*Id.* at 70.

5. Copying without inclusion of the copyright notice which appears on the printed copy.

The new copyright law also contains provisions dealing with reproduction or copying by libraries:

> ... it is not an infringement of copyright for a library or archives, or any of its employees acting within the scope of their employment, to reproduce no more than one copy or phonorecord of a work, or to distribute such copy or phonorecord, under the conditions specified by this section, if
>
> (1) the reproduction or distribution is made without any purpose of direct or indirect commercial advantage;
>
> (2) the collections of the library or archives are (i) open to the public, or (ii) available not only to researchers affiliated with the library or archives or with the institution of which it is a part; but also to other persons doing research in a aspecialized field;
>
> (3) the reproduction or distribution of the work includes a notice of copyright.

COPYING IN THE LIBRARY

Copying in the library is considered fair use provided the following standards are observed:[50]

1. The library is making a reproduction without any purpose of commercial advantage.
2. The library collection is open to the public.
3. The library reproduces no more than one copy of a work.
4. The reproduction includes a notice of copyright.

If the library follows the four standards, it can make copies for the following purposes:[51]

1. To preserve in facsimile form an unpublished work currently in the library or for another library (such as putting a copy of a doctoral dissertation on microfiche).
2. To replace in facsimile form a published work that is damaged, lost, or stolen if the library has, after reasonable effort, determined that an unused replacement cannot be obtained at a fair price.
3. In response to a request by a user or by another library on behalf of a user. (This exemption only applies if the copy becomes the property of the

[50]L. Fischer, D. Schimmel, and C. Kelly, *Teachers and the Law,* 2d ed. (New York: Longman, 1987), p. 101. Citing Notes of Committee on the Judiciary, H.R. No. 94–1476, 94th Cong., 210 Sess. 68–70 (1976) at Sec. 108.

[51]*Id.* at 102 citing at Sec. 108 (f) (1).

user, the library has no reason to believe that it will be used for purposes other than private study or research, and the library displays a copyright warning notice.)

Libraries are required to post copyright restrictions in a conspicuous place. The recommended format is as follows:[52]

NOTICE

WARNING CONCERNING COPYRIGHT RESTRICTIONS

The copyright law of the United States (Title 17, United States Code) governs the making of photocopies or other reproductions of copyrighted material.

Under certain conditions specified in the law, libraries and archives are authorized to furnish a photocopy or other reproduction. One of these specified conditions is that the photocopy or reproduction is not to be "used for any purpose other than private study, scholarship, or research." If a user makes a request for, or later uses, a photocopy or reproduction for purposes in excess of "fair use," that user may be liable for copyright infringement.

This institution reserves the right to refuse to accept a copying order if, in its judgment, fulfillment of the order would involve violation of copyright law.

Copying Restrictions with Videocassette Recorders

The increase in the use of videocassette recorders (VCRs) in the classroom raises the question of copyright restrictions. In 1981, the House Subcommittee on the Courts, Civil Liberties, and the Administration of Justice ratified the "Guidelines for Off-the-Air Recording of Broadcast Programming for Educational Purposes." As is the case with the other guidelines presented, the VCR guidelines do not have the force of law. However, they are persuasive and are used by the courts in analyzing facts for a determination of fair use. As the title of the guidelines implies, teachers should follow the standards whenever they tape a commercial television program with the intention of showing it to a class at a later date. The guidelines specify nine standards:[53]

1. Videotaped recordings may be kept for no more than *45 calendar days* after the recording date, at which time the tapes must be erased.

---

[52]Warning Concerning Copyright Restrictions, 42 Fed. Req. 59, (1977), pp. 264–265.
[53]Helm, p. 40.

2. Videotaped recordings may be shown to students only within the *first 10 school days* of the 45-day retention period.

3. Off-air recordings must be made only *at the request* of an individual teacher for *instructional* purposes, not by school staff in anticipation of later requests by teachers.

4. The recordings are to be shown to students no more than two times during the 10-day period, and the second time only for necessary instructional reinforcement.

5. The taped recordings may be viewed after the 10-day period only by teachers for evaluation purposes—that is, to determine whether to include the broadcast program in the curriculum in the future.

6. If several teachers request videotaping of the same program, duplicate copies are permitted to supply their request; all copies are subject to the same restrictions as the original recording.

7. The off-air recordings may not be physically or electronically altered or combined with others to form anthologies, but they need not necessarily be used or shown in their entirety.

8. All copies of off-air recordings must include the copyright notice on the broadcast program as recorded.

9. These guidelines apply only to nonprofit education institutions, which are further "expected to establish appropriate control procedures to maintain the integrity of these guidelines."

Many of the programs that teachers tape for their students are aired on public television, not on commercial television. The guidelines for taping programs from public television are different. Even before the Copyright Act was passed, the four major public television stations came together to develop guidelines for educators interested in taping programs. The guidelines are as follows:[54]

1. The recordings may be made only by students, faculty, or staff members in accredited, nonprofit education institutions.

2. The recordings may be used only for instruction or educationally related activities in a classroom, laboratory, or auditorium.

3. The recordings may be used only in the school for which they were made; they may not be made available outside that school.

4. The recordings may be used "only during the seven-day period of local ETV [Educational Television] and other educational broadcast licensed by the distribution agency, and will be erased or destroyed immediately at the end of that seven-day period except to the extent specifically authorized in writing in advance."

It should be noted that the same guidelines should be followed whether teachers tape the program at school with school equipment or at home with their own equipment.

[54]*Id.* at 41–42.

Copyright Law and Computers

In 1980, Congress passed an amendment to the Copyright Act. Known as Public Law 96-517, the amendment specifically addressed the use of computers in connection with copyright law. Section 101 legally defines the term *computer program* as "a set of statements or instructions to be used directly or indirectly in a computer in order to bring about a certain result." Section 117 provides a description of how a computer program may be used without copyright infringement.

> Notwithstanding the provisions of section 106, it is not an infringement for the owner of a copy of a computer program to make or authorize the making of another copy or adaptation of that computer program provided:
>
> > (1) that such new copy or adaptation is created as an essential step in the utilization of the computer program in conjunction with a machine and that it is used in no other manner, or
> >
> > (2) that such new copy or adaptation is for archival purposes only and that all archival copies are destroyed in the event that continued possession of the computer program should cease to be rightful.
>
> Any exact copies prepared in accordance with the provisions of this section may be leased, sold, or otherwise transferred, along with the copy from which such copies were prepared, only as part of the lease, sale, or other transfer of all rights in the program. Adaptations so prepared may be transferred only with the authorization of the copyright owner.

Two important conditions of Section 107 merit emphasis:

1. It is illegal to make copies of a computer program for use in the classroom by anyone other than the owner of the master copy.
2. It is illegal to make a copy from a program that was acquired for the purpose of previewing.

Penalties for Copyright Infringement

The penalties for violation of the Copyright Act are severe. They can involve money damages or imprisonment, or both, as well as the destruction of the product of the illegal copying.

Money damages.   The amount of money the copyright owner may recover depends on the facts of the case. The court may award between $250 and $10,000, depending upon how much the infringer knew about having broken the law at the time. If it is clear that the infringer *willfully* broke the law, the award can be as high as $50,000. In order to receive these amounts, the owner does not have to show actual damages. These awards are part of what is called *statutory damages*. They exist to deter infringement. If owners of copyrights believe that the infringer has made sums of money that exceed $50,000 from illegally copying their works, they can sue for *actual damages*. This would allow for the recovery of profits of which they were deprived, regardless of the amount. Whether the court uses the statutory-damages or the actual-damages approach is up to the suing copyright owner. Under the statutory approach, the court can award as little as $100 if it finds that the infringer had no reason to believe that a copyright law was being broken.

Educators were given special consideration by the Congress when penalties were developed. Teachers, librarians, archivists, public broadcasters, and nonprofit organizations are provided with a general "innocent infringer clause."[55] This provision requires the courts to use the statutory-damages approach when a member of this special category is being sued. The owner of the copyright may not sue an educator for actual damages.

Imprisonment

The law provides for a jail sentence of up to one year for willful violation of copyright.

Copy Destruction

At the time a copyright infringement suit is filed, the court may issue an injunction to prohibit further reproduction or distribution of the work in question. In addition, the court may order that all allegedly illegal copies be impounded until the trial is over. If the court finds for the plaintiff, the illegally made copies could be ordered destroyed.

SUMMARY

There are a number of areas within the school curriculum that may have legal impact for the principal. While school officials have broad powers in controlling the instructional program, this power is not unlimited. If parents can show a court of law that they have a legiti-

---

[55]17 U.S.C. Sec. 504 (c) (2) (Supp. II 1978).

mate religious objection to a certain course of study, for example, their children may be exempt from that class.

Panoch and Barr differentiate between legal and illegal instructional activities involving religion.[56]

1. The school may sponsor the *study* of religion,   but may not sponsor the *practice* of religion.
2. The school may *expose* students to all religious views,   but may not *impose* any particular view.
3. The school's approach to religion is one of *instruction*,   not one of *indoctrination.*
4. The function of the school is to *educate* about all,   not to *convert* to any one religion
5. The school's approach to religion is *academic*,   not *devotional*
6. The school should *study* what all people believe,   but should not *teach* a pupil what he should believe.
7. The school should strive for student *awareness* of all religions,   but should not press for student *acceptance* of any one religion.
8. The school should seek to *inform* the student about various beliefs,   but should not seek to *conform* him to any one belief.[57]

A student may be punished for misbehavior, but the punishment may not include denying promotion or an earned grade for a course. Academic penalties should be applied to academic failures, not to misbehavior.

The school may require MCT, but it must ensure that students are given sufficient notice, adequate preparation, and opportunities for remediation. Homework may be required of students as long as the school does not impose the time during off-school hours that students must use for doing the assignments.

Principals can censor material that is obscene or inappropriate to the educational mission of the school. However, the principal may not censor student views simply because they are controversial or in discord with his own opinions. Specifically, the censorship of school library books can take place only at the acquisition stage. Once the book has made it to the library shelf, authorities may not remove it (unless it is found to be obscene). Principals should note that their personal definitions of obscenity are not a criterion. The US Supreme Court in *US* v. *Roth* suggested that obscenity is work created for the prurient interest. The alleged obscene work cannot be judged by counting the number of four-letter words. Only after the thematic intent of a work "as a whole" has been examined can obscenity be determined.

[56]Smith, p. 4.

[57]J. Panoch and D. Barr, *Religion Goes to School* (New York: Harper and Row, 1968), p. 15.

SELECTED BIBLIOGRAPHY

FISCHER, L., D. SCHIMMEL AND C. KELLY, *Teacher and the Law* (2nd ed.), New York: Longman, 1987.

GUTHRIE, JAMES W. AND RODNEY J. REED, *Educational Administration and Policy: Effective Leadership for American Education*, Englewood Cliffs, NJ: Prentice-Hall, Inc., 1983.

HELM, V. M., *What Educators Should Know About Copyright, Fastback 233*, Bloomington, IN: Phi Delta Kappa, 1986.

HUDGINS, H. C. JR. AND RICHARD S. VACCA, *Law and Education: Contemporary Issues and Court Decisions*, Charlottesville, VA: Michie Co., 1985.

KIMBROUGH, RALPH, *Ethics: A Course Study for Educational Leaders*, Arlington, VA: American Association of School Administrators, 1985.

KIRP, DAVID L. AND DONALD JESSEN, *School Days, Rule Days: The Legalization and Regulation of Education*, New York: Taylor and Francis, 1986.

KIRP, DAVID L. AND MARK G. YUDOF, *Educational Policy and the Law: Cases and Materials* (2nd ed.), Berkeley, CA: McCutchan, 1982.

MONKS, ROBERT L. AND ERNEST I. PROULX, *Legal Basics for Teachers*, Bloomington, IN: Phi Delta Kappa, 1986.

NOLL, JAMES W., *Taking Sides: Clashing Views on Controversial Issues* (4th ed.), Guilford, CT., Dushkin Publishing Group, Inc., 1987.

NOLTE, M. CHESTER, *How To Survive as a Principal: The Legal Dimension*, Chicago, IL: Teach'em, 1983.

O'REILLY, ROBERT C. AND EDWARD T. GREEN, *School Law for the Practitioner*, Westport, CT: Greenwood Press, Inc., 1983.

REUTTER, E. EDMUND JR., *The Law of Public Education* (3rd ed.), Mineola, NY: Foundation Press, 1985.

SERGIOVANNI, THOMAS J., MARTIN BURLINGAME, FRED S. COOMBS, AND PAUL W. THURSTON, *Educational Governance and Administration*, Englewood Cliffs, NJ: Prentice-Hall, Inc., 1987.

VAN GEEL, TYLL, *The Courts and American Education Law*, Buffalo, NY: Prometheus Books, 1987.

9

Business Management in the Principalship

This book has focused on the principal in the role of instructional leader. Perhaps the idea of business management seems foreign to instructional matters. It is not. Without a sound knowledge of the principles of business management, the principal will have neither the time nor the peace of mind to act as an instructional leader because the school will be in chaos. The dictates of the central office require that the principal run an efficient building that stays within budget, and that he keep the physical plant safe and in good repair. If the principal can manage the building efficiently, then the potential for assuming the role of instructional leader increases. On the other hand, a poorly run building will interfere with the main purpose for the school's existence: instruction.

This chapter will discuss some of the important features of school management. Budgetary processes, accounting procedures, and physical plant management can assist the principal in developing a strong instructional program. No instructional program can survive without the support of needed resources. The business side of the principalship must be mastered if the instructional program is to be successful.

DEVELOPING THE SCHOOL BUDGET

Before we discuss the actual development of the budget, we should mention the overall budgeting process. The budgeting process involves planning, writing, presenting, administering, and evaluating. The planning and writing of the budget can be a great opportunity for the principal to involve the teaching staff. This phase allows the professional staff to set instructional goals for the following year in the hope that they will be financially supported. When the principal presents the budget to the superintendent, it will be an opportunity to "sell" the school. Administering the budget can help the school reach its instructional goals by ensuring that the money is placed where it is needed. Finally, the budget must be evaluated to determine whether it adequately supported the program for which it was intended.

Defining the Budget

Webster's defines *budget* as "a financial report containing estimates of income and expenses."[1] However, the simplicity of this definition belies the full impact of the budget in the life of a school. Several experts have realized a more accurate perspective in their definitions

[1]*Webster's Third New International Dictionary* (New York: Merriam, 1966), p. 290.

of *budget.* For example, Campbell has said that "the school budget is often defined as a school program expressed in fiscal terms."[2] Roe defined the school budget as follows:

> the translation of educational needs into a financial plan which is interpreted to the public in such a way that when formally adopted it expresses the kind of educational program the community is willing to support, financially and morally, for a one-year period.[3]

Planning the Budget

Budget planning usually follows a schedule that is determined, in part, by state statutes. School districts typically use a calendar to plot the events that must take place in order to meet the statutorily imposed deadlines. It is common for the budget calendar to begin as early as September. Table 9-1 gives an example of a typical calendar.

Lipham has suggested that the initial planning phase of the budgetary process involves considerations[4]

1. assessing community, school, and student needs, problems, and issues
2. identifying and reviewing existing goals and priorities
3. translating general goals into measurable performance objectives
4. developing a program structure and format to achieve the objectives
5. analyzing alternative approaches and options to achieve the objectives
6. recommending and selecting the most cost-effective alternatives for attaining the objectives

Budgetary planning should be driven by the academic program, not the other way around. The idea that the budget should exist to support the educational program is not a new one. DeYoung first represented the school budget as an equilateral triangle.[5] The base of the triangle is the educational program (Table 9-1). One side represents the cost to support the program. The other side is the revenue plan (how to get the money needed).

The triangle represents a philosophy that says that the educational programs should be planned for the specific needs of the students without letting the available funds dictate the nature of education. Unfortunately, the reality of limited funding in many school

---

[2]R. F. Campbell, J. E. Corbally, Jr., and J. A. Ramsazer, *Introduction to Educational Administration,* 3d ed. (Boston: Allyn & Bacon, 1966), p. 124.

[3]W. H. Roe, *School Business Management* (New York: McGraw-Hill, 1961), p. 81.

[4]J. M. Lipham, R. E. Rankin, and J. A. Hoeh, Jr., *The Principalship: Concepts, Competencies, and Cases* (New York: Longman, 1985), pp. 239-240.

[5]P. E. Burrup and V. Brimley, Jr., *Financing Education in a Climate of Change,* 3d ed. (Boston: Allyn & Bacon, 1982), p. 318.

TABLE 9-1.   Typical Budget Calendar.

DATE	ACTIVITY	RESPONSIBLE AGENT
Sept. 1	Approval of proposed budget calendar	Superintendent's council
Sept. 15	Approval of proposed budget calendar	Board of education
Sept. 30	Distribute capital Budget request materials	Business manager
Sept. 30	Distribute operational budget request materials	Principal
Sept. 30	Distribute general maintenance budget request materials	Principal
Nov. 1	All capital project requests and general maintenance requests returned to unit administrator	Department heads
Nov. 5	Department furniture and equipment requests due in unit administrator's office	Department head
Nov. 15	Submission of new program proposals to director of curriculum	Various
Nov. 20	Operational budget request due in unit administrator's office	Department head
Nov. 20	Review of proposed capital projects	Business office Maintenance and operations supervisor
Nov. 30	Capital project requests to maintenance and operations division for costing	Business Manager
Dec. 1	Vehicle, athletic, furniture and equipment requests due in business office	Director of transportion Athletic director Various
Dec. 20	Costed projects due in business office	Purchasing devision Maintenance and operations division
Jan. 15	Requests for additional staffing to be submitted to personnel director	Unit principals Unit administrators
Jan. 20	All certificated and classified staff requests to business office	Personnel director
Jan. 20	Review of new program proposals	Superintendent's council
Jan. 30	All operational budgets due in business office	Principals
Feb. 15	Preparation of operational budget	Business office
Feb. 22	Review of operational budget with superintendent's council	Business office
March 10	Board study, session and review of capital budget, transportation, and new program proposals	Board of education
March 17	Board approval of partial budget relative to capital outlay and transportation	Board of education
March 24	Board study session and review of operational budget	Board of education
April 5	Board review study session of 1984–85 proposed budget	Board of education
April 15	Deadline for personnel rehiring	Personnel director

May 2	Board meeting to sign proposed budget and notice of hearing	Board of education
May 17	Advertise proposed budget and notice of hearing (must be no later than 15 days prior to the hearing)	Business manager
May 27	Advertise second notice of hearing	Business manager
June 3	Board meeting and public hearing to adopt budget	Board of education

From D. E. Orlosky et al., *Educational Administration Today* (Columbia, OH: Merrill, 1984), p. 242.

districts causes reverse planning to take place. In other words, after available revenue is determined, school officials look for programs that can be purchased with the limited funds. The obvious danger in reverse planning is that the school district can find itself purchasing goods that do not meet the needs of the pupils. In education, the wrong programs are as negative as no programs. It is far better for the school district to do with less of what is right than to have a lot of what is wrong.

Writing the Budget

The school building-level budget will be incorporated into the overall district budget later in the year. In preparing the building budget, the principal must be thoroughly familiar with the forms and instructions given by the central office. With increasing frequency, school districts are allowing teachers and staff to participate in the budgeting process. Teachers are asked to list the materials, supplies, and related resources they will need for the following year. The listed

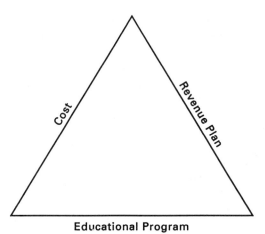

Educational Program

FIGURE 9-1. School budget triangle.

materials should be intended to further the educational program goals determined at the planning stage.

Some schools also ask teachers to participate in the budgeting process by suggesting additional categories for program support. The principal can ask teachers to submit requests for those supplies and facilities that would provide a *superior* program or an alternative program. Even though such requests may not ultimately be supported in the overall district budget, the experience of forecasting what it would take to create the best possible program has benefits for future planning.

The principal should check the teachers' request forms for completeness and for accuracy. Duplications of requests should be spotted. The requests are then combined for the building and submitted to the central office, where the building budgets will be combined into a single school-district budget. The initial budget is called the *tentative* budget. It is so called because it has not yet been made available for public inspection and input (usually a requirement set by state statute). It also has not yet been approved by the board of education, which is the final stage of the budgeting process. That part of the budgeting process which involves examination by the public and the board is called the *budget hearing*.

Presenting the Budget

In addition to assigning costs to each item, the principal should develop a rationale in defense of the school budget. Rarely are questions not asked once the budget arrives at the central office. Since the superintendent will ultimately be required to defend the budget before the board and public, it is likely the principal will be called to task by the superintendent. Once the superintendent is satisfied that individual school budgets are reasonable and defensible, the principal should be prepared to answer questions at the annual budget hearing.

The budget hearing is a formal meeting at which the superintendent and staff present the tentative budget for the board's and the public's consideration. The superintendent will typically attempt to summarize the main features of the budget in a way that can be understood by board members and citizens. Many schedules and supplemental information accompany the budget document in order to clarify the district's educational goals. Ovsiew and Castetter have suggested that the following be included as part of the supplement material:[6]

[6]L. Ovsiew and W. Castetter, *Budgeting for Better Schools* (Englewood Cliffs, NJ: Prentice-Hall, 1960), p. 52.

- Letter of transmittal
- Statement of introduction, especially relating to the school philosophy
- Justifications
- Curriculum review, by unit, divisions, and departments
- Audited statements of funds
- Bonding schedule
- Recapitulations of sections of the budget
- Salary schedules
- Statistical summary of salary program, showing experience, training, and classifications
- Statistical summary of other pertinent data, such as
  - Enrollment, showing trends and projections
  - Numerical adequacy of staff
  - Average daily attendance
  - Pupil–teacher ratio in instruction
  - Per pupil costs by budget categories
  - Enrollment by curriculum in the high school
- State-aid provisions, indicating changes
- Insurance in force
- Transportation schedules
- Property tax experience, including relationship to assessments, market values, percent of collection, and millage limits
- Nonproperty tax experience, by type levied and by potential
- Cost experience, by trends in prices of selected items
- Retirement and social security schedules
- Expenditure and revenue items for two to three previous years
- Policy statements mandating expenditures
- Unmet needs report
- Items mandated by new laws or official directives
- Inventory report
- Budget transfers during previous year
- Summary of germane committee reports
- Comparative costs data with selected school district

The presentation may evoke questions and requests for justification. It is at this time that the principal may be called upon to assist the superintendent with an explanation.

Once the budget has been approved, the work has just begun. The principal must now be prepared to administer the budget.

ADMINISTERING THE SCHOOL BUDGET

The approved budget now becomes the daily guide for the expenditure of money in support of the educational program. If the central office has not provided the school with request forms of some sort, the principal should develop a simple system for teachers to submit requests for funds. Purchase orders, which include a description of the item, quantity, and cost, are commonly used. It is wise for the principal to ask that a rationale accompany all requests for funds. Figure 9–2 provides an example of a budget request that the principal might consider.

The principal should keep in mind that the purpose of the budget is not to save money. The purpose is to spend money when necessary, but as wisely as possible.

There are a number of ways to administer the school budget. Deciding on the proper form for requesting funds is only a small mechanical part of the process. Administering the budget is an exten-

FIGURE 9–2. Sample budget request.

Department _____	Budget Code _____				
Priority	Item	Vendor	Quantity	Cost/Item	Total Cost

	Total	Shipping*	Grand Total
Priority 1	_____	_____	_____
Priority 2	_____	_____	_____
Priority 3	_____	_____	_____
Total	_____	_____	_____

*Multiply total by 10%.

Priority 1: We must have this next year.
Priority 2: We need this next year, but, if necessary, we could wait another year.
Priority 3: It would be nice to have this, but it is not essential.

sion of the philosophy of school authorities as it relates to ideas about participation and control.

Methods of Budget Administration

Some principals use the "benevolent despot" method of budget administration, whereby they maintain a firm hold on all of the money and require teachers to strictly justify each request. Another approach is to allocate money to each department, and allow teachers to spend as they wish as long as they stay within the amount given.[7]

Regardless of the style that the principal adopts for managing the budget, an up-to-date budget encumbrance system is necessary for determining the financial status of each account at any particular point. The principal cannot exercise responsible control over the budget and make decisions to accept, reject, or modify a request for funds unless the amount of money available is known.

The balance of a fund is different from the amount of money "available" in that fund. Fund balances are reduced only when the money is actually paid out to a vendor. However, several months can pass between the day an item is ordered and the day it actually arrives with the bill. Until the bill is paid, the money that *will be* used is "encumbered," and it should remain unavailable for use even though it is technically still in the account. Unless the principal makes decisions on encumbered balances, the school may be avalanched by bills that exceed the budget limit.

Evaluation of the Budget

The final phase of the budgetary process is the evaluation of the budget. How well did the budget serve the educational goals it was meant to accomplish? This question is the bottom line for any school budget. Regardless of the dollar amount that was given, unless that money met the needs of the pupils, the budget was not effective. Evaluating the school budget's effectiveness is one of the primary ways in which the principal can make recommendations for changes in next year's budget. Each program should be examined to determine whether it reached forecasted goals. The principal must also decide whether increased funding of the same program would have resulted in greater achievement of educational objectives. A program's budget should not be judged effective or ineffective merely on its own merit; it must be compared to what an alternative might cost and accomplish.

[7]M. L. Bowman. "Allocating Money for Priority Items: Easier with Participative Budgeting," *NASSP Bulletin* (November 1986):5.

The following standards could be used to assist the principal in comparing programs:

1. instructional costs per pupil
2. costs per pupil by grade level, subject area, or school building
3. capital outlay or debt service costs per pupil
4. testbooks, library books, and instructional supplies per pupil
5. administrative, guidance, and teacher costs per pupil
6. maintenance and custodial costs per building
7. cocurricular costs per program per participant[8]

Another aspect of budget evaluation is *efficiency*. To what extent were the goods and services purchased with the budget actually used? How were they used? Any product or service that is underutilized or wasted is inefficient. The principal needs to look into underutilization of equipment and inappropriate use of time and personnel in evaluating budget efficiency.

Frohreich has suggested that the following questions be asked when evaluating the school budget:[9]

1. What goals and objectives was the school attempting to achieve with the budget?
2. What standards and measures shall be used to determine if the goals and objectives were achieved?
3. Who will determine what constitutes an acceptable goal achievement standard?
4. What costs (personnel and material resources) were necessary to achieve each goal and objective?
5. Were the goals adequate in light of acceptable educational standards and community needs?
6. Should educational programs be added, eliminated, reduced, increased, or otherwise altered?
7. Were the resources adequate for achieving the goals and objectives?
8. What additional resources are needed and how might they be obtained?
9. What effect will securing additional resources have on those who must share the burden of providing the resources?
10. How should existing or additional resources be distributed among programs in the next budget so that goals and objectives are achieved efficiently and economically?

[8]Lipham, p. 245.
[9]L. E. Frohreich, *The School Budgeting Cycle* (Winneconne, WI: Wisconsin Association of School Boards, 1983), p. 49, as cited in Lipham, *The Principalship,* p. 244.

ACCOUNTING AND THE PRINCIPALSHIP

Accounting can be defined as the act of recording, classifying, summarizing, interpreting, and reporting the results of financial activities.[10] In a practical sense, accounting is the vehicle that keeps spending at a level consistent with the budget.

School districts typically uses an accounting system known as *fund accounting.* A fund is a district accounting category that exists to support a particular area of activity. The largest and most active fund is usually the education fund. In some states, the education fund is known as the general fund. In either case, the education fund is where all of the accounts pertaining to teaching and curriculum, such as teaching salaries, textbook purchases, and teaching supplies, are placed. There are other funds that represent the necessary support areas. Some of these are the building and maintenance fund and the capital outlay fund. The resources that supply the money for these funds come from state aid and local property taxation.

The funds that are normally the accounting responsibility of the school principal are those that arise from money generated through various student activities within the building. The area of student-activity accounting has been the source of many headaches for principals over the years.

Student-Activities Accounting

Depending upon the size of the school and the extent of its activities, large sums of money may be collected every year from fees charged for such activities as athletic events, concerts, plays, dances, the student newspaper, the annual yearbook, and any number of fundraising events by students, the PTA, or boosters. In general, what the principal purchases with these funds is a matter of individual discretion. Since the allocation of these funds is so flexible, principals often use them for expenditures that normally would not be approved as part of the district education fund. Some of these areas might include a class trip, special awards for students or teachers, new athletic uniforms, and even school beautification purchases (furniture, paintings, or plants).

The principal should use restraint in spending funds from the

[10]R. W. Rebore, *Educational Administration: A Management Approach* (Englewood Cliffs, NJ: Prentice-Hall, 1985), p. 120.

student-activity accounts, however. Legally, the proceeds from these activities belong to the board of education and must be accounted for in the same way as are other funds within the school district.

The accounting system that the principal uses for student-activity accounts should involve at least the following activities: (1) journalizing transactions, (2) reporting, and (3) auditing.

The overall system should include the following characteristics"[11]

1. School board authorization for the collection of student-activities fees.
2. The involvement of students and teachers in determining the establishment and size of student activities fees and in decisions about how monies are to be spent.
3. The maintenance of school records of monies collected and disbursed, showing that the procedures enumerated below are being followed:
   a. a receipt is issued to the individual from whom money is received,
   b. a deposit receipt is obtained from the bank, indicating that all monies have been deposited upon being received,
   c. the amount which is deposited is recorded in a student activities account under the appropriate fund,
   d. a requisition form, requiring the signature of the activity sponsor, is used to initiate purchases, with purchases involving large sums of money requiring the approval of the principal additionally,
   e. school checks are used to expend monies and to pay student activities bills,
   f. all expenditures are recorded in the student activities ledger, under the appropriate fund.
4. The provision of a budget-status report for each activity sponsor and for the school administrator, on a monthly basis.
5. A yearly audit and review of the purposes for which student activity monies have been spent, conducted by the district office with the involvement of the school administrator and activities' sponsors.

If the school district does not require a specific accounting system for the activity accounts, the principal might consider using a simple "T account" for each activity. A T account is nothing more than a journal that includes all the transactions for an activity. The debits are recorded on the left side of the T. The right side is for credits. In accounting, a debit is an *increase* in funds, and credit is a *decrease*. Figure 9–3 lists several entries to a T account for the school drama club.

[11]R. A. Gorton, *School Administration and Supervision,* 2d ed. (Dubuque, IA: Wm. C. Brown, 1983), p. 143.

DATE	ACTIVITY	DEBITS	DATE	ACTIVITY	CREDITS
9/10	Previous balance	$800.00	9/17	Posters for play	$10.00
9/15	Gift from PTA	$200.00	11/15	Costumes for play	$700.00

FIGURE 9-3. T account for a drama club.

Reporting

It is recommended that the balance of each activity account be reported monthly. The report should show the opening balance at the beginning of the month, the receipts and disbursements throughout the month, and the closing balance on the last day of the month.

Bank deposit slips should be reconciled with the receipts in the journal. A similar report for each activity would be reported at the end of the year.

Auditing

It is important that the accuracy of the information in the activity accounts be checked periodically. In the world of accounting, checking for accuracy is called *auditing*. In addition to checking for accuracy, the audit attempts to determine whether procedures used comply with all statutory provisions and board policies. The audit can also recommend improvements in methods and procedures.

The audit can be conducted by school district employees (called an internal audit) or by people hired outside the school district (referred to as an external audit). Larger school districts tend to conduct more internal audits than smaller districts, which generally lack expertise and school personnel of sufficient organizational distance to maintain objectivity.

Whether internal or external, the principal should view the audit as helpful rather than intimidating. Audits are an excellent way to maintain credibility and show accountability.

Following Guidelines

The Association of School Business Officials has recommended twelve specific areas to guide in the management of student-activity accounts:[12]

[12] D. E. Orlosky, L. E. McCleary, A. Shapiro, and L. D. Webb, *Educational Administration Today* (Columbia, OH: Merrill, 1984), p. 256.

1. All money received should be acknowledged by issuing prenumbered receipts or prenumbered tickets to the person from whom the money is received.
2. Deposits should be made daily if possible. Cash should never be left in the school over the weekend or holidays.
3. Receipts should be issued to the person making the deposit. Deposit slips should be retained by both the depositor and the school accountant or bookkeeper.
4. Purchase orders or requisitions should be initiated by the person in charge of the activity fund.
5. Payments should be made by check, prepared and mailed from the business office to the payee.
6. The principal should designate two or more persons in addition to himself or herself who will be authorized to sign checks. Two of the three authorized signatures should also be required for all withdrawals.
7. No payment should be made unless supported by a written purchase order and by a signed invoice certifying receipt of merchandise and accuracy of prices.
8. Student-activity funds should not be used for any purpose which represents a loan or accommodation to any school district employee or other nonstudent. Emergency loans may be made to students for lunches, carfare, and the like on written permission of the principal. Individuals may not make purchases through the student body in order to take advantage of better prices.
9. Student bodies may enter contracts for the purchase of supplies, equipment, and services from an approved vendor provided the term of the contract is within the tenure of the students of the school (usually three years).
10. The student body should operate on a budget reflecting past experience and future plans; like the school and school district budget, the student budget should serve as a guide to the year's financing activities.
11. Student activity books and financial procedures should be subjected to periodic internal and external audits. An annual examination by outside, independent accountants is also recommended.
12. Regular reports (monthly and annual) should be prepared and submitted to the principal, business office, or any others responsible for the supervision of student activity funds.

FACILITIES MANAGEMENT

In many ways, the expression "clothes make the person" applies to the school plant. Visitors to a school are quick to pass judgment on the school based on its physical appearance. Indeed, the environment in which we work can influence how we feel. The condition of the school building and grounds can shape the morale of teachers and the attitudes of students, and will ultimately affect the instructional program.

Therefore, even the principal, whose main focus is on instruction, must attend to the physical plant.

The most direct link to the physical plant is through the custodial staff. Therefore, we will now discuss how the principal can improve relationships with the custodial staff in order to maintain and improve the physical plant.

Cleanliness is often a problem in the school cafeteria. In order for the principal to have a positive impact on the school environment, he must attend to the school's food-service program. We will discuss this area as well.

Managing the Physical Plant

The extent to which the principal is expected to supervise the custodial staff varies from district to district. However, the principal should assume some general responsibilities. Gorton has suggested five:[13]

1. Keep informed about the work schedule and specific responsibilities of each member of the custodial staff.
2. Tour the school building and grounds regularly to observe the extent to which they are being kept clean, neat, energy efficient, and in good repair.
3. Conduct, with the assistance of appropriate personnel, a comprehensive audit of the energy needs and excesses of the school and design and implement energy-conservation practices.
4. Design some method or procedure for students, teachers, or others to bring to the attention of the head custodian or the school administrator any problems in plant and grounds maintenance, appearance, or energy loss.
5. Develop a good working relationship with all of the custodial staff, particularly the head custodian.

Some school buildings suffer from neglect. In such a case, the principal may have to take a more active role in improving the situation.

The principal may need the support of the central office in order to create an atmosphere that will draw attention to the need for improvement. An administrative regulation or even a school board policy which establishes physical plant cleanliness will help to communicate that the school district wants cleaner buildings.

As the demand for cleanliness becomes known, the principal must

[13]Gorton, *School Administration,* pp. 146–147.

not make the mistake of assuming that the solution is to ask for more custodians. An expanded staff may not be the answer. In order to know whether existing staff can handle the job, a formula for assigning staff for a particular work load should be established.

The most commonly used criterion for custodian–work load formula is the square-footage approach. In other words, each custodian will be expected to clean a certain square footage of the building within a certain period of time. For example, Orlosky suggests 660 square feet for every 20 minutes of custodian time. Others have suggested that a custodian should be able to clean 14,850 square feet in an 8-hour shift.[14]

Other factors to consider are how many students, teachers, and staff members use the building, how many extracurricular activities take place in the building, and to what extent the building is used by the community. Only after making such an assessment can the administration know whether the existing staff is adequate and should therefore be made to work harder to improve the school's condition.

Once the appropriate custodial staff size is determined, the principal should ensure that all custodians have job descriptions. Job descriptions for custodians should include:

1. specific tasks to be performed
2. responsibilities for daily or routine inspections
3. responsibilities for conducting preventive maintenance
4. responsibilities for notifying the principal regarding hazards
5. compliance with regulatory requirements
6. maintenance of inventory
7. handling emergencies[15]

Unless job descriptions are provided, there can always be some argument about who should have done what when a maintenance area "falls through the cracks."

The principal must make sure that the custodians have the right kind of cleaning equipment to do the job. Skimping on cleaning supplies can lead to low morale among custodians, not to mention a dirty building. The vendors who supply the school with cleaning products can be helpful in establishing whether the current use of certain cleaning supplies is meeting the building's needs. In addition, the vendor can instruct custodians on the proper use of the products.

The principal should realize that the custodial staff needs recog-

---

[14]A. Steller and C. Pell, "Clean Up Your School Custodial Program," *Updating School Board Policies*—National School Boards Association (December 1986):2.
[15]*Ibid.*

nition. Perhaps a special luncheon or afterschool gathering can be arranged from time to time for this purpose. Giving each custodian a chance to "shine" can go a long way toward improving performance.

SUMMARY

In this chapter, we have explored the role of the principal as business manager. We noted that in order for the principal to be an instructional leader, he must maintain certain business functions. A well-run school is the prerequisite for instructional leadership.

The principal should understand how the school budget is developed. There are three phases of budget development with which the principal must become skilled: planning the budget, writing the budget, and presenting the budget to the central office.

The responsibility for the administration of the budget can be carried out by a number of methods; some are highly authoritarian, while others are highly participatory. Regardless of the method by which the principal administers the budget, the budget itself must be evaluated at the end of the year to determine whether it has served the school in meeting its educational program.

Certain accounting procedures should be familiar to the principal. The use of the simple T account can suffice to fulfill the responsibility for monitoring student-activity funds. The principal should use caution in administering student-activity accounts.

Last, the principal should be able to maintain a clean school building. A poorly maintained building sends a negative message to the community. Beyond impressions, a clean, well-maintained environment is important for teaching and learning. Good relationships with the custodial staff can go a long way toward improving the appearance of the school building.

SELECTED BIBLIOGRAPHY

AUGENBLICK, JOHN, *Public Schools: Issues in Budgeting and Financial Management,* New Brunswick, NJ: Transaction Books, 1985.

BERNE, ROBERT AND LEANNA STIEFEL, *The Measure of Equity in School Finance: Conceptual Methodological and Empirical Dimensions,* Baltimore, MD: Johns Hopkins University Press, 1984.

BURRUP, P. E., AND V. BRIMLEY, JR., *Financing Education in a Climate of Change,* (3rd ed.), Boston, MA: Allyn and Bacon, 1982.

CAMBRON, McCABE, NELDA H., AND ALLAN ODDEN, *The Changing Politics of School Finance,* Cambridge, MA: Ballinger Publication, 1982.

CANDOLI, I. CARL., ET AL., *School Business Administration: A Planning Approach,* (3rd ed.), Wolfeboro, NH: Longwood Publication Co., 1984.

COCHRANE, ALLAN, ED., *Developing Local Economic Strategies: Some Issue and Ideas,* New York: Taylor and Francis, 1987.

DENNISON, W. F., *Educational Finance and Resource,* New York: Routledge Chapman and Hall, Inc., 1984.

GOLDSTEIN, WILLIAM, *Selling School Budgets in Hard Times,* Bloomington, IN: Phi Delta Kappa, 1984.

GUTHRIE, JAMES W., *School Finance Policies and Practices: The Nineteen-Eighties: Decade of Conflict,* Cambridge, MA: Ballinger Publishing Co., 1981.

GUTHRIE, JAMES W., WALTER I. GARMS, AND LAWRENCE C. PIERCE, *School Finance and Education Policy: Enhancing Educational Efficiency, Equality and Choice,* (2nd ed.), Englewood Cliffs, NJ: Prentice-Hall, Inc., 1988.

JOHNS, ROE L., EDGAR MORPHET AND KERN ALEXANDER, *Economics and Financing of Education,* (4th ed.), Englewood Cliffs, NJ: Prentice-Hall, Inc., 1983.

LIPHAM, J. M., R. E. RANKIN AND J. A. HOEH, JR., *The Principalship, Concepts, Competencies, and Cases.* New York: Longman, 1985.

McMAHON, WALTER W., AND TERRY G. GRESKE, *Financing Education: Overcoming Inefficiency and Inequity,* Champaign, IL: University of Illinois Press, 1982.

ORLOSKY, D. E., L. E. McCLEARY, A. SHAPIRO AND L. D. WEBB, *Educational Administration Today,* Columbia, OH: Merrill Publishing Co., 1984.

REBORE, R. W., *Educational Administration: A Management Approach,* Englewood Cliffs, NJ: Prentice-Hall, Inc., 1985.

WILLIAMS, MARY F., *The Public School and Finances,* New York: Pilgrim Press, The United Church Press, 1980.

10

School–Community Relations for Instructional Leadership

With the increase in accountability and the public's growing interest in education, positive school–community relationships have become important to the success of the instructional program. The training of school principals must include the development of skills necessary to carry on a successful school–community relations program. Studies conducted by a number of professional education organizations have shown that school administrators have consistently ranked courses in school–community relations among those courses they wish they had taken more of when they were preparing for their administrative careers.[1]

This chapter will deal with the important aspects of the school–community relations program as well as with those skills that the principal must develop in order to be successful in school–community relations. First, it is necessary for the principal to know how to develop a program. The school–community relations effort should not be left to chance. Rather, activities should stem from a well-planned program. Beyond program development, the principal will need to know how to (1) get support from the community, (2) communicate effectively with the community; and (3) work effectively with groups.

DEVELOPING A SCHOOL–COMMUNITY RELATIONS PROGRAM

The development of the school–community relations program requires that the principal first "get a feel" for the community. Copies of the most recent census as well as any demographic studies that have been conducted can help orient the principal. A community that has a large senior-citizen population, for example, would require a different kind of public relations program than a community in which young families predominate. Knowledge of other factors, such as the number of single-parent families and the general socioeconomic status of the community, can be helpful in planning for the right kind of program. Once the principal has a feel for the community, specific analysis must begin.

ANALYZING THE COMMUNITY

Community analysis should attempt to answer two questions: (1) What are the issues of concern to the community? (2) Who are the people in the community most responsible for shaping opinions?

[1]L. W. Kindred, D. Bagin, and D. R. Gallagher, *The School and Community Relations*, 3d ed. (Englewood Cliffs, NJ: Prentice-Hall, 1984).

There are a number of ways in which the principal can gain insight into the issues concerning the community. The most precise information can be obtained through the use of *surveys*.

Surveys

There are generally four survey methods to be considered. The amount of time, money, and volunteer help available will dictate which of the four methods is used. The methods include (1) the mail questionnaire, (2) the drop off–pick up questionnaire, (3) the personal interview, and (4) the telephone interview. Table 10–1 compares the four methods in terms of cost, time needed, and amount of volunteer help available to the principal.

The mail questionnaire has the advantage of requiring very little volunteer help. A few volunteers to stuff envelopes and to open returns is about all that is needed. In addition, the mail questionnaire can reach parent groups that are usually inaccessible and can provide answers that are more candid than those provided by other survey techniques. However, the mail questionnaire is costly and generally provides few returns compared with other methods.

The drop off–pick up method requires that a volunteer drop off a questionnaire to the respondent's home or place of business. The volunteer then returns in a few days to pick up the completed questionnaire. The costs associated with this method are minimal since there is no postage involved. However, the number of volunteers needed is high. The volunteers would also have to be asked to contribute their travel expenses in addition to their time if the costs of this method are to remain low.

The personal interview has the advantage of being inexpensive. The disadvantage is that a great deal of time is needed to personally interview community members. In addition, volunteers would need training in interview techniques. Personal interviews do provide a high level of return, however. This aspect might be important if the public is likely to have trouble understanding the questionnaire.

TABLE 10–1. Comparison of Four Survey Methods.

METHOD	COST	TIME NEEDED	NUMBER OF VOLUNTEERS NEEDED
1. Mail questionnaire	high	moderate	low
2. Drop off–pick up	low	moderate	high
3. Personal interview	low	high	high
4. Telephone interview	low	low	high

The telephone interview has two major advantages: It is inexpensive, and it requires little time compared to other methods. In order to use this method, however, the principal must have many volunteers available to make phone calls.

Regardless of the survey method used, the questions that are posed to the public should attempt to measure attitudes and opinions about the school. The principal should keep in mind that there are two distinct school publics: the parents and the community at large. Survey questions should be designed to address issues that are important to both groups. The community at large are likely to want to express opinions about student disciplines, drugs, and the condition of the school building and grounds. Parents' interests are more complex. In addition to the issues that are of concern to the general public, parents are concerned about the curriculum, the quality of teaching, and the human growth and development of their children. Figure 10-1 provides a sample of some questions that could be included in a parent survey.

Part I–District Reaction	Agree Strongly	Agree	Disagree	Disagree Strongly
1. This district places enough importance on basic skills.	————	————	————	————
2. Given the resources available, the schools have been managed effectively.	————	————	————	————
3. The school facilities (building, equipment, play areas, etc.) meet my child's needs.	————	————	————	————
4. Parents have an opportunity to become informed about school programs through school publications, the local press and meetings with teachers and administrators.	————	————	————	————
5. As a parent, I have opportunities to express my feelings about my child's education.	————	————	————	————
6. Student bus services are satisfactory.	————	————	————	————
7. The student lunch program meets my child's needs.	————	————	————	————

8. This district places enough emphasis on vocational skills. _____ _____ _____ _____

9. Having art and music classes meets my child's needs. _____ _____ _____ _____

10. Having physical educations classes meets my child's needs. _____ _____ _____ _____

Part II – Building Reaction

1. My child likes school this year. _____ _____ _____ _____

2. My child has effective teachers. _____ _____ _____ _____

3. My child is learning skills at a satisfactory rate in the basic areas of:

   Mathematics _____ _____ _____ _____

   Science _____ _____ _____ _____

   Social studies _____ _____ _____ _____

   Writing _____ _____ _____ _____

   Oral communication _____ _____ _____ _____

   Music _____ _____ _____ _____

   Art _____ _____ _____ _____

   Physical education _____ _____ _____ _____

   Foreign language _____ _____ _____ _____

   Reading _____ _____ _____ _____

4. Class sizes have ensured sufficient individual attention for my child. _____ _____ _____ _____

5. I am satisfied with the amount of homework assigned to my child. _____ _____ _____ _____

6. My child's teachers seem sincerely concerned about how well he or she is doing. _____ _____ _____ _____

7. Parent–teacher conferences have provided me with helpful information about my child's progress _____ _____ _____ _____

8. The student discipline standards are acceptable. _____ _____ _____ _____

9. The report card used is helpful in communicating my child's progress. _____ _____ _____ _____

10. Existing classroom exposure to family life and health education information meets my child's needs. _____ _____ _____ _____

11. Additional student services (i.e., speech therapy, learning disabilities and psychological counseling) are meeting my child's needs. _____ _____ _____ _____

12. I am satisfied with the school's physical facilities and the maintenance of them. _____ _____ _____ _____

Part III – Personal Reaction

1. Describe aspects of this school that you like and would like to see continued.

2. Describe aspects of this school that you would like to see changed.

3. If you have any other comments about this school, please write them here.

FIGURE 10-1. Sample parent survey. From Thomas J. Martin, "Community Relations and External Forces," in J. Kaiser, ed., *The Principalship* (Minneapolis: Burgess, 1985), pp. 228–229.

Kindred provides seven suggestions to keep in mind when writing the survey questions:

1. Be as concise as possible.
2. Use words and language that respondents understand. For example, a question such as "What is your attitude toward year-round schools?" is likely to be misunderstood. The phrase "year-round" may have different meanings to different people. Does it mean forty-five weeks of school and fifteen days off? Or does it mean two semesters of classes and a semester off? Or does it mean school every week of the year? Most citizens would be unable to respond to this question with a valid response.
3. Structure questions to provide you with the exact information, not answers, you desire. For example, in the question "How long have you lived here?" you may get answers such as "A long time," "Not too long," or "A good while." These answers are of little value. In such a question, list alternative answers, such as "less than one year; one to five years; six to ten years; over ten years."
4. Avoid leading questions. An example of a leading question is "If your taxes were reduced, would you favor light industry locating in the school district?" The phrase "If your taxes were reduced" is leading. Many people will answer "yes" to any question that will indicate their taxes will be reduced.

5. Avoid double-barreled questions, such as "Do you work full- or part-time? Yes–No–" If the respondents work full-time, how do they answer it?
6. Avoid ambiguous questions. The question "Don't you think reading should be emphasized in the high school?" is impossible to answer. What does a "yes" answer mean? "Yes, I don't think . . ." or "Yes, I do think . . ."
7. Pretest all questions on a small group similar to the one to be surveyed.[2]

It would be wise for the principal to include citizens and parents in the development of the questionnaire. Their participation will enhance the quality and the acceptance of the survey.

Another way to analyze the community is through the use of advisory committees.

Advisory Committees

If it is to be effective, the advisory committee must represent a cross-section of the community and parent groups. The assumption is that a committee that is reflective of the community will provide opinions that can be generalized back to the community. The recommendations of the advisory committee can be accepted or rejected by the principal. However, it is important that the committee members know in advance that their role will be strictly advisory. In using the advisory-committee method, there is always the danger that the group will not accurately represent the opinions of the larger community.

Handling the Results

When the results are tabulated, they should be made available to the public. A brochure that explains the results in easy-to-understand language can be sent to parents and to community members upon request. The ample use of tables and graphs usually helps make the results understandable.

A news release with a summary of the results would enhance public awareness of the project. Finally, detailed answers to each question in the questionnaire should be highlighted in a school newsletter.

Before the results are distributed to the public and to parents, the teachers, superintendent, and school board should be made aware of the results. The principal should be prepared to make a presentation at a school board meeting as well as at faculty and staff meetings.

Once information about attitudes has been collected, it is impor-

[2]Kindred, p. 33.

tant for the principal to discern which individuals in the community and among parents are primarily responsible for shaping attitudes. In other words, the principal should identify the "power brokers" in the school and in the community.

Identifying the Power Brokers

Power brokers are those individuals in the community who exercise control over matters of basic public policy. The way in which the school is run is, of course, a matter of public policy. The power brokers are the individuals to consult before any major community project is launched.

Lipham has suggested three possible approaches for determining *subpublics*.[3] A subpulic is a sociological term for an influential group and is synonymous with "power broker" in the present discussion. Power brokers can be identified by using role-position, issue-analysis, or reputational techniques. The role-position technique identifies influential people in terms of their formal roles or positions in the local community. For example, the principal would identify the mayor, the presidents of civic organizations, little league organizers, and PTA officers. It is not always true that the individuals who hold these offices also hold the power. However, using the role-position technique is a good way to start the identification process. Although it is not a foolproof method, it is generally accurate.

The issue-analysis technique for identifying the power brokers requires that the principal explore the history of the major issues in the community and identify the major "players" involved in those issues.

The reputational method is a bit more involved than the other approaches. A panel of individuals would be selected from those who hold formal positions of influence. Each of the panel members is asked individually to name persons whom they believe have the most influence in the community. Those who are named by the panel members are then approached and asked the same question. As the field of names begins to narrow, the power hierarchy in the community is revealed.

With the issues identified and the people most involved in those issues recognized, the principal is ready to begin putting together a model school–community relations program.

[3]J. M. Lipham, R. E. Rankin, and J. A. Hoeh, Jr., *The Principalship: Concepts, Competencies, and Cases* (New York: Longman, 1985), p. 263.

STARTING A SCHOOL–COMMUNITY RELATIONS PROGRAM AT THE BUILDING LEVEL

It is important that the principal develop a varied program. The National School Public Relations Association has suggested twelve elements to be contained in a school–community relations program:[4]

1. Determine with whom you need to communicate. Don't forget the need to communicate effectively with central administration. Often they can help considerably in getting your message to a wider audience.
2. Plan your program on a yearly basis.
3. Prepare a varied program. Publications from the National School Public Relations Association can be very helpful in suggesting new and valuable techniques of communicating with one's public.
4. Inservice for the secretarial staff in telephone manners, greeting student and adult visitors, office organization. Make certain you meet new students and their parents.
5. Organize your parents night, open house, back-to-school night programs so that they meet parents needs. Provide for parent evaluations at these programs.
6. School newsletters are popular with parents. Provide balance between articles about programs and those about students. If time and resources are limited, enlist PTA members or community volunteers to produce a newsletter for you.
7. Find ways to develop two-way communication. Don't be satisfied with just telling parents about school—learn to listen also.
8. Host Parent Visitation Days where parents sign up to come to school when students are there. Limit guests to manageable number (15–20). Prearrange classroom visitations for them. Be certain to notify teachers in advance. Then sit down with guests and discuss what they saw and heard.
9. Initiate coffees in the homes of parents. Don't wait for parents to call and ask.
10. Call 5 to 10 parents a month whom you do not know to discuss their concerns about their children or school in general.
11. Include post cards in report cards or newsletters surveying parents about current issues at school.
12. Provide as many opportunities as possible for parents to volunteer in school.

[4]*Building Public Confidence for Your Schools* (Arlington, VA: National School Public Relations Association, 1978), pp. 175–176.

OBTAINING COMMUNITY SUPPORT

The primary vehicle for obtaining community support is *involvement*. The extent to which people feel involved in the school can dictate the response that the principal can expect when there is a need for support. While there are many ways in which the principal can involve parents, four approaches are common: formal parent organizations, committee memberships, school volunteers, and parent education.

Parent–Teacher Organizations

There are many types of parent–teacher organizations, including the PTA (Parent–Teacher Association), PTO (Parent–Teacher Organization), room mothers, mothers' and fathers' clubs, and the home and school association. Regardless of the name of the organization, support will come by the group's focus on what they want for the young people of the community.

The oldest and largest parent organization is the PTA. Organized in 1897, it has local chapters in every state and annually hosts a very large national convention. The objectives of the PTA are stated in their bylaws:

1. To promote the welfare of children and youth in home, school, church, and community.
2. To raise the standards of home life.
3. To secure adequate laws for the care and protection of children and youth.
4. To bring into closer relation the home and the school, that parents and teachers may cooperate intelligently in the education of children and youth.
5. To develop between educators and the general public such united efforts as will secure for all children and youth physical, mental, social, and spiritual education.[5]

The scope of the parent organization is mostly in the hands of the principal. For the principal who wastes the opportunity to obtain support for the school through the parent organization, it will be little more than a coffe-and-cookies group that meets several times a year to hear speeches and to discuss buying equipment for the school. In the hands of a wise principal, however, the parent organization can do

---

[5]T. J. Martin, "Community Relations and External Forces," in J. Kaiser, ed., *The Principalship* (Minneopolis: Burgess, 1985), p. 219.

many things. For example, the organization can run parent visitation nights as well as a community open-house week. They can sponsor informal coffees to spread good will. The coffees could include parents as well as members of the community. At these meetings, the principal and even teachers could serve as spokespersons to answer questions about the school or talk about needed support for planned programs.

Parent–Community Committees

The principal can consider forming an advisory committee composed of parents and citizens. There are two types of advisory committees: special, or ad hoc, and standing. The special or ad hoc, committee is formed to accomplish a specific task, and it ceases to exist after the task is completed. For example, the principal may wish to adopt a new student discipline code. An ad hoc advisory committee of parents and citizens that can help the principal with shaping the code will provide greater assurance that the new program will be accepted by parents and by the community.

A *standing* advisory committee is part of the organizational structure of the school. The committee would have members who serve for a specified term and are then replaced by others. The standing advisory committee can assist with any number of projects that the principal deems necessary. The committee might assist with curriculum development, extracurricular activities, fund raising, or the organization of seasonal events.

Selection of Members

Whether ad hoc or standing, the membership of the advisory committee must be chosen with care. The principal can obtain names of interested parties from the PTA, teachers, or other already-existing groups. Certainly the principal will be aware of certain persons who have come to his attention during his tenure in office. Regardless of the method used for selection of members, it is important that the committee be truly representative of both the parents and the community. Representation is best ensured when populations are taken into account in drawing up the qualifications of members. The principal should try for a mix of citizens, taking into consideration gender, race, age, occupation, and the neighborhoods in which the member would reside. In addition to the criteria mentioned for citizens at large, parent members should represent the various grade levels within the school. The principal should be careful not to include too many persons who appear to be "in the principal's corner." The public must sense that the committee serves as a voice of the people, not as a means for the principal to legitimate his ideas.

Size and Terms of Office

An advisory committee should be large enough to represent the community and the parents and small enough to encourage informal, efficient work relationships among the members. Some advisory committees can be as small as five, while others are as large as twenty-five. The ideal size will depend upon the heterogeneity of the community and the nature of the problem given to the committee for their input. Greater diversity in population and problem complexity tends to require larger membership.

The terms of membership should be a matter of policy. Typical terms range from one to three years.

Meetings and the Role of the Prinicipal

Meetings should be held monthly. Special meetings can be held as often as necessary. At the initial meeting for the year, a chairperson, vice-chairperson, and secretary should be elected. Since the committee exists to advise and assist the principal, the principal should not be an officer of the committee. In fact, the ideal role for the principal is to serve as ex-officio with no voting power. The length of each meeting should be kept to under two hours. Longer meetings tend to discourage attendance.

To be sure, there are problems associated with advisory committees. Because of these problems, some principals would rather not bother with the arrangement. The biggest problems tend to occur when the committee lets the power "go to their heads." Even though the advisory nature of their duties is made clear to them in the beginning, some committee members become overinvolved in their assignments.

Gorton has suggested six guidelines for minimizing problems with advisory committees:[6]

1. *Don't* establish an advisory committee or council *unless* you sincerely believe that parents and other community members have something important to contribute, and you are prepared to implement those recommendations which are not in violation of school board policy or state or federal law. (In situations where committees or councils are mandated by

[6]R. A. Gorton, *School Administration and Supervision,* 2d ed. (Dubuque, IA: Wm. C. Brown, 1983), pp. 447–448.

law, the first part of this guidelines does not, of course, apply.) Unless you are willing to provide and facilitate meaningful citizen participation on important issues and problems, you are better off not establishing a committee or council, thereby avoiding citizen and administrator frustration and disillusionment.

2. If you establish a citizen advisory committee or council, then clearly define and communicate to all members, in advance, the objectives, function, scope, and authority of the committee or council. If it is only an advisory committee to develop recommendations to submit to the administrator, then that function should be made clear to all participants.

3. Provide *training* to members of the committee or council on how to function effectively in a group. Many citizens have had little or no experience or training in this kind of activity.

4. Keep all members of the committee or council well informed before, during, and between meetings, as to what is transpiring. Advance agendas and minutes of each meeting are minimum requirements.

5. Utilize to the greatest extent possible the individual interests and talents of the members of the committee or council. There is little to be gained by either the school or the participants if the latter's potential contributions are not fully utilized.

6. Reward members of the committee or council for their individual and total contributions at every available opportunity. Committee and council work is frequently tedious, and periodic recognition of the value of the group's work by the administrator will pay important dividends.

The advisory committee can be a source of major support for the school's programs. Whether the committee provides this support or becomes a problem will depend on the skills of the principal.

SCHOOL VOLUNTEERS

Among the four ways to gain support, school volunteers may provide the widest range of support. School volunteers can come from every neighborhood and every walk of life. They can be male, female, old, young, professionals, or just interesting people. For elementary schools, even high school students can be used as volunteers. College students can be volunteers for high schools.

The principal can recruit volunteers in a number of ways. A sign-up sheet sent home with students at the beginning of the year is a good way to get parent volunteers. The principal can recruit volunteers by making personal appeals at club meetings or senior citizens centers. Even advertising in the local newspaper can bring positive results.

Once the volunteers are recruited, some form of inservice training should take place. The nature of the training will depend on the duties the volunteer is expected to perform. The following is a list of the wide range of jobs volunteers can do:

Audiovisual operator
Classroom monitor
Field trip supervisor
Library aid
Story reader

Special resource (cartoonist, photo-
    grapher)
Teacher aid, clerical
Teacher aid, instructional
Tutor

There are some disadvantages to using school volunteers. For example, the faculty may feel uncomfortable having "outsiders" in the school, especially in their classrooms. The principal can combat this problem by providing inservice for teachers on how to use school volunteers.

PARENT EDUCATION

Another way to get support is to include parents in the job of educating their children. A program of parent education typically includes special courses and workshops on such topics as how to tutor your child, how to deal with home discipline, and how to deal with potentially negative influences such as peers, television, or drugs.

While the benefits of parent education are many, the principal should be aware that faculty may resist attempts to institute such programs. In addition, the parents themselves may feel that teaching their children is the job of the "professional." These obstacles can be overcome by the leadership of the principal.

Using Communication

Kindred has said about the job of communication:

It is the result of careful planning regarding the kind of information that needs to be disseminated, the particular audience that is to be reached, and the choice of tools that are best fitted for the job. The job itself is that of bringing about understanding, gaining acceptance, and stimulating supportive action for ideas of proposals.[7]

There are two types of communication: informal and formal. Informal communication takes place every time someone walks into the school building. The cleanliness, noise level, decor, and welcome

[7]Kindred, p. 78.

given by the office all say something to the public. Even the principal's clothing communicates a message. It is important that the principal be aware of such messages. Otherwise, it will be difficult to control informal communication.

Formal communication is what will be discussed in the next section. It is by properly handling the tools of communication that the principal stands the best chance of sending the kind of message to the public that will best support the school program. For the principal as instructional leader, formal communication is an indispensable ally. In this section, we will explore the ways in which various communication tools can be used. In addition, we will discuss dealing with the media and its potential for enhancing communication.

THE TOOLS OF COMMUNICATION

The tolls available to the principal for formal communication are many. There are a wide variety of printed materials that should be considered. The principal can also use a few novel communication techniques, such as a school "hot line."

Printed Material

The kinds of printed material that can be used are endless. Bagin and colleagues list thirteen different publications that the principal might use:[8]

1. Rumor control bulletin: To help quell rumors with facts. Sent to opinion leaders and key communicators.
2. Welcome leaflet: To welcome new residents into the district with school facts and registration procedures.
3. Report card stuffers: To provide parents with information and special announcements.
4. Wallet-size calendar: To familiarize residents with important dates and vital school information.
5. Recruitment brochure: To attract high-quality faculty and administrators to the district.
6. Parent handbook: To acquaint parents with important school information.
7. Guidance booklet: To suggest to parents how to help children adjust to important educational periods in their lives.

[8]D. Bagin, F. Grazian, and C. Harrison, "PR for School Board Members," *AASA Executive Handbook Series* (Arlington, VA: American Association of School Administration, 1976), pp. 31–33.

8. Curriculum and special-service brochure: To explain to residents the various programs offered.
9. Work-study report: To familiarize prospective employers with the vocational and career-oriented programs in the high school or vocational school.
10. Special-purpose publications: To solve specific problems as they arise. This category might include a drug abuse booklet, a brochure on busing, etc.
11. Annual report: To acquaint the board, staff, and public with the district's efforts for the year.
12. Budget and bond issue publications: To gain public and staff acceptance for budgets and building programs.
13. Facts and figures booklet: To provide in pocket-size format vital facts about the district.

All forms of printed materials should be handled in a way that addresses the following questions: Who is the audience? Who should write the publication? How will it be printed? How will it be distributed?

The Audience.   The publication should be written with the audience in mind. School information is too often full of jargon—words like *stanines, mods,* and *learning stations.* While theses words have meaning to the educator, they sound like nonsense to the lay public. The writer who is not sensitive to readers risks alienating them. What is worse, the reader will be left with the impression that school people are removed from the public and have no real interest in communicating.

The Writer.   The writing should be done by a person who knows how to put facts and ideas together in a persuasive way. The message sent to the audience should evoke positive thoughts about the school and thus move the reader to be supportive. The writer must be able to translate education language into something that will have meaning to the audience.

Optimally, the writer is also the principal, but the principal must be realistic about his own writing ability. If the principal does not possess the required skills, the job should be assigned to someone who can do justice to this important task. Usually someone on the faculty (perhaps an English or journalism teacher) will have the requisite skills. The person who assumes the task of writing publications for the school should be given extra compensation—preferably compensatory time. Asking a teacher to write as a favor to the principal would be an unfair approach to getting the job done.

Getting It Printed.   Poor printing can diminish the impact of even the best-written publication. Publications printed on ditto paper convey a dull, lifeless message. A four-color glossy appears extravagant. The answer is somewhere between these extremes.

The principal should investigate the cost of photocopying as compared to mimeographing. With the advances in photocopy technology, what was once an expensive process is becoming affordable. Surprisingly, offset printing can be affordable, depending upon the volume to be printed. The principal should also investigate the possibility of having publications printed by outside professional printers. Most school districts use outside printers to print some of their publications. Some districts use them for all publications. The principal should compare the costs, taking time and effort into account. If the principal does decide to use an outside printer, Kindred offers some basic guidelines:[9]

- Get at least two quotes on every printing job. Some legal requirements will dictate that formal bids be received on printing over a certain cost. Be sure someone on the staff knows enough about printing to write specifications that all printers will understand and abide by.
- If some printers are guilty of missing deadlines, insert a penalty clause. If the schools have met all the deadlines for submitting copy, reading proofs, etc., then the printer must produce the job on time or suffer a penalty for every day of lateness. This if often a small percentage of the cost of the job.
- Realize that not all printers are experts when it comes to layout and design, legibility of type faces, and other important areas. Some printers do have experts available for these areas; most do not. Thus, giving the copy to the printers and asking them to return the printed publication could guarantee mediocrity at best, especially if the printers are extremely busy.
- Keep a copy of all material submitted. Printers seldom lose copy, but it has happened. The time and cost of making a copy are little when contrasted with the difficulty associated with having to redo the material.
- Make a copy of corrected proofs that are returned to the printer. If the printer forgets to make a requested change and 10,000 copies of a newsletter are printed with a spelling error, the school will have clear proof that the error was the printer's.
- Realize that changes made at the proof stages (after printer has set the type) are expensive. Too often someone in the administration decides to rephrase a statement merely because it flows a little better and insists on the change being introduced to the publication at the proof stage. This

[9]Kindred, pp. 265–266.

means the printer must reset the copy and perhaps much of the material that follows. Corrections, of course, should be made at this point; wholesale changes should not—unless the district can afford large bills for alterations.

- Be honest with printers. Occasions will arise when they are under tremendous pressures for other jobs and the school's job is not needed immediately. If school officials cooperate with printers in these instances, printers will undoubtedly reciprocate by helping in deadline situations caused by some unexpected problem.

The most common method of distributing school publications is also the least effective—*sending them home with the students*. Studies have shown that after fifth grade, very few students give the publications to parents.[10] The most effective distribution is through the mail. While the cost seems high, it is actually low when compared to the cost of wasted publications that are thrown away by students. The school can use its nonprofit status to use bulk mail rates. This will reduce mailing costs considerably.

It is important to include citizens in the mailing list. School officials too often send newsletters to parents on a regular basis but send them to other residents only before a school finance election. When using direct mail, the time and effort expended by school employees must be weighed against the cost of employing an outside firm to handle the mailing.

In addition to the use of the mail, the principal can place publications in stores and other centers where citizens gather. It is a good idea to give publications to local real estate agencies, chambers of commerce, and welcome wagon organizers.

The School Hot Line

The school hot line (also known as an "informaphone" or telecom) is a recorded-message service. Interested citizens can dial a telephone number and receive recorded information about school news. Hints on how to make a hot line work are offered in a book called *Building Public Confidence For Your Schools,* published by the National School Public Relations Association.[11] Some of these hints are as follows:

- Keep the recorded messages to 90 seconds or less. About 80 percent of the messages are 60 seconds or less.

[10]*Ibid.,* p. 276.
[11]*Building Public Confidence for Your Schools* (Arlington, VA: National School Public Relations Association, 1978), p. 77.

- Attempt to include only news of areawide or districtwide interest, although a smaller district could consider including local school items.
- Include agendas of area advisory committees, agendas of board of education meetings, and brief summaries of news releases issued from the central office, as appropriate.
- Change the message two to three times a week.
- Prerecord tapes announcing school closings in bad weather which can be put on early (5-6 A.M.) to notify area news media.
- Consider carrying the daily elementary school lunch menus. The volume of calls picked up sharply when we started carrying the menus.

The media include newspapers, magazines, television, and radio. The school principal will spend most of the time dealing with the news media and the press. Rebore has provided a number of suggestions for dealing with the media.[12]

1. Maintain all elements of a professional relationship with the news media. Get to know your local editors and broadcast news directors. In a small town this will normally be a relatively simple procedure. In larger areas it is considerably more difficult but still well worth the effort.
2. Whenever possible, deliver news releases and other information to the media personally. This will permit you to get to know the editors and news directors, building good rapport and credibility.
3. On the first visit, make an effort to sit down with the editor or news director and mutually decide on operating policy, preparation of news stories, deadlines, types of photos needed, and other necessary information. From then on, a planned program for keeping on good terms with the news media is essential.
4. Learn as much as possible about the newspaper or broadcast facility, politically and philosophically. Get to know the personal idiosyncrasies of those you will be working with.
5. Know deadlines and be prompt in meeting them. Bring news items in advance. They will have a better chance of being used.
6. Use good glossy back and white photos with your news releases whenever possible. Articles with good accompanying pictures will get better use.
7. Be fair among the news media. Don't play favorites.
8. Be the only person from your group to contact the news media. Two people calling the same editor or news director will only cause confusion.
9. Try to understand the journalistic temperament. Like educators, they are professionals and should be treated as such. Qualities of candidness, frankness, honesty and openness will go far in establishing your credibility and in obtaining fair and accurate news coverage for your group. Don't try to "cover up" for the press. Stress the positive. Tell what's right

[12]R. Rebore, *Educational Administration* (Englewood Cliffs, NJ: 1985), pp. 104-105.

with education. However, if a journalist asks a question about a "sticky" subject, give an honest answer. If you can't answer a question, send them to the person who can or the place where they can research the topic.

10. Respect the journalist's time, especially around deadlines.

11. Publicity is not news to a journalist. Therefore, don't ask for "publicity" about a given topic. Explain that you have some information and you think it might make a good story.

12. Keep in mind, members of the press are always invited guests. Never ask them to buy tickets or pay admission. Arrange a special press table for large events.

13. Use the telephone to report information that is extremely timely. When time or logistics do not permit you to take news releases to the media personally, it is acceptable to use the mail.

14. Write in journalistic style. If a story is not in journalistic style, it must have content that is extremely important or the editor will file it in the wastebasket. Stories written in journalistic style are many times set in type "as is." If the information is not extremely important to the editor, it still may get into the paper because it took minimum effort to get it ready for print.

15. There are basically two kinds of stories—straight news and feature. Straight news answers who, what, when, where, why, and how. A feature gives the facts, but adds the human interest angle. Write simply. Use a minimum of adjectives and few superlatives.

16. Check facts, figures, dates, grammar, spelling, and titles in your stories. Be concise, clear, timely, and objective. Attribute subjective statements.

School officials and news people (especially the press) are often at odds. School officials complain about the lack of interest the press has in school events. School activities are reported with reluctance or not at all. Unfortunately, much of the problem lies with the school administration's not understanding the job of the press. Perhaps a bigger problem is that school officials do not understand what is newsworthy or how to present information to the press in a way that they can use it.

School news can be defined as information that is of interest to the public. It may be information that people wish to know about the school as well as information they *should* know in order to judge intelligently the value of the institution and its work.

Newsworthiness means that the information contains elements that make it readable—news that the press will accept and the public will read. The principal should not make the mistake of confusing newsworthiness with free publicity. The press does not exist to give the school free publicity. This confusion may be the reason that events that the principal thinks should be covered are of no interest to the press. It is the job of the principal to "convert" a piece of information that is otherwise not newsworthy into an item of interest.

The principal should remember that a personal relationship must be developed with the press. Principals should not expect that the press will come to them; nor should they send a standard news release and expect attention. Instead, the principal should make personal appearances at the news office with the facts that reporters can use to create a story. A school event can be newsworthy if

it is unusual
it names names
it is innovative
it is about money
it is about new positions
it is controversial

For the principal, it is important to know where to look for newsworthy events. There are more places to look than might be imagined. The following list of news sources provides areas for the principal to consider.[13]

Checklist of News Sources

Administrative Activities
Board meetings
Board actions
Board members
Board elections
Board officers
Speaking engagements
Programs under consideration
Addresses made
Recognition recieved
New administrators
Surveys conducted
Changes in organization
Cost of education
Record systems
School budget
Decline in number of employees
Interviews with board members
Interviews with administrators
School calendar
Slogans adopted
Research studies

Educational needs
Long-range challenges
Attendance at conferences
Participation in community
    projects

Classroom Activities
Field trips and excursions
Methods of teaching
Curriculum study
Curriculum changes
Testing program
Results of testing
Special study projects
Exhibits
Demonstrations
New instructional materials
Textbook selection
Library references
New equipment
Trends in teaching practices
Promotion policies
New techniques and devices

[13]Kindred, pp. 228–230.

Work of supervisors
Homework policies
Evaluating pupil progress
Parent participation
Provision for handicapped children
Guidance suggestions
Course offerings
Educational objectives
Humorous incidents
Unusual happenings
Success stories of individual children
Character development

Community Activities

Services to community
Use of community resources
Citizen participation in school program
Special lay committees
School–community projects
Staff participation in community affairs
Cooperation with community groups
Community surveys and opinion polls

Activities of Graduates

Business success
Special awards and honors
Reunions
Acts of valor
Success in college

Contributions to school
Alumni programs
Marriages and births
Opinions on school questions
Citizenship activities
Participation in community affairs
Services to community
Vocational outlook
Work after school

Staff activities

Scholarships, awards, and special honors
New members
Exchange teachers
Summer activities
Acts of bravery
Leaves of absence
Professional interests
Avocational interests
Weddings
Births in family
In-service education
Attendance at conferences
Activities in community
Retirement
Visiting educators
Rewards of teaching
Special talents
Offices in professional organizations
Books and articles written

Perhaps the greatest mistake that school administrators make in dealing with the media is the failure to understand the job of the reporter. Gorton listed a number of proposals for improving understanding of the role of the reporter.[14] Ten guidelines are provided for consideration

1. Don't wait for reporters to call you. Take the initiative and call the reporter first, especially when there is a crisis.

[14]Gorton, pp. 476–477.

2. Regularly and systematically offer news and feature story ideas to the press. Don't be discouraged because your first half-dozen or dozen ideas are brushed off with no coverage or only a few lines. Keep trying. Not only is the law of averages on your side, but if you are alert, you will be sharpening you skills in identifying what makes a good story. Also, don't limit yourself to the newspaper. Initiate contact with radio and television sources of news as well.

3. Get to know the reporters and editors covering your school. If you don't have a speaking relationship with them, pick up the phone and introduce yourself. Let them know that you would be happy to discuss educational issues with them.

4. Find out the reporter's time-deadline requirements and try to cooperate. You need not drop everything for the press and, indeed, often you have more pressing responsibilities. But perhaps you can spare sixty seconds before his deadline, or assign someone else to help, or decide when you have time for the press before it's too late.

5. Be patient with reporters so that you know they have all the facts and understand them in context of your interpretation.

6. If you don't know an answer, say so. If you know who does know, refer the reporter to the source, but don't shuttle him just because you don't want the responsibility for the answers. If you don't know and don't know who does, agree to try to find out and call back, and do it.

7. Spend as much time as necessary explaining an idea or program to get it understood. A percentage of the people who feel they are misquoted are really people who didn't make clear what they were trying to say.

8. Be credible. Don't distort the facts even if they hurt. The media will usually believe what you say until you give them cause not to believe you.

9. Keep your head about errors. If a story has an error, decide whether the error invalidates the main idea of the story. If it doesn't invalidate the whole thing, you would probably still want to let the reporter know about it so the mistake won't reoccur on subsequent articles—but don't make a federal case out of it. A correction or a retraction on this level does more harm than good. If the mistake does serious harm (says the school play will be Friday when it is Thursday) or makes the whole story erroneous (say the school board is thinking of closing down one of the high schools when they have decided not to do so), ask for a correction. You'll probably get it. If a reporter does a good job on a story, tell him.

10. Maintain your composure. Even though the reporter might call you during a crisis, be "calm, cool, and collected." This type of image helps create credibility and a favorable impression of the administrator and the school.

It may seem that the blame has been laid on school administrators for failing to establish sound working relationships with the media, and much of that blame is deserved. Principals must remember that the media have a job to do: They must report the news. If school events are to receive the publicity they deserve, they must be newsworthy from the media's perspective, not the principal's.

WORKING WITH PARENT AND COMMUNITY GROUPS

The school's success in gaining the support of the community will largely depend on the effectiveness of the principal in working with groups. Many groups come in contact with the school. Some of the major groups are room parents, alumni, neighborhood associations, and even extremist groups. School volunteers and the PTA are also important groups. These two groups were discussed earlier in this chapter.

The groups being examined in this section all have a different purpose, and the principal should recognize the uniqueness of each group.

Room Parents

The term *room parent* refers to two or more parents of students in a particular grade or classroom who help the teacher during special occasions. Parents become room parents in a number of ways. Often the PTA will arrange for placement of room parents by soliciting names from the PTA membership list. Since the usual number of room parents to a room is two, it may not be possible to place all parents who wish to help. In this case the PTA may hold an election to decide who will be the room parents. Teachers may also be the ones to decide who will be their room parents. In this event, teachers may wish to approach individual parents with whom they are familiar in order to find the right people.

Specific responsibilities of room parents vary. In some schools room parents volunteer during holiday seasons to help teachers with parties and plays. In other schools the room parent may act more like a teacher's aide.

The influence of room parents on public relations should not be underestimated. The room parent is in the unique position of being more familiar with the teacher's work than perhaps any other member of the community. Therefore, the room parent becomes the school's chief ambassador to the community for that class. The principal should spend time with the room parents. They should be given the latest information about the school and its plans for the future. It is important that the room parents know something about the curriculum and the instructional program. The principal should arrange for periodic informal meetings with the room parents as a way to keep them briefed and to show the principal's continual support and appreciation.

Alumni

Former students can be a powerful public relations tool for the principal. The principal should consider forming an alumni association if one does not already exist. It is important that alumni not be thought of only as sources of money. Schools too often abuse their relationships with alumni by constantly asking them to donate. It should be remembered that the *welfare* of former students must be one of the reasons for having an alumni group. This concern for the alumni as "people" should be clearly communicated.

Kindred has provided nine suggestions for the kinds of services alumni groups can perform:[15]

- sponsoring social affairs for the opportunity they afford to meet faculty and pupils
- sending congratulatory letters to former pupils
- mailing an annual inventory card for information concerning their work, marital status, family, and so forth
- disseminating this information through publication to former pupils
- issuing periodic newsletters concerning individual graduates
- providing counseling services for personal problems and vocational placement
- publishing honors won by former pupils
- mailing district publications to alumni whose addresses are known
- developing any particular services that seem appropriate in the local situation.

Neighborhood Associations

Common in urban settings, the neighborhood association is another group about which the principal should have some knowledge. The members of a neighborhood association are residents living in a specific geographic area. They have a keen interest in the conditions of the neighborhood. The neighborhood association might monitor activities such as housing, recreation, community improvements, and especially education. So powerful are neighborhood associations in certain cities that school boards consult with them in the hiring of the building principal.

[15]Kindred, p. 146.

The principal can involve the neighborhood association in the school in the following ways:

1. Invite members to serve on advisory committees.
2. Structure an on-going two-way communication process.
3. Work with universities in providing the group with leadership training.

It would be wise for the principal to keep the neighborhood association informed on the school's major activities. It would certainly be helpful for the principal to actually become a member of the neighborhood association.

Extremist Groups

As society becomes more complex, even extremist groups find their way into the school. Groups such as the John Birch Society, the Communist party, and the American Nazi party are examples of extremist groups. The best way for the principal to deal with these groups is to be calm, factual, and candid.

School is a place where children learn through a school board–approved curriculum. If extremists are interested in reaching children with a particular ideology, they would have to persuade the school board to adopt their literature as part of the curriculum. Otherwise, the principal has every right to deny school access to these groups.

SUMMARY

The success of the instructional program may hinge on the extent to which the principal is able to develop a strong school–community relations program. To develop a program, the principal must first analyze the community by learning what the issues are and who is most responsible for shaping opinions surrounding those issues.

Once the principal analyzes the community, the process of getting support from the community can begin. The primary vehicle for getting support is to involve the community in the school. Through involvement, community groups can feel a sense of "ownership" in the school. Therefore, they will be more apt to support the instructional program.

In order to carry out the school–community relations program, the principal must become skilled in the tools of communication. Printed material, such as the school newsletter, can be effective. The principal must learn to work with the media so that school publicity becomes newsworthy.

Being able to work with groups is an essential element in carrying out a sound school–community relations program.

SELECTED BIBLIOGRAPHY

BIKLEN, DOUGLAS, *Community Organizing: Theory and Practice,* Englewood Cliffs, NJ: Prentice-Hall, Inc., 1983.

COLCON, ELIZABETH, *Community Efforts to Improve Local Schools: Pt. I, A Case Study of District Planning,* New York: Community Service Society, NY, 1983.

DECKER, LARRY E. AND VIRGINIA A. DECKER, *A Home-School-Community Involvement,* Arlington, VA: American Association of School Administrators, 1988.

GOVAN-KLECKLEY, ROBYN, *Community Efforts to Improve Local Schools: Pt. II, An Inventory of Programs and Resources in New York,* New York: Community Service Society, NY, 1983.

HUYLEN, JEAN W., *Communications is a "People Process" for School Districts,* Denver, CO: Education Commission of the United States, 1981.

KINDRED, LESLIE, DON BAGIN, DONALD GALLAGHER, *School and Community Relations* (3rd ed.), Englewood Cliffs, NJ: Prentice-Hall, Inc., 1984.

LEICHTER, HOPE, *Families and Communities as Educators,* New York: Columbia University Teachers College, Teachers College Press, 1979.

LEWIS, ANN E., *Partnerships Connecting School and Community,* Arlington, VA: American Association of School Administrators, 1986.

LITWAK, EUGENE AND HENRY MEYER, *School, Family, and Neighborhood,* New York: Columbia University Press, 1974.

MARTIN, T. J., "Community Relations and External Forces," J. Kaiser, ed., *The Principalship,* Minneapolis, MN: Burgess Publishing Company, 1985.

SAXE, RICHARD W., *School-Community Relations in Transition, rev. ed.,* Berkeley, CA: McCutchan, 1984.

WILLIAMS, MICHAEL F., *Neighborhood Organizing for Urban School Reform,* New York: Columbia University Teachers College, Teachers College Press, 1988.

WOLFENDALE, SHEILA, *Parental Participation in Children's Development and Education,* New York: Gordon and Breach Science Pubs., Inc., 1983.

11

The Principal
and
Educational Change

Regardless of how knowledgeable the principal is about an educational innovation, no change will take place unless the teachers and staff are willing to change. While the principal may have the power to "legislate" a change, the staff may respond by merely *appearing* to cooperate. No lasting change will take place unless the teachers can call the change their own.

In this chapter we will examine the details of producing change. First, the principal must have a *plan* that maps the way in which the change will occur. Second, the principal should know which *model* for change will be used. Third, the *phases* of the change process must be monitored. Finally, the role the principal play as *change agent* must be explored.

PLANNING FOR CHANGE

Planning for an educational change requires that the principal assess the situation and identify the purposes for the change. Without an effective plan, the probability of successful change becomes doubtful.

Situation Assessment

The principal must gain information about the extent to which teachers are ready for change. Are there specific areas of dissatisfaction that could be corrected by the change? Who among the faculty are most dissatisfied? Most ready for change? Are the teachers—those who have the respect of the others—ready for change? Can they be made ready? Unless the principal spends sufficient time identifying the problem, he risks using the wrong solution.

Identifying the Purpose

In order for any change to take place, there must be a broad base of support. Support can be obtained by systematically identifying the *purpose* for the change. McCoy and Alfred have developed what they call a Purpose Identification Model (PIM), shown in Figure 11-1, which can be useful to the principal.

Notice that the PIM suggest that a number of people be involved in the identification process. The principal should not attempt this important stage in a vacuum. To summarize the planning step in the

1. Select a steering quality assurance committee to guide identification activities and make recommendations.

↓

2. Survey all affected population groups to assess their feelings about what is currently being done and what needs to be done in the future.

↓

3. Analyze what is actually being done and why it is done that way.

↓

4. Examine suggestions for improvement from affected populations. Use research and other "experts" as they relate to current or projected purpose.

↓

5. Assimilate all input and revise operational processes of the institution as necessary to teach institutional outcomes.

↓

6. Evaluate periodically the perceived effectiveness of processes in goal attainment.

FIGURE 11-1. Purpose identification model. From J. W. McCoy and W. E. Allred, "Balance Purposes, Processes to Achieve Effective Change," *NASSP Bulletin* (January 1985):4.

change process, Neagley and Evans have developed 10 propositions that the principal should keep in mind:[1]

Proposition 1: Planning and initiating change will be more effective when the objectives and policies of the organization are clear, realistic and understood.

Proposition 2: Change efforts will be more effective when they are carefully planned, have definite goals, and incorporate some functional method of problem-solving to attain the desired ends.

Proposition 3: The effectiveness of change efforts will be enhanced when the people who are to be affected are involved in the planning and decision-making.

[1]R. L. Neagley and N. D. Evans, *Handbook for Effective Supervision of Instruction,* 3d ed. (Englewood Cliffs, NJ: Prentice-Hall, 1980), pp. 164–166.

Proposition 4: Change efforts will be more effective if they are supported by an appropriate, systematic, and comprehensive strategy.

Proposition 5: Change will be more effective when the choice of a strategy is consistent with the focus of the change effort.

Proposition 6: Change will be more effective when, at the appropriate point in the change process, the change agent's efforts shift from "selling" to "diffusion."

Proposition 7: Change will be more effective within groups that do not see themselves in competition with each other.

STRATEGIES FOR CHANGE

There are four basic strategies or models of change that should be examined: the social interaction model, the linkage model, the organizational development model, and the research-development-diffusion model. While there may be other models for change, these four represent the best choices for the principal.

The Social Interaction Model

This model was originally developed in 1943 for the purpose of getting farmers to accept new methods of agriculture.[2] The model focuses on using information about the benefits of a change in order to effect a change in behavior. There are four stages in the social interaction model: *awareness* of the new behavior; creation of *interest* in the new behavior; *evaluation*, which leads to a decision about the new behavior; and finally, *confirmation* from peers that the decision to adopt or reject was sound.

The model suggests that information about the change be provided through face-to-face contact. Printed material can be used as a back-up. The principal would act as the facilitator of information, attempting to be as persuasive as possible in introducing the idea of change. Lipham has suggested that the social interaction model works best when the following conditions exist:[3]

1. There is financial support to establish outside sources of information.
2. There is a cosmopolitan orientation among the staff.
3. There are opportunities for traveling, attending conferences, and buying journals.

[2]B. Ryan and N. Cross, "The Diffusion of Hybrid Seed Corn in Two Iowa Communities," *Rural Sociology* (August 1943):15–24.

[3]J. M. Lipham, R. E. Rankin, and J. A. Hoeh, Jr., *The Principalship: Concepts, Competencies, and Cases* (New York: Longman, 1985), p. 111.

4. There is time available for teachers to talk with one another.
5. Teachers have a desire to gain status, recognition, or influence.
6. There are funds to purchase products.
7. There is proximity to sources of new ideas.

It is clear that the social interaction model would not work well for principals who do not have the time or social skills to engage in one-to-one contact with teachers. Likewise, the model does not appear to be well suited to schools with tight budgets.

The Linkage Model

The linkage model is concerned with establishing communication networks between the people undergoing change and sources of information about the innovation.[4] The linkage is done through a *linking agent,* who could be the principal. This role requires that the principal thoroughly understand the change behavior expected of the teachers. The principal's key function in serving as linking agent would be to facilitate the work of the teachers involved in the change by providing them with relevant ideas and materials.[5] Crandall has suggested ten roles for linking agents.[6]

product peddler	resource arranger
information linker	information linker
program facilitator	technical assister
process enabler	action researcher/data feedbacker
provocateur/doer	educator/capacity builder

Lipham believes that the linkage model is particularly useful to a principal who must link to the larger educational community and who must serve as the key internal change agent for the school.[7]

[4] D. Paul, "Change Processes at the Elementary, Secondary, and Postsecondary Levels of Education," in N. Naoh and J. Culbertson eds.) *Linking Processes in Educational Improvements: Concepts and Applications* (Columbus, OH: University Council for Educational Administration, 1977), pp. 26–27.

[5] W. L. Rutherford, S. M. Hord, L. L. Huling, and G. E. Hall, *Change Facilitators: In Search of Understanding Their Role* (Austin, TX: Research and Development Center for Teacher Education, 1983), (ERIC Document Reproduction Service No. ED 250 801), p. 58.

[6] D. P. Crandall, "Training and Supporting Linking Agents," in N. Nash and J. Culbertson (eds.) *Linking Processes in Educational Improvements.*

[7] J. M. Lipham, "Change Agentry and School Improvement: The Principal's Role," *Interorganizational Arrangements for Collaborative Efforts: Commissioned Papers* (Portland, OR: Northwest Regional Educational Laboratory, 1980).

The Organizational Development Model

Organizational development (OD) had its beginning in the business world. During the 1960s it was adapted for use in the schools largely through the work of Schmuck and his associates.[8]

The concept of OD is that the nature of the school "as an institution or group" is the source for change, not the personalities of individuals (teachers). As Schmuck notes, "It is the dynamics of the group, not the skills of individual members, that is both the major source of problems and the primary determiner of the quality of solutions."[9]

Twelve approaches to OD strategy have been proposed by French and Bell.[10] The summary of these approaches should be considered by the principal:

1. diagnostic
2. team-building
3. intergroup
4. survey-feedback
5. education and training
6. technostructural or structural
7. process consultation
8. grid organization development
9. third party peacemaking
10. coaching and counseling
11. life and career planning
12. planning and goalsetting

The Research–Development–Diffusion Model

According to the research-development-diffusion (RD&D) model, change is an orderly, planned sequence of events. It begins with identification of the need for change, follows with recognition of the specific behavior or program that will satisfy the need, and ends with diffusion of the new program. The new program is created by researchers, or "experts." The adopter (teacher) is seen more as a passive consumer.

For the RD&D model to be successful, Havelock and Havelock have suggested the following:[11]

[8]R. A. Schmuck, P. J. Runkel, J. H. Arends, and R. I. Arends, *The Second Handbook of Organizational Development in Schools* (Euguene, OR: Center for Educational Policy and Management, 1977).

[9]*Ibid.*, p. 9.

[10]W. L. French and C. H. Bell, *Organizational Development*, 2d ed, (Englewood Cliffs, NJ: Prentice-Hall, 1978).

[11]R. G. Havelock and M. C. Havelock, *Training for Change Agents* (Ann Arbor, MI: Institute for Social Research, Center for Research on Utilization of Scientific Knowledge, 1973).

1. There should be a rational sequence in the evaluation and application of an innovation.
2. Research, development, and packaging of a program change should occur before distributing the program.
3. Planning on a massive scale is desirable.
4. A rational division of labor and coordination of jobs is essential.
5. The proponents of the innovation should be willing to accept high initial development costs prior to any distribution activity.

Clearly, the drawback to the RD&D model is that all efforts are concentrated on the research, development, and diffusing functions. Little attention is paid to helping the teacher implement the change. The model describes the national curriculum movements of the 1960s, wherein materials were developed with such a high degree of confidence that they were thought to be "teacherproof."

Lipham has suggested eight requirements for the use of the RD&D model in the school setting:[12]

1. Cooperative institutional arrangements between developers, distributors, and users.
2. Leadership that remains abreast of current research and encourages its use.
3. Perceiving products of research and development as legitimate solutions to actual problems.
4. Clear communication between researchers and users.
5. Attentive and receptive audiences for messages and materials from developers.
6. Time to discover and implement new products.
7. Funds for learning about and purchasing new products.
8. Local political support for change.

Of the four models described, no one model can be singled out as the best. Each model has strengths and weaknesses. Principals should study each model carefully and use the approach that seems best suited to their schools.

THE CHANGE PROCESS

The process of implementing change has been a topic of discussion since the early 1970s. Hage and Aiken viewed the change process as involving four steps: evaluation, initiation, implementation, and

---

[12]Lipham, p. 112.

routinization.[13] Others have conceived of the process in terms of initiation, implementation, and incorporation.[14] Still others have looked at the change process as requiring awareness, commitment, changeover, refinement, and renewal.[15]

Most recently, Lipham has synthesized previous work to develop the seven phases of the change process: awareness, initiation, implementation, routinization, refinement, renewal, and evaluation.[16] In this section we will discuss Lipham's seven phases in some detail.

Awareness

In this first phase of the change process, the principal becomes aware that the current state of affairs is inadequate. This revelation comes about because of failures pointed out by observers, who are either internal or external to the school. The deficits are frequently identified as a result of an accreditation visit.

Once the need for a change becomes known to the principal, searching reveals the nature and causes of the inadequacies. Alternative approaches to address the inadequacies begins. During the awareness phase, the principal may consult with experienced members of the faculty to obtain their assistance in accurately identifying the problem. The senior faculty may also be asked to help the principal decide on an initial plan for the expected change that will be necessary.

Initiation

During the second phase, the principal will reveal the problem and the need for change to the entire faculty. At this time all faculty are asked to evaluate their performance and the status of the current programs. The principal is now trying to involve the entire group in the process and to encourage them to share the feeling that a change is needed.

Implementation

During the third phase, the principal engages the entire staff in change activities. The principal must ensure that everyone under-

[13]J. Hage and M. Aikes, *Social Change in Complex Organizations* (New York: Random House, 1970).

[14]P. Bergman and M. W. McLaughlin, "Implementation of Educational Innovation," *Educational Forum* 40 (1976):345–370.

[15]H. J. Klausmeier, M. L. Karges, and W. E. Krupa, "Outcomes of IGE and Performance Objectives for Implementation," in H. J. Klausmeier, R. A. Rossmiller, and M. Sailey (eds.), *Individually Guided Elementary Education* (New York: Academic, 1977), pp. 334–358.

[16]Lipham, pp. 114–118.

stands the new goals and specifically what new behaviors are required of the staff. The necessary permission and administrative support from the central office must now be in place. The principal must be prepared to arrange for staff training to ensure that the change is effective.

Routinization

The principal is now faced with the fourth phase. It is time for the faculty to receive maximum support from the principal as they attempt to adapt to their new roles. Some faculty may begin to resist the change at this point, as they begin to feel the discomfort that accompanies any change. The principal must be on guard for these resisters and must be prepared to work with them individually.

Refinement

During the fifth phase, the principal concentrates efforts on handling any individual problems that might come up within the faculty. The change has now become reality. Some "fine tuning" is always necessary.

Renewal

During the sixth phase, the principal should consider stepping back and taking a fresh look at the change. It is time for the principal to renew interest in and enthusiasm about the change. In order for the change to be permanent, the principal must keep up the momentum.

Evaluation

During the seventh and final phase, the principal must stress systematic evaluation of the change and look for ways to improve it. If the evaluation produces favorable results, then the principal can be resolute in defending the change against critics. Favorable evaluations can also help promote higher levels of morale for the staff and support a positive school climate.

Unfavorable evaluations can mean a number of things for the principal. Rarely is an evaluation totally unfavorable. A more realistic situation is that an evaluation reveals weaknesses in the new program. These weaknesses can be converted into new goals for the school. If an evaluation produces more weaknesses than strengths, however, the principal may have to rethink whether the change was prudent.

As mentioned at the beginning of this section, a number of theorists have proposed steps that can be taken to produce change. Lipham's seven-phase synthesis brings many of the approaches together. Gorton has also developed a synthesis of change-process theories. He has suggested that there are seven distinct stages to the introduction of change.[17]

Stage I.   Conduct a needs assessment
    A. Identify the need for change. Examine the *present* system to ascertain which aspects need to be improved.
    B. Develop or evaluate and select a new approach or system which will replace the former method.

Stage II.   Orient the target group to the proposed change
    A. Create an awareness and interest in the proposed innovation on the part of the target group, e.g., teachers.
    B. Institute with the target group an examination of the strengths and weaknesses of the proposed change. Test and refine the new system prior to its introduction.
    C. Identify with the help of the target group the commitments which will need to be made in terms of additional resources, inservice training programs, and/or building modifications.

Stage III. Decide whether to introduce the proposed change
    A. Identify those who should participate in the decision.
    B. Decide on the process by which the decision will be made.
    C. Decide whether to proceed with the implementation of the proposed change.

Stage IV.   Plan a program of implementation
    A. Plan and carry out a program of inservice education for those involved in the proposed change.
    B. Provide the resources and facilities which are necessary for successfully introducing the change.
    C. Anticipate and attempt to resolve in advance the operational problems which may be encountered in implementing the proposed innovation.

Stage V.   Implement the proposed innovation

Stage VI.   Conduct in-process evaluation
    A. Design and institute an system which will provide feedback on the extent to which the proposed change is accomplishing its objectives.
    B. Diagnose those aspects of the program or its implementation which need improvement.

---

[17]R. A. Gorton, *School Administration and Supervision* 2d ed. (Dubuque, IA: Wm. C. Brown, 1983), pp. 294–295.

Stage VII. Modify, refine, and institutionalize the innovation
  A. Revise the innovation and, if necessary, provde additional orientation, training, resources, facilities, etc.
  B. Gain the acceptance of the innovation (if it is successful) as a regular and permanent part of the total educational program in the school or school district.

THE PRINCIPAL AS CHANGE FACILITATOR

From the discussion of the factors associated with effective change, it should now be clear that the principal is key to the success of any planned school change. The principal's style as a change agent has been examined by Hall and Hord.[18] Principals should be aware of the various styles that they might assume as facilitators. Each principal should determine the style most suited to his personal beliefs and to the particular school before launching a major change. Facilitator styles, as outlined by Hall and Hord, include those of initiator, responder, and manager.[19]

The Initiator

Perhaps the key in describing the initiator style is *vision*. Principals who display this style have definite ideas about what a good school should look like. They have a well-defined vision of their roles and of those of teachers, students, parents, and the principals. Initiators *push*. They have high expectations for everyone, including themselves. They are goal-oriented. Initiators will seek change whenever they feel it is in the best interest of the school.

The Responder

The responder style is typified by principals who are concerned about others' perceptions of the school. Because of this disposition, they will solicit as much input as possible before making a decision. It is important for them to be able to say that everyone has had a chance to participate. For the responder, change does not come easily. They believe that their role is to keep the school running smoothly. Change threatens the status quo.

When the responder makes changes, it is in order to keep peace

[18]G. E. Hall and S. M. Hord, *Change in Schools* (Albany, NY: State University of New York Press, 1987).
[19]*Ibid.,* pp. 230–232.

within the school. This principal is likely to initiate change in response to angry parents or teachers who express their dissatisfaction. Therefore, decisions tend to be made one at a time and to be influenced by the last person to complain.

The Manager

Managers pride themselves on running their schools efficiently. They are responsive to the needs of their teachers, even to the point of being protective. The manager would initially question any suggested change for the school. This resistance would be predicated on a view that changes would mean more demands on the teachers. However, once managers understand the change and are convinced of its necessity, they become very involved with helping teachers work through the change.

Managers feel uncomfortable delegating. When forced to delegate, they monitor the activities of the subordinate as opposed to letting go.

THE IDEAL STYLE?

There is no ideal change-facilitator style. Each style has strengths and weaknesses. Principals should attempt to use the style that best suits the school and their own personal attributes.

SUMMARY

The principal is the key factor in any change within the schools. Without support from the principal, it is unlikely that change will occur. On the other hand, when the principal acts as change agent with some degree of skill, change is possible.

In order to effect change in a school, the principal must begin with a plan. The plan should be the result of an accurate assessment of the situation and proper identification of the purpose for the change.

Once a plan is developed, the principal should consider employing a change strategy. There are four basic change strategies or models: the social interaction model, the linkage model, the organizational development model and the research-development-diffusion model.

With the proper change model selected, the principal can begin the change process. The change process involves seven steps: awareness, initiation, implementation, routinization, refinement, renewal, and evaluation.

As change facilitators, principals must consider adapting a style that is best suited to the school and to their personal characteristics. Three recognized facilitator styles are those of initiator, responder, and manager.

SELECTED BIBLIOGRAPHY

BALDRIDGE, J. VICTOR AND TERRANCE DEAL, *Dynamics of Organizational Change in Education,* Berkeley, CA: McCutchan, 1983.

CARLSON, ROBERT V. & EDWARD R. DUCHARME, *School Improvement: Theory & Practice: A Book of Readings,* Lanham, MD: University Press of America, 1987.

CETRON, MARVIN, *Schools of the Future,* Arlington, VA: American Association of School Administrators, 1985.

CUNNINGHAM, WILLIAM, *Systematic Planning for Educational Change,* Mountain View, CA: Mayfield Pubs, 1982.

HALL, G. E. AND S. M. HORD, *Changes in Schools,* Albany, NY: State University of New York Press, 1987.

HEWTON, ERIC, *Rethinking Educational Change,* New York: Taylor & Francis, 1983.

LIPHAM, J. M., "Change Agentry and School Improvement: The Principal's Role," *Interorganizational Arrangements for Collaborative Efforts: Commissioned Papers,* Portland, OR: Northwest Regional Educational Laboratory, 1980.

MCKENZIE, JAMIESON A., *Making Change in Education: Preparing Schools for the Future,* Westbury, NY: Wilkerson, U.L., Publishing Co., 1987.

NEAGLEY, R. L. AND N. D. EVANS, *Handbook for Effective Supervision of Instruction (3rd ed.),* Englewood Cliff, NJ: Prentice-Hall, Inc., 1980.

OWENS, ROBERT G., *Organizational Behavior in Education (3rd ed.),* Englewood Cliffs, NJ: Prentice-Hall, Inc., 1987.

RUTHERFORD, S. M. HORD, L. L. HULING, AND G. E. HALL, *Change Facilitators: In Search of Understanding Their Role,* Austin, TX: Research and Development Center for Teacher Education, 1983.

WALKER, STEPHEN, *Changing Policies, Changing Teachers: New Directions for Schooling,* New York: Taylor & Francis, 1987.

JENCKS, CHRISTOPHER M., M. SMITH, H. ACCLAND, M. BANE, D. COHEN, H. GINTIS, B. HEYNO, AND S. MICHELSON, *Inequality: A Reassessment of the Effect of Family and Schooling in America,* New York: Basic Books, 1972.

HERZBERG, FREDERICK, BERNARD MAUSNER, AND BARBARA SNYDERMAN, *The Motivation to Work (2nd ed.),* New York: John Wiley and Sons, Inc., 1959.

KAISER, JEFFREY, *The Principalship,* Minneapolis, MN: Burgess Publishing Co., 1985.

LEZOTTE, LAWRENCE, RON EDMONDS, AND G. RATNER, *A Final Report: Remedy for School Failure to Equitably Deliver Basic School Skills,* East Lansing, MI: Michigan State University, 1974.

MASLOW, ABRAHAM, *Motivation and Personality,* New York: Harper & Brothers, 1954.

MCGREGOR, DOUGLAS, *The Human Side of Enterprise,* New York: McGraw-Hill Book Company, Inc., 1960.

RUTTER, M., B. MAUGHAN, P. MORTIMORE, J. OUSTON, AND A. SMITH, *Fifteen Thousand Hours: Secondary Schools and Their Effects on Children,* Cambridge, MA: Harvard University Press, 1979.

SERGIOVANNI, THOMAS AND FRED CARVER, *The New School Executive: A Theory of Administration (2nd ed.),* New York: Harper and Row, 1980.

SQUIRES, DAVID, WILLIAM HUITT, AND JOHN SEGAR, *Effective Schools and Classrooms: A Research-Based Perspective,* Alexandria, VA: ASCD, 1985.

U.S. Department of Health, Education, and Welfare, *Violent Schools-Safe Schools: The Safe School Study Report to the Congress, Vol. 1,* Washington, D.C.: Government Printing Office, 1978.

Index

Ability tests, 142–43
Academic emphasis, principal's role in, 35–39
Academic freedom, 212–13, 241
Academic visibility of principal, 126–27
Access to records, right of, 151–53
Accounting, 267–70
Achievement, academic, 2, 51–53
Achievement testing, 143–45
Adapted physical education teacher, 173
Ad hoc committee, 285
Administrative Style Analysis (ASA), 31–32
Administrative Theory (Griffiths), 85–86
Adverse impact due to race, 197–98
Advice, evaluation of legal, 188–94
Advisors, faculty, 133
Advisory committees, 281, 285–87
Age discrimination, 203–5
Age Discrimination in Employment Act
    (ADEA), 197, 203
Aikes, M., 309–10
Alfred, 304
Alienation, 9
Allsion, G., 83
Alumni, 298
American Association for Health, Physical Ed-
    ucation, and Recreation, 137
Analysis in clinical supervision, 61
Anderson, Lorin, 58
Apathy, student, 131–33
Appley, 26
Appraisal service, 142–47
Aptitude tests, 142–43
Arbitrariness, 8
Argyris, Chris, 12, 18
Armor, D., 4, 5
Assessment. *See also* Evaluation
    of curriculum needs, 105–9
    procedures, 9
    situation, 304
    special-education, 174–81
Association of School Business Officials, 269
Athletic program, 127, 134–37
Attorney, school, 192–94
Audit, legal, 225
Auditing, 269
Authority for curriculum, legal, 230–34
Autocratic leadership style, 12
Awareness of need for change, 310

"Back to basics" movement, 100
Bagin, D., 289

Barnard, C., 80, 86
Beck, J.J., 65, 69
Behavior, teaching proper, 54–55
Behavioral disorders (BDs), 172, 173
Behavioral-objective curriculum format, 102
Behavior theory, 12–18
Bell, C.H., 308
Blake, 18
Block, James N., 56, 58
Bloom, B., 47, 53
*Board of Education, Island Trees Union Free
    School District* v. *Pico,* 242
Board of Regents v. *Roth,* 207
Boards of education, 213–14, 231–32
Bona fide occupational qualification (BFOQ),
    204, 205
Bona fide seniority systems or benefits plan,
    205
Bonds, C.W., 181
Boothe, David, 219
Bornstein, R., 136
Bossert, S., 40
Brady, M.E., 50, 51, 52
Brainstorming, 87
Brennan, W.J., Jr., 242
Brightman, H., 92, 93
Brookover, W., 4, 5, 6
Brophy, J.E., 46, 53
Brown, L., 224, 225
Buckley Amendment, 146–53
Budget, school, 258–66
Budget calendar, 259, 260–61
Budget hearing, 262
Budget triangle, 259, 261
Building Public Confidence for Your Schools,
    292
Burns, R.B., 56
Burnside v. *Byars,* 218
Business management, 257–74
    accounting, 267–70
    facilities management, 270–73
    school budget, 258–66

Calculative model of decision making, 81–82
Calendar, budget, 259, 260–61
Cambron-McCabe, N., 214
Campbell, R.F., 259
Carnine, D., 38–40
Carver, Fred, 26, 29
Case studies of effective schools, 4
Castetter, W., 262
Censorship, 240–44

Champagne-Morgan conference strategy, 62, 63
Change, educational, 303–16
    planning for, 304–6
    principal as change facilitator, 313–14
    process of, 309–13
    resistance to, dealing with, 71–77, 89
    strategies for, 306–9
Charisma model of decision making, 84
Civil Rights Act of 1964, 197–203
Civil rights of the handicapped, 162
Classroom, fair use of copyrighted material in, 245–47
Classroom management, 46–47, 53–55
Classroom materials, censorship of, 240–41
Classroom visits, 126
Climate, school, 42
Clinical supervision, 59–65
Coaches, athletic, 134, 135, 136
Coffer, 26
Cogan, M., 60
Cohen, M., 84
Coleman, J., 2
Collegial model of decision making, 82–83
Communication, 112–13, 182, 288–89
    tools of, 289–97
Community. See School-community relations
Competency testing, minimum, 100, 234–37
Computers, copyright law and, 252
Conceptual mapping, 102–4
Congress, 163, 164, 203, 245, 248
Consensus building role, 36–37
Constitutional rights. See also US Constitution
    of students, 216–24
    of teachers, 194–96, 211–12
Content goals, congruence with tests, 50
Contextual requisites, 40–42
Coons, 13
Copyright Act, 244–45, 251, 252
Copyright law in education, 244–53
Core curriculum, 101
Counseling service, 154–56
County court, 191
Court system, federal and state, 191–92
Crandall, D.P., 307
Crime, school, 7–9
Criteria for decision making, 87
Curriculum, 97–123
    assessment, 105–9
    basis for, 98–104
    core, 101
    defining, 98
    design, 111–12
    development, 104–19
    evaluation of, 119–21
    freedom of religion and, 237–40
    guides, 50
    implementation, 112–14
    involving others in development, 114–19
    legal authority for, 230–34
    parents and, 118–19, 230–34
    principal's direct involvement in, 126–27
    proposal, 112–13
    statement of goals, 110–11
    statement of philosophy, 106–10
Curriculum committee, 116–18

Curtis, J., 208–10
Custodial staff, supervising, 271–73

Damaged learner, 48
Damages, copyright infringement, 252–53
Data, pupil, 146–54
Data collection, decision-making process and, 87–88
Dauer, F., 224, 225
Davis, W.E., 181
Davis v. Page, 238
Decisional leadership roles, 93
Decision making, 79–95
    defined, 80
    group, 90–91
    models of, 80–85
    principal's role in, 91–93
    process, 85–91
Delberg, 91
Delon, Floyd, 208, 209
Delphi technique, 90
Democratic leadership style, 12
Design, curriculum, 111–12
Dewey, J., 85, 98, 99–100, 101
DeYoung, 259
Diagnosis phase of clinical supervision, 62–64
Dill, 82
Direct-instruction model, 55–56, 57
Directory information, rights to, 151
Discipline, 7–8, 168
Discrimination, employment, 196–205
Dismissal, teacher, 206–15
Disparate treatment, 197, 198–99, 203, 204
Dissatisfiers, 24, 25
Districtwide approach to curriculum development, 115, 116
Duden, 83
Due process, 161, 166
    concept of, 206
    parents and, 169–70
    procedural, 216–17
    substantive, 217–20
    teacher dismissal and, 206–11
Dunn, Kenneth J. and Rita S., 49
Dwyer, D., 40, 42

Eclectic learner, 48
Edmonds, R., 4, 5, 11
Education
    general, 101
    gifted, 167
    liberal, 99
    low-incidence handicap, 173
Educational rights, family, 146–53
Education for All Handicapped Children Act (Public Law 94–142), 160, 162, 163–68, 179, 181
Effective schools, 2–11
    clear and focused mission of, 9
    high level of expectation in, 5–6
    leadership theory and, 18–20
    principal's role as leader in, 34–42
    safe and orderly environment of, 7–9
    strong leadership in, 10–11

Effective teaching practices. *See* Teaching practices, effective
Elias, 52
Employment discrimination, 196–205
Engagement time, pupil, 51–53
English, F.W., 50
Entrance phase of clinical supervision, 62
Environment
    least restrictive, 166, 179
    safe and orderly, 7–9, 35–39
Equal Access Act (PL 98-377), 223–24
Equal Employment Opportunity Commission (EEOC), 201
Equal Pay Act, 197
Erickson, D.A., 145
Essentialism, 99–100
Establishment Clause of First Amendment, 223, 238
Evaluation
    appraisal service, 142–47
    of budget, 265–66
    of change, 311–13
    of curriculum, 119–21
    of legal advice, 188–94
    for special education needs, 178–79
Evans, N.D., 305
Existentialism in education, 99, 101–2, 104
Expectation(s)
    follow-up on, 54–55
    level of, 5–6
    of privacy, 221
    for success, 36–39
Experience, personal, 41, 42
Experimentalism, 99, 100–101
Expulsion, student rights in, 216–20
Extra-classroom variables, 69–71
Extracurricular activities, 127–39
    athletic program, 127, 134–37
    problems associated with, 130–33
    student government, 137–39
    supervision of, 128–30
Extremist groups, dealing with, 300

Facilitator, principal as change, 313–14
Facilities management, 270–73
Facts comparison, legal, 189–90
Faculty advisors, 133
Faculty involvement in curriculum development, 116, 117
Fair-use doctrine in copyright law, 245–51
Fair warning, standard, 218, 219
Family, deterioration of, 155
Family Education Rights and Privacy Act (Buckley Amendment), 146–53
Federal courts, 191–92
Federal legislation for special education, 162–68
Federal statutes, 191–92
Feedback role, 37–38, 39
Fifth Amendment, 161. *See also* Due process
First Amendment, 196, 202, 211, 218, 221–24, 237–40, 242
Fisher, B. and L., 48, 53
Follow-up on expectations, 54–55
Fourteenth Amendment, 206, 218, 235, 236

Fourth Amendment, 220
Freedom. *See also* Rights; Students' rights; Teachers' rights
    academic, 212–13, 241
    religious, 223–24, 237–40
    of speech and expression, 194–96, 211, 222–23
Free-exercise clause of First Amendment, 202, 238, 239
French, W.L., 308
Frohreich, L.E., 266
Frustration, student, 8
Functional requisites, 38–40
Fund accounting, 267
Fundamental fairness standard, 218–19
Fundamental skills/literacy approach, 99–100
Fund balances, 265

Galveston Independent School District v. *Boothe,* 219
Garbage-can model of decision making, 84–85
Gebert v. *Hoffman,* 223
General education, 101
Gersten, R., 38–40
Gifted education, 167
Givhan, Bessie, 196
Givhan v. *Western Line Consolidated School District,* 196
Glickman, C.D., 98
Goals
    for athletics, 134, 135
    content, congruence with testing, 50
    instructional, 9
    statement of curriculum, 110–11
Goldhaber, G.M., 15, 18
Goodlad, J.I., 51, 52
Gorton, R.A., 75–76, 86, 89, 105, 119, 271, 286, 296, 312
Goss v. *Lopez,* 216-17
Government, student, 137–39
Grade and course placement, 233
Grade equivalents, 143
Grade reports, 127
Graduation, legal aspects of, 100, 233–37
Griffiths, D., 85-86, 91
Group decision making, 90–91
Groups, parent and community, 298–300
Grove v. *Mead School District No. 354,* 239
Guidance services, 140–42

Habit, resistance due to, 71–72
Hage, J., 309–10
Hall, G.E., 313
Halpin, A., 13, 18
Handicapped students, 160. *See also* Special education
    defined under P.L. 94-142, 167
    minimum competency testing for, 236
    related services for, 164–66
    types of handicaps, 172–73
Harassment, sexual, 200, 201
Harvard Committee on General Education in a Free Society, 101

Havelock, M.C. and R.G., 308
Hazelwood School District v. *Kuhlmeier,* 243
Heidegger, M., 101
Hemphill, 13
Herzberg, Frederick, 24, 25, 27–30
Hierarchy of needs, 23–24, 26–27
Homework, legal status of, 237
Honor roll, 126
Hord, S.M., 313
Hornischfeger, A., 51
Hot line, school, 292–93
How We Think (Dewey), 85
Huitt, W., 6, 8, 10, 34, 39, 51, 52, 59, 60, 62
Human Side of Enterprise, The (McGregor), 24
Hygienes, 24, 25, 27–30
Hygiene seekers, 29–30

Idealism, 99
Immaturity-maturity continuum, 18
Immorality as cause for dismissal, 210
Impersonality, school, 7
Incentive, resistance and use of, 72
Incompetency, 210
Incremental model of decision making, 83
Individual education plan (IEP), 160, 165–66,
     168, 170, 175–76, 179–81
Informaphone, 292–93
Informational leadership roles, 93
Initiation of change process, 310
Initiation of structure, leader behavior indica-
     tive of, 15
Initiator style, 313
In loco parentis concept, 215
Inservice, teacher, 113–14
Institutional context, 41–42
Instructional Dimensions study, 51
Instructional leadership
     contextual requisites, 40–42
     effective-schools research on, 2–11
     functional requisites, 38–40
     motivation techniques in aiding, 20–34
     personal requisites, 34–38
     principal's role as leader in effective
        schools, 34–42
     theories supporting, 11–22
Instructional organization, 42
Instructional program. *See* Legal aspects of in-
     structional program
Instruction planning, 114
Insubordination, dismissal and, 210–11
Intelligence quotient (IQ), 142–43
Interpersonal leadership roles, 93
Interviews to survey community, 277–78
Intuitive perception, 92
Irwin, C.C., 69
Issue-analysis technique, 282

Jencks, C., 2
Johari window, 73–74
Jones, 100–101
Judgment, types of, 92
Jung, Carl, 92
Jurisdiction, legal, 190–92

Kaiser, Jeffrey, 15, 30, 32
Kaskowitz, D., 52
Keefe v. *Geanakos,* 212–13
Kierkegaard, S.A., 101
Kindred, L.W., 288, 291, 299
Knezevich, S., 80

Laissez-faire leadership approach, 12
Law, principal and the, 186–227. *See also* Le-
     gal aspects of instructional program
     employment discrimination, 196–205
     evaluation of legal advice, 188–94
     legal literacy, 186–94
     preventive school law, 224–25
     students' rights, 215–24
     suspension and expulsion, 216–20
     teacher dismissal, 206–15
     teachers' rights, 194–215
Leader Behavior Description Questionnaire
     (LBDQ), 13–15
Leadership, 10–11, 93. *See also* Instructional
     leadership
     theory, 11–22
Leadership forces hierarchy, 19–20
Learning
     mastery, 56–58
     prior, 47–48
     styles, 48–50
Learning disabilities (LDs), 172–73
Learning for mastery (LFM), 56
Least restrictive environment, 166, 179
Lee, O., 40
Legal advice, evaluation of, 188–94
Legal aspects of instructional program, 229–55
     authority for curriculum, 230–34
     censorship, 240–44
     copyright law, 244–53
     homework, legal status of, 237
     minimum competency testing, 234–37
     religious freedom and curriculum, 237–40
Legal audit, 225
Legal jurisdiction, 190–92
Legal literacy, 186–94
Leinhardt, G., 55–56, 57
Lezotte, L., 3, 4, 5
Liberal education, 99
Liberty interest, 206, 207
Library, school
     censorship in, 242–43
     copying in, 249-50
Lindblom, C., 83
Lindsey, J., 181
Lines, P.M., 219–20
Linkage model for change, 307
Lipham, J.M., 259, 282, 306, 307, 309, 310,
     312
Lippitt, Ronald, 75, 77
Literacy, legal. *See* Legal literacy
Literacy rationale for curriculum, 99–100
Local involvement, 11
Low-incidence handicap education, 173
Luft, Joseph, 74

McCarthy, M., 214
McCoy, 304

McDonald, 52
McGregor, D., 24–25
McPherson, R.B., 145
Management. *See* Business management
Manager style, 314
Mapping, conceptual, 102–4
March, J., 82
Martin, Thomas J., 280
Maryland State Department of Education, 3
Maslow, A., 23–24, 26–27
Mastery learning, 56–58
Mastery Learning in Classroom Instruction Planning (Block & Anderson), 58
Maternity leave, 200–201
Mathematics, pupil engagement time for, 51, 52
Mausner, Bernard, 25
Media, dealing with, 293–97
Meetings, advisory committee, 286–87
Menacker, J., 187
Mills v. *Board of Education of the District of Columbia*, 161–62
Minimum competency testing (MCT), 100, 234–37
Minor physical handicaps, 173
Mintzberg, 92, 93
Mission, clear and focused, 9
Modeling behavior role, 34–36
Money damages for copyright infringement, 252–53
Monitoring student progress, 10
Motivation and Personality (Maslow), 23
Motivation checklist, 33
Motivation-hygiene theory, 24, 25, 27–30
Motivation of teachers, 20–34
Motivation seekers, 29–30
Motivation to Work, The (Herzberg), 24
Motivators, 24, 25, 27–30, 32–33
Mouton, 18
Mozert v. *Hawkins County Board of Education*, 239–40
Mt. Healthy City School District v. *Doyle*, 195–96
Multidisciplinary team, 168, 176, 178
Music, copying, 248–49

National Association of School Psychologists, 170
National Association of Secondary School Principals, 32, 33, 70
National Association of Social Workers, 171
National Institute for Education, 46, 230
National Organization on Legal Problems of Education (NOLPE), 187–88
National School Public Relations Association, 283, 292
Neagley, R.L., 305
Needs hierarchy, 23–24, 26–27
Negative feedback, 38
Neighborhood associations, 299–300
Neill, S., 208–10
New Jersey v. *T.L.O.*, 220
News media, dealing with, 293–97
Newspaper, censorship of school, 243–44
New York State Department of Education, 3
Nominal group technique (NGT), 91

Nondiscriminatory evaluation, principle of, 165
Nonrenewal, 206, 207
Nontenured teachers, dismissal of, 207–8

Observation, 60–61, 65–69
O'Hanlon, James, 135
Oliva, P., 106
Organization, instructional, 42
Organizational development (OD) model for change, 308
Orientation service, 140–42
Orlosky, D.E., 261, 271
Outlier studies of effective schools, 3–4
Ovsiew, L., 262

Parent-community committees, 285
Parent education, 145, 288–89
Parents
  curriculum and, 118–19, 230–34
  due process and, 169–70
  family educational and privacy rights, 146–53
  referral conference and, 178
  religious objections of, 238–40
  room, 298
  special education and, 166, 169–70, 176–77, 182
  survey of, 278–80
Parent-teacher organizations, 110, 113, 284-85, 298
Partin, R., 87–88
Pascarella, E., 187
Pennsylvania Association for Retarded Children (PARC) v. *Commonwealth of Pennsylvania*, 160–61, 162
Percentiles, 143
Perception, types of, 92
Personal beliefs, influence of, 41, 42
Personal interview, 277
Personalized system of instruction (PSI), 56
Personal requisites, 34–38
Philosophy, curriculum and, 99–104
Philosophy statement, 106–10
Physical education teacher, adapted, 173
Physical plant, managing, 271–73
Pickering, Marvin, 195
Pickering v. *Board of Education*, 194–95
Pierce, 100–101
Place Called School, A (Goodlad), 51
Placement, 179, 233
Planning
  of budget, 259–61
  for change, 304–6
  instruction, 114
Plato, 99
Political-bargaining model of decision making, 83–84
Porter, L.W., 26, 28
Positive feedback, 38
Posner, G.J., 103–4
Postconference, 61–62
Potter, Glenn, 135
Power brokers, identifying, 282
Preconference, 60

Pregnancy, discrimination due to, 200–201
Pregnancy Discrimination Act, 197
Presentation of budget, 262–63
Prevention vs. remediation, 53–54
Preventive school law, 224–25
Primary parental initiative, theory of, 232
Principal, roles of
　clinical supervision, 59–65
　in decision making, 91–93
　in effective classroom, 59–71
　as leader in effective schools, 34–42
　as motivator, 33–34
　observation instrumentation, 65–69
Printed material, 289–92, 306
Prior learning, 47–48
Privacy rights, 146–53, 220–21
Privilege doctrine, 194
Problem, analyzing and evaluating, 86–87
Procedural due process, 216–17
Professionalization of education, 91
Progressive Education Association, 98
Promotion, legal aspects of, 233–34
Property interest, 206
Property loss, 7–9
Property right, 235
Psychologist, school, 170–71
PTA (Parent-Teacher Association), 110, 113, 284, 285, 298
PTO (Parent-Teacher Organization), 284
Public law 93–112, 162–63
Public law 94–142, 160, 162, 163–68, 179, 181
Public law 96–517, 252
Public television, taping programs from, 251
Pupil data, 146–54
Pupil engagement time, 51–53
Purkey, S., 3
Purposefulness, conveying, 54
Purpose Identification Model (PIM), 304–5

Questionnaires, community survey, 277–78

Race discrimination, 197–99
Ratner, G., 4, 5
Read, H., 92
Reading, pupil engagement time for, 51, 52
Reagan, Ronald, 223
Rebore, R., 293
Records, student, 146–54
Referral conference, 178–81
Referral (special education), 171, 176–77
Rehabilitation Act, 197
Reintegration phase in clinical supervision, 65
Related services for the handicapped, 164–66
Religion, freedom of, 223–24, 237–40
Religious discrimination, 202–3
Remediation, 53–54, 236–37
Reporter, understanding role of, 296–97
Reporting of account activities, 269
Report on the Core Curriculum, 101
Reputational method, 282
Research-development-diffusion model (RD&D) for change, 308–9
Resistance, dealing with, 71–77, 89
Resource method of teaching, 172–73

Responder style, 313
Results-only curriculum format, 104
Retarded children. See Special education
Reward structure of school, 8–9
Rights. See also Students' rights; Teachers' rights
　due process, 161, 166, 169–70, 206–11, 216–20
　family educational and privacy, 146–53
Roe, W.H., 295
Role-position technique, 282
Room parents, 298
Rosenshine, B.V., 55
Rossow, L.F., 218
Routinization of change, 311
Rowan, B., 40
Rudnitsky, A.N., 103–4
Rules, school, 218–20
Rutter, M., 4, 5, 38

Sartre, J.P., 101
Satisfiers, 24, 25
Schmuck, R.A., 308
School, effective. See Effective schools
School Administration and Supervision (Gorton), 75–76
School building-level committee (SBLC), 176, 178
School climate, 42
School-community relations, 275–301
　analyzing community, 276–82
　communications and, 182, 289–97
　community resources, 40–41
　curriculum development and, 118–19
　obtaining community support, 284–89
　parent and community groups, working with, 298–300
　program of, 276–83
School hot line, 292–93
School law. See Law, principal and the
School news, 294–96
School psychologist, 170–71
School rules, 218–20
School-site approach to curriculum development, 115–16
School size and impersonality, 7
School social worker, 171–72
Searches and seizures, unreasonable, 220
Segars, J.K., 6, 8, 10, 34, 39, 51, 52, 59, 60, 62
Seifert, E.H., 65, 69
Seniority system, bona fide, 205
Sensing perception, 92
Sergiovanni, T.J., 11, 18–20, 26–29, 73, 81
Sex discrimination, 136, 199–201
Sexual harassment, 200, 201
Simon, H., 80, 82
Situation assessment, 304
Smith, M., 3
Snyderman, Barbara, 25
Social growth/general education approach, 100–101
Social interaction model for change, 306–7
Social worker, school, 171–72
Socioeconomics status, achievement and, 2
Spartz, J., 4, 5
Special education, 159–84

assessment process, 174–81
discipline of students, 168
increasing communication about, 182
law of, 160–70
minimum competency testing for, 236
parents and, 166, 169–70, 176–77, 182
personnel, principal and, 170–74
regular education relationship, 181–82
Special-education director, 174
Speech and expression, freedom of, 194–96, 211, 222–23
Speach pathologies, 172
Speech therapist, 173–74
Sports and sportsmanship, 134–37, 138
Squires, D., 6, 8, 10, 34, 39, 59, 60, 62
Stallings, J.A., 46, 52
Standardized achievement test, 143–45
Standards of judgment, setting, 87
Standing advisory committee, 285
State court system, 191
State statutes, 190–91
State textbook commission, 231
Statutes
federal and state, 190–92
tenure, 208, 209
Statutory analysis, 189–90
Stogdill, R., 12
Strategies for change, 306–9
Structure-Consideration Intersect Instrument (SCII), 16–18
Student(s)
apathy, 131–33
behavior in excellent schools, 20
engaged time, 51–53
experience at success, 53
frustration of, 8
participation in extracurricular activities, 131–33
teacher attention to characteristics of, 47–50
testing and evaluation of, 142–47
Student-activities accounting, 267–70
Student government, 137–39
Student observation form (SOF), 65–69
Student records, 146–54
Students, principal's relationship with, 125–58
appraisal service, 142–47
athletic program, 134–37
counseling service, 154–56
direct involvement in subject-related curriculum, 126–27
extracurricular activities, 127–39
guidance services, 140–42
pupil data, 146–54
student government, 137–39
Students' rights, 215–24
First Amendment, 221–24
privacy, 146–53, 220–21
in suspension and expulsion, 216–20
Study of School Evaluation, 110
Stufflebeam, 120, 121
Subpublics, 282
Substantive due process, 217–20
Success
consensus building for, 36, 37
expectation of, 36–39
student experience at, 53
Sullivan, C., 60

Supervision
clinical, 59–65
of extracurricular activities, 128–30
Support, obtaining community, 284–89
Support services to facilitate communication, 113
Surveys of community, 277–81
Suspension
student rights in, 216–20
of teachers, 209

T-account, 268, 269
Tanner, D. and L., 117
Task Force on Education for Economic Growth, 100
Teachers
basic needs of, 28
behaviors for effective management, 54
expectations of students, 5–6
motivation of, 20–34
principal acting as, 127
referral for special education from, 176–77
resistance of, 71–75, 89
special-education, 172–73, 182
Teachers' rights, 194–215
constitutional, 194–96, 211–12
in dismissal, 206–15
employment discrimination, 196–205
Teaching practices, effective, 45–78
attention to content goals and testing, 50
attention to student characteristics, 47–50
classroom management, 53–55
direct-instruction model, 55–56, 57
mastery learning, 56–58
principal's roles in, 59–71
pupil engagement time, 51–53
resistance to, dealing with, 71–75, 89
student experience at success, 53
"Teaching the test," 144–45
Technical success phase in clinical supervision, 64
Telecom, 292–93
Telephone interview, 277
Tenured teachers, dismissal of, 208–11
Tenure statutes, 208, 209
Termination, 206
Testing
appraisal service, 142–47
congruence with content goals, 50
minimum competency, 100, 234–37
for special education needs, 178–79
Test validity, 144–45
Textbook commission, state, 231
Theoretical outlook, resistance due to, 72–74
Theory X and theory Y, 24–25, 30–34
Thompson, 83
Time as incentive, 72
Tinker v. *Des Moines Independent Community School District*, 215, 222
Title IX of the Education Amendments of 1972, 136, 200
Title VII of the Civil Rights Act of 1964, 197–203
Training for faculty and staff, 10
Trans World Airlines v. *Hardison*, 202
Tripart test, 238

Tyler, R.W., 98, 112
Tyler rationale, 111–12

Unwed parenthood, 201
US Constitution, 206, 220, 237–40
  Fifth Amendment, 161
  First Amendment, 196, 202, 211, 218,
    221–24, 237–40, 242
  Fourteenth Amendment, 206, 218, 235, 236
  Fourth Amendment, 220
US Department of Health, Education, and
  Welfare, 7
US Department of Labor, 203
US District Court, 192
US Supreme Court, 187, 191, 204
  on academic freedom, 212
  on censorship, 242, 243
  on student rights, 215, 216–17, 220
  on teachers' rights, 194–96, 200, 202

Validity, test, 144–45
Van de Ven, 91
Videocassette recorders, copying with, 250–51

Violence, factors affecting, 7–9
*Violent Schools, Safe Schools: the Safe School
  Study Report to the Congress,* 7–9
Virgilio, I.R. and S.J., 113
Vocational Rehabilitation Act of 1973 (Public
  Law 93–112), 162–63
Volunteers, school, 287–88
Vornberg, J.A., 131, 132

Walberg, H., 3
Wandzilak, Thomas, 135
Webbing format for curriculum, 102–4
Weber, Max, 84
Weiss, 52
West Virginia Board of Education v. *Barnette,*
  221
Wiley, D.E., 51
Wood, C.L., 129

Zero reject, principle of, 165
Zirkel, P.A., 186–87
Zykan v. *Warsaw Community School,* 240–41